FRIENDS AND THE GOLDEN AGE OF THE SITCOM

FRIENDS AND THE GOLDEN AGE OF THE SITCOM

JOANNA HAGAN

WHITE OWL

AN IMPRINT OF PEN & SWORD BOOKS LTD.
YORKSHIRE – PHILADELPHIA

First published in Great Britain in 2024 by
PEN AND SWORD WHITE OWL
An imprint of
Pen & Sword Books Ltd
Yorkshire – Philadelphia

ISBN 978 1 39905 285 6

A CIP catalogue record for this book is available from the British Library.

Typeset in Times New Roman 11.5/14 by
SJmagic DESIGN SERVICES, India.
Printed and bound in the UK by CPI Group (UK) Ltd, Croydon, CR0 4YY.

Pen & Sword Books Limited incorporates the imprints of Atlas, Archaeology, Aviation, Discovery, Family History, Fiction, History, Maritime, Military, Military Classics, Politics, Select, Transport, True Crime, Air World, Frontline Publishing, Leo Cooper, Remember When, Seaforth Publishing, The Praetorian Press, Wharncliffe Local History, Wharncliffe Transport, Wharncliffe True Crime, White Owl and After the Battle.

For a complete list of Pen & Sword titles please contact

PEN & SWORD BOOKS LIMITED
George House, Units 12 & 13, Beevor Street, Off Pontefract Road,
Barnsley, South Yorkshire, S71 1HN, England
E-mail: enquiries@pen-and-sword.co.uk
Website: www.pen-and-sword.co.uk

or
PEN AND SWORD BOOKS
1950 Lawrence Rd, Havertown, PA 19083, USA
E-mail: uspen-and-sword@casematepublishers.com
Website: www.penandswordbooks.com

Contents

The One with the Question

What is a sitcom? Technically, 'sitcom' is short for 'situation comedy'. It's comedy derived from odd situations: aliens living as humans on earth, a straight woman living with a gay man, a fastidious psychiatrist moving to his home town to host a radio show, or sometimes just a group of friends that enjoy spending time together. The better answer, though, is that sitcoms are a form of storytelling like no other. They're funny – or at least they're supposed to be. Sometimes they're poignant, heartbreaking, or too clever for their own good. A sitcom is simply a vehicle for telling a story, or stories, and making the audience laugh along the way.

How does a sitcom become more than just a TV show? How does a comedy that ended twenty years ago become worth billions of dollars? How does a show become so beloved that it remains a cultural touchstone, years after it aired on television? How does a sitcom survive?

Friends did it. (If not, this would be a much shorter book.) How, though? *Friends* was a hit, but it wasn't the only one from its time. In those ten years that *Friends* was on the air, countless sitcoms rose and fell. Some were giants, dominating ratings and the cultural conversation. Some lasted just weeks before executives looked at the numbers and deemed them unworthy of airtime. Many fell somewhere in between, lasting a few seasons and loved by a few people. The world, and the world of television, changed dramatically in that one decade. The landscape of television in which *Friends* first appeared was almost unrecognisable by the time the show ended. Still, unlike any of the others, *Friends* lives on. That's not to say it's the only beloved show from its era, the only one still remembered and quoted, or even the only one still binge-watched with regularity. *Friends*, does however, stand in a league of its own. No other show from that era has quite the same kind of current, active fanbase, or exists as such a distinct cultural shorthand. No matter which streaming service has the rights to *Friends*, the show will still be watched by new and old fans, over and over again. It remains a touchstone, still quoted and alluded to, a shared language of jokes and nods. It's so distinctly a part of modern culture that just the sight of an orange sofa, of purple walls and a yellow picture frame, of reclining chairs and a stuffed penguin toy, bring up memories of this television giant.

Alongside that cultural significance comes valid criticism. *Friends* was not, and is not, by any means a perfect show. It was, however, in a perfect storm of a peak TV era, with a perfect place on a perfect network, and so became perfectly adored. So although there were plenty of shows from the nineties, none of them have retained the same cultural significance. How, out of all those sitcom giants of that single decade, has this one show remained so important, so popular and so loved? That's the question I want to answer. Why *Friends*?

Chapter Zero

The One Before it all Began

Forty-seven years into the twentieth century, the first American television sitcom began. Forty-seven years later, *Friends* graced American screens for the first time. The sitcom format previously existed on radio, but it wasn't until 1947's *Mary Kay and Johnny* that four cameras and a laughing audience started to become the norm for viewers across America. The show had a simple premise: a charming portrayal of the domestic lives of a newly married couple. *Mary Kay and Johnny* was created by Mary Kay and Johnny Stearns, who also played their fictional counterparts. It aired on the now-defunct Dumont Television network before moving first to CBS, then NBC; two of the 'big three' networks that would dominate American television for the next forty years (the third being ABC). The show was a far cry from the sitcoms we know today. Episodes were just fifteen minutes long, broadcast live to the East Coast and recorded on kinescope for later time zones. *Mary Kay* broke plenty of new ground. Not only was it the first sitcom, but it existed in a time before any kind of formal television ratings system. It was the first show of any kind, not just comedy, on television to show a couple sharing a bed – the medium was so fresh that networks hadn't learned to be wary of scandal yet. Other married couples on television would continue to be shown sleeping in separate beds until as late as the 1960s.

Sadly, very little footage of *Mary Kay and Johnny* is left in the world. In the seventies, when the Dumont network was taken over by another company, there was some debate over who exactly would be responsible for Dumont's extensive library of kinescope recordings. Kinescopes were expensive to hold onto, as they need to be kept in a temperature-controlled space, and no company wanted to pay the cost of preservation. In 1997, during a public hearing before the Panel of the Library of Congress on Television and Video preservation, comedian Edie Adams revealed the fate of those recordings. According to Adams, a lawyer offered to 'take care' of the situation and all parties agreed. The lawyer then arranged for a few trucks to collect the entire content library from its temperature-controlled warehouse in the middle of the night, and dump the kinescopes in the Upper New York Bay. Only a single episode of *Mary Kay and Johnny* remains in any format, in possession of the Paley Center for Media.

America's first on-screen sitcom might have met an undignified end in the waters surrounding the Statue of Liberty, but the genre lived on. In the fifties, Lucille Ball dominated on CBS in *I Love Lucy*, not only an iconic comedy but one of the first television shows to be shot on film. The fifties also saw the beginning of Nielsen Media Research's work to collect and compile television ratings. Initially, ratings were collected and compiled via an 'Audimeter' – a device connected to televisions in randomly selected households across America that recorded the channels viewed onto a film cartridge that was sent weekly to Nielsen headquarters. The technology grew more sophisticated over time, and Nielsen ratings became the main source of television audience data in America. Those ratings measured the success of shows, their worth with advertisers and became an invaluable part of the US television industry.

In the sixties, sitcoms still tended towards domestic life, but there was a fantasy slant as both *Bewitched* on ABC, and *I Dream of Jeannie* on NBC became hits. One of the most important sitcoms to come out of the sixties was *The Dick Van Dyke Show*, created by Carl Reiner for CBS. It was one of the first sitcoms to focus on the workplace, rather than domestic life, and was lauded for its honest portrayal of television production and the world behind the curtain. Among the stars of *The Dick Van Dyke Show* was Mary Tyler Moore. In 1970, Moore went on to create *The Mary Tyler Moore Show*, one of the first female-driven workplace sitcoms. This was the era of second-wave feminism, and showing a woman taking more interest in her career than her love life was a huge breakthrough in television.

In 1967, before *The Mary Tyler Moore Show*, its eponymous star appeared in *Holly Golightly,* a stage adaptation of Truman Capote's

Breakfast at Tiffany's, and a man who would become vital to American sitcoms entered the scene. *Holly Golightly* was a resounding flop, but during its run Moore and her husband, Grant Tinker, befriended a young assistant stage manager named James Burrows. In 1974, Burrows caught an episode of *The Mary Tyler Moore Show* and realised that this theatrical thing on camera was something he wanted to be a part of. Burrows wrote to Mary Tyler Moore who, with Tinker, convinced Jay Sandrich – director of both *Mary Tyler Moore* and *The Bob Newhart Show* – to mentor Burrows. A career was launched that went on to span over fifty years of sitcoms. Burrows went on to become the in-house director for *Taxi* in 1978, directing a total of seventy-six episodes of the ABC show. It was there that Burrows met the writers Glen and Les Charles, and a trio was formed that would go on to create one of the biggest shows of the following decade.

By the beginning of the eighties, network television had settled into a comfortable rhythm. The season began every year in September and ended in May the following year, leaving the summer months clear for reruns and specials. Nielsen Media Research was collecting viewing figures, and those numbers would in turn inspire advertisers to spend vast numbers in order to sell their products during the most popular shows on air. In September 1982, *Cheers* premiered to an unimpressed public. The show set in a Boston bar, created by James Burrows and the Charles brothers, was loved by critics from the off, but the audience's eyes were clearly elsewhere. *Cheers* finished seventy-fourth in the ratings out of seventy-seven shows. At this point in time, NBC was struggling as a network. The previous season had been an unmitigated failure and the network's current slogan, 'Just Watch Us Now', sounded like a desperate plea for attention from then-Entertainment President Brandon Tartikoff. In 1983, after looking at the dismal ratings for *Cheers*' first season, Tartikoff and Warren Littlefield, his head of comedy, found themselves debating whether to give the show another chance or quietly cancel it. Grant Tinker, by this point CEO of NBC, asked if they had anything better to replace it with. The answer was a resolute no. *Cheers* got a stay of execution, found an audience in the summer reruns, and went on to run for a further ten years.

Eventually, the network would find something better, or at least just as good. In the sixties and seventies quality sitcoms were abundant, but by the eighties the well looked like it was running dry and entertainment critics were making dire predictions about the death of half-hour comedy. These predictions have continued showing up fairly regularly for the last forty years, and yet somehow the sitcom lives on. In 1984, two years after the start of *Cheers*, *The Cosby Show* premiered on NBC. It was immediately popular and hit incredibly high viewing figures from the beginning. The legacy of *The Cosby Show* has been deeply tarnished since the show's run due to the many assault allegations levelled at Bill Cosby. At the time, however, it simply represented a major turnaround for both NBC and sitcoms in general. The success of both *Cheers* and *The Cosby Show* reminded networks that there was plenty of money to be made from sitcoms, and reminded audiences that there was plenty of joy to be found in that half-hour format; and that NBC was the place to look for it.

By the end of the eighties, sitcoms had once again risen to popularity, but the format had started to grow formulaic. In 1989, a new show came along that promised to disrupt that format. *Seinfeld*, the brainchild of Jerry Seinfeld and Larry David, had a rocky start. The show began as a pilot called *The Seinfeld Chronicles* – one of the weakest-testing pilots in NBC's history. The testing process involved showing the episode to small sample audiences and compiling the feedback into a single 'Test Report'. The report for *The Seinfeld Chronicles* was brutal, simply ending with 'Pilot Performance: Weak'. The pilot aired in July 1989 during summer reruns in a process called 'burning-off', i.e., when a contract demands a pilot has to be aired, but the network doesn't want to develop the show further, they 'burn off' that pilot by airing it just once at an inconsequential time outside of the main September–May season. *The Seinfeld Chronicles* received a surprisingly decent number of viewers for a burnt-off pilot – around fifteen million.

There were still people at the network who had faith in what *Seinfeld* could be. One was Rick Ludwin, who had taken charge of developing the show for the network. Ludwin found room in the budget to order just four episodes of the newly renamed *Seinfeld*, one of the smallest series ordered in sitcom history. Those four episodes, treated as unique comedy specials rather than the beginning of something, aired in the summer of 1990. They did well in the ratings, airing after reruns of the now-huge *Cheers*, and *Seinfeld* finally began to find its audience. In 1990, NBC finally ordered thirteen episodes – half the length of a full season – and began airing *Seinfeld* as a mid-season replacement for another cancelled show in January 1991, almost two years after the pilot episode aired. Larry David originally wanted to turn down the offer from the network, claiming he was out of ideas. He would go on to write or co-write 137 episodes of *Seinfeld*. That same year, Brandon Tartikoff left NBC to become chairman of Paramount Pictures, and Warren Littlefield stepped up to become the network's president of entertainment. A new era of television was beginning.

When a new competitor for the 'big three' networks launched in 1986, very few top executives at NBC, ABC or CBS were concerned that Fox was serious competition. They would be proven wrong, and eventually the big three became a bigger four. In the early nineties Fox began to challenge its competitors on their biggest nights. The network began airing *The Simpsons* – by far its most successful show – at 8 pm on Thursday nights, challenging both NBC's reign over Thursday evening programming and *The Cosby Show*'s place in the ratings. In 1991, *The Cosby Show*'s ratings were dwindling, and so were those of its spin-off *A Different World*. *Cheers* was airing in the Thursday 9 pm slot, and was followed by a relatively new show – *Wings*. Created by David Angell, Peter Casey and David Lee – previous showrunners of *Cheers* – and part of the *Cheers* cinematic universe, *Wings* had potential, but was often referred to as *Cheers*-lite at NBC, and couldn't quite stand on its own two feet in the ratings without a big show as a lead-in. In 1992, *The Cosby Show* came to an end and Ted Danson announced that the current season of *Cheers* would be his last, effectively forcing an end to the hit sitcom.

NBC was struggling, and the competition from Fox was just the tip of the iceberg. *Seinfeld* was struggling to hold its own against ABC's *Home Improvement* on Wednesday nights, new domestic sitcom *Mad About You* hadn't yet found its audience and now *Cheers* was about to end. In an article for *Time* magazine, Richard Zoglin wrote that 'NBC, the onetime kingpin of primetime, has seen its fortunes turn sour almost overnight ... The network is desperately in need of a miracle.' NBC looked like it was scrambling for that miraculous win. *Seinfeld* moved to Thursdays for the first time halfway through the 1992/1993 season, *Cheers* reruns seemed to be a bigger draw than anything else the network had, and new shows that hadn't immediately found a decent-sized audience were being rapidly cancelled. NBC largely pinned this on Warren Littlefield, apparently struggling to follow in his predecessor's footsteps. The network brought in Don Ohlmeyer as president of its West Coast division, placing him quite literally above Littlefield in both hierarchy and the office itself. Ohlmeyer and Littlefield's relationship was, as a result, consistently contentious throughout their years working together, but it led to a truly great time for the network.

With *Cheers* coming to an end, NBC needed a solid replacement, and the idea of a true spin-off was floating around. Casey, Angell and Lee of *Wings* had originally created the character of Frasier Crane for *Cheers*. Frasier seemed the best character for a spin-off and they were the obvious candidates to create it. *Frasier* had rough beginnings: Kelsey Grammer didn't want to reprise the role and the writing trio didn't want to be known just for spin-offs. Instead, Casey, Angell and Lee spent a long time working on a pitch for a show that involved Grammer playing a man running his business empire from his bed after a terrible motorcycle accident. Eventually they realised that the show was a non-starter and instead, with some trepidation, the *Cheers* spin-off *Frasier* was born and the titular character was transplanted to Seattle. James Burrows was the obvious choice to direct the pilot, and became a regular in the director's chair during the first four seasons of *Frasier*.

As the 1993/1994 season approached, Don Ohlmeyer was determined that NBC would once again become the home of Thursday night appointment television. Advertising dictated everything in the television industry in the nineties, including schedules, and advertisers were willing to spend the most for slots on Thursday evenings. This was the night when young professionals with disposable income were most likely to be watching primetime television. Thursdays were a particular hotspot for movie advertisers, showing off their trailers to the demographic most likely to be headed out on a Friday night to catch the latest releases. In the eighties, NBC Thursdays were a 'Night of Bests'. In the nineties, the network was looking for a better tagline. It was Dan Holm, a promotional producer at NBC, who suggested the slogan 'Must See TV'. There was no focus grouping, no market research. An iconic era of television began with the off-hand suggestion of a slogan that happened to rhyme, and a handful of shows that looked solid enough to find audiences. Constant promos during summer repeats in 1993 pushed the block of shows, urging viewers to 'get home early for Must See TV Thursday'.

It was the eighteen to forty-nine demographic that NBC were after, so *Seinfeld* became the centrepiece of the two-hour block of essential viewing, taking the 9 pm slot. That age group formed the bulk of *Seinfeld*'s audience, and that season saw the show shoot up to rank third in the overall ratings for the season. For the rest of *Seinfeld*'s run, it remained in either first or second place. *Mad About You*, still growing its audience, kicked things off at 8 pm, followed by *Wings*, and *Frasier* finished everything off – carrying enough clout from *Cheers* and retaining enough of *Seinfeld*'s audience to rank seventh in the season ratings. The promotion, the slogan and above all the quality of the content revived a flagging NBC and created a powerhouse.

While sitcoms and television networks were rising and falling, a creative partnership was forming. In the late seventies, David Crane and Marta Kauffman met at Brandeis University, co-starring in a Tennessee Williams play as a street urchin and a prostitute, respectively. They became close friends later, taking a directing class together and co-directing a production of *Godspell*. The friendship became professional, and the pair eventually went out to LA together and worked to break into the TV business. After spending much of their early days in television selling scripts that never made it to screen, they eventually got a break on cable television when HBO brought *Dream On*, which began airing in 1990. The show was a New York-based sitcom interspersed with black-and-white clips from HBO's extensive film archives. It was a high-concept show, created almost entirely to answer the question 'what can we do with all of this old footage?' Despite it being the television equivalent of a pot of soup knocked together to use up flagging leftovers, *Dream On* earned Crane and Kauffman critical acclaim, professional attention and Crane's first Emmy nomination. It was also the first step in the pair becoming a trio. The two of them hit it off with Kevin Bright, their executive producer, going on to form Bright/Kauffman/Crane productions with him and striking a development deal with Warner Brothers television.

By 1993, just as 'Must See TV' was becoming a must see, Crane and Kauffman were preparing to pitch a new pilot to the networks. Drawing on the lives of their post-college friendship group, the idea was for an ensemble show about 'that time in your life where your friends are your family'. When driving down Beverly Boulevard, Marta Kauffman spotted a coffee shop called 'Insomnia Cafe'. She borrowed the name, and it became the title of the pilot – a show about six friends drinking coffee together. Must See TV indeed.

Chapter One

The One with the Pilot

Before *Dream On*, and long before *Insomnia Cafe*, David Crane and Marta Kauffman sold their very first script. It was for a sitcom almost completely lacking in concept called *Just a Guy* – the premise of which was that the main character was just a guy. The show was never made, and they've spoken disparagingly of the script since, but the idea of a low-concept series would eventually lead to their biggest success.

The sitcoms of the late eighties and early nineties often clung to concepts. Whether it was the Boston bar setting of *Cheers* that allowed for an ever-evolving roster of characters to walk through the door, or the show-within-a-show of *Home Improvement*, the emphasis was on the situation as much as the comedy. *Seinfeld* was one of the first shows to start making cracks in the mould with the writer's insistence on no learning or hugging at the end of an episode, centring the comedy on a group of characters who refused to learn a single life lesson. In the early nineties, family-centric sitcoms were still going strong, while the 'hang-out' sitcom, focused on a group of friends spending their time at say, a diner or a coffee shop, was still comparatively new. It was in this landscape that David Crane and Marta Kauffman would find themselves returning to their earlier idea of a low-concept show. They wanted a group of twenty-somethings, that friends-forming-family age, and they wanted this comedy to be a true ensemble; without a single star pulling focus. The now-famous sofas of Central Perk began as a set piece for the Insomnia Cafe, a place to perch their group of youngsters.

There would have been no way for Crane and Kauffman to know that this pilot was the one that would go all the way, and at the time they were pitching it to NBC the pair had another piece in the works – *Reality Check* for Fox. In an interview for the Television Academy, Marta Kauffman described this single-camera show about a teenager and his family life – with Hilary Swank briefly attached to play the mother – as 'arduous'. Crane and Kauffman were worried for a while that the wrong show was about to become their working life. Even before NBC picked up *Friends* under the show's working title, the creators had faith in that pilot script. Of course, a network picking up a show and ordering episodes, and a network showing faith that the show could succeed, are two very different things. When NBC opted to add *Friends* to the Thursday 'Must See' line up, it was a demonstration of the latter, a huge vote of confidence in this new sitcom.

In 1994, the year *Friends* began, the 'Must See' umbrella spread to Tuesdays, moving *Frasier* and *Wings* earlier in the week and freeing up room on Thursdays. With the *Friends* pilot filmed and submitted to NBC just days before the announcement of the Fall schedule, the creators of the show were delighted to find out it was slated to land on Thursday night. *Friends* would be airing straight after *Mad About You* – now becoming a runaway hit – and just before *Seinfeld*, which would go on to be the top-rated show of the 1994/1995 season. The network only ordered twelve episodes of *Friends* to begin with, but that time slot was almost a guarantee of high ratings for that half a season. Those ratings were the key to the show getting a full-season order of twenty-four episodes and, eventually, longevity. The title of the show stayed up for debate right down to the wire. *The Insomnia Cafe* became *Six of One* and *Friends Like You* before eventually being shortened to *Friends*. However, the title was far from everyone's main priority. Kevin Bright told *Rolling Stone* that if the show was on Thursday nights, they could name it 'Kevorkian' for all he cared.

The other additions to the 'Must See' banner that season showed that comedy might not be everything, and a time slot was no guarantee of success. *Madman of the People*, another new sitcom, took the 9.30 pm slot, airing right after *Seinfeld*. Like *Friends*, *Madman* managed decent ratings. It couldn't, however, quite hold on to *Seinfeld*'s massive audience. The show only survived until January 1995, making it one of the highest rated shows ever to end in abrupt cancellation. The network hadn't forgotten the ratings struggles at the beginning of the decade, and wasn't willing to risk giving a show time to build an audience – not in a precious 'Must See' slot. In the past, NBC's marketing had focused on the two hours between 8 pm and 10 pm, and centered entirely on comedy. In 1994, NBC began to push a third hour and a new drama. *E.R.* successfully debuted at 10pm, post *Madman*, and with the power of George Clooney, managed to hold on to audience attention; it became the second highest rated show for the season.

This was the NBC that *Friends* became a part of. A network at the top of its game with, in Warren Littlefield, a President of Entertainment that truly wanted to make the best possible home for good television. A network, however, that had only recently fallen from grace, with the president of its West Coast division more than ready to cancel a show that couldn't immediately deliver stunning ratings. The *Friends* creators were walking a tightrope, but doing so with a lot of support. Not only had they bagged the Thursday time slot that could make or break the show, but the already-legendary James Burrows had signed on to direct the pilot, and would go on to direct over half of the first season.

That opening episode began with a perfect introduction to the ensemble of characters. Each one of the friend's key personality traits were established through a set of short, coffee shop vignettes. The first scene opened with Monica Geller, played by Courtney Cox (arguably the biggest name attached to the series at that point), interrogated by a few of the group about an upcoming date. Before *Friends*, Cox was most famous for her appearance in Bruce Springsteen's 'Dancing in the Dark' music video, pulled up on stage to dance by the Boss himself. Shortly before *Friends*, Cox appeared in both *Ace Ventura: Pet Detective* and a single episode of *Seinfeld*, in which she played one of the many women Jerry Seinfeld miraculously managed to date. It was Cox's time on *Seinfeld* that helped set the tone among the six stars of *Friends*. She noticed that the *Seinfeld* actors often suggested little things their co-stars could do to improve their performances and make the show funnier. According to Lisa Kudrow in Warren Littlefield's book *Top of the Rock*, Cox told her fellow actors 'feel free to tell me. If I could do anything funnier, I want to do it.' It wasn't usually the done thing for actors to give each other notes, but Cox's permission bonded the group, giving them a real reason to be open and honest with each other.

Courtney Cox was originally offered the role of Rachel Green, but preferred the character of Monica. In *Top of the Rock*, Marta Kauffman mentions that the original Monica was imagined as 'darker, edgier and snarkier'. Crane and Kauffman originally had Janeane Garafolo, a well-known stand up and part of *The Larry Sanders Show*'s cast, in their minds. Garafolo went on to play another of Seinfeld's out-of-his-league girlfriends, but never made it on to *Friends*. Instead, Courtney Cox as

Monica brought a softer side to the role. Early episodes regulated her character's personality to be mostly maternal. Also, a chef. Six episodes in, she also got the character trait of 'tidy'. Who says women can't have it all? There was some debate among NBC executives over whether her character would also be considered 'slutty'. In a run-through of the pilot episode for the network, Don Ohlmeyer gave the note that Monica got what she deserved after sleeping with 'Paul the Wine Guy' on the first date. Ohlmeyer insisted on a questionnaire being handed out to the audience asking if Monica falling for a lie and sleeping with a man made her a slut, a whore or a trollop. Thankfully, the old-fashioned ideals seemed to be Ohlmeyer's alone; the rest of the audience were unbothered. Television had come a long way from those married couples and their separate beds.

As the pilot moves on to its second vignette, Chandler Bing – the sarcastic one, played by Matthew Perry – describes a nightmare of being back in high school with a phone in place of his genitals (a mental image we could all live without). Perry was one of the first names on the list for Chandler, but almost didn't join the *Friends* cast due to already being attached to another pilot – *LAX2194*. The landscape of nineties sitcoms could have been very different if this show – about baggage handlers in the year 2194 and starring Ryan Stiles of *Whose Line Is It Anyway* – had made it to series. Unfortunately, or fortunately, all that remains of *LAX2194* now is a few minutes of footage on YouTube. Imagine *Red Dwarf* with a smaller budget and Ryan Stiles with a truly incomprehensible accent, and you'll get the idea.

The creators of *Friends* were certain that Chandler would be the easiest part to cast – it was the character with the best jokes. Instead, casting Chandler turned out to be an unexpected challenge. With Perry unavailable, the casting process dragged on, with the writers growing more and more concerned that the character that they'd created just didn't work. For a large city, Hollywood was a small town and many of the actors in the running for Chandler were close friends of Matthew Perry. Perry had formed something of a gang with David Pressman, Craig Bierko and Hank Azaria, describing them in his autobiography *Friends, Lovers and the Big Terrible Thing*, as a 'mini-Rat Pack'. When the pilot script for *Friends Like Us* was going around, Perry was certain that Chandler would be the perfect for him, if only he was available for the job. Hank Azaria auditioned for *Friends* twice, both times for the part of Joey. He didn't make the core cast, but later won an Emmy for his performance as David, Phoebe's love interest. Perry, meanwhile, was coaching friend after friend on how best to play Chandler, but no actor seemed quite right. The writers were even worried that the character just didn't work and had to be rewritten. Eventually, the producers settled on Craig Bierko, and offered him the role. In his book, Perry recalled a lunch with Bierko and Azaria. Bierko had to make the choice between *Friends* and the lead role in a show called *Best Friends*. Against his friend's advice, Bierko took the latter role, wanting to be a solo star rather than part of the group. The role of Chandler Bing remained up for grabs.

After a long and frustrating casting process Jamie Tarses, one of the producers developing *Friends Like Us* at NBC, asked her then-husband Dan McDermott – a producer at Fox, the network producing *LAX2194* – if the futuristic baggage-handlers show had any chance of being picked up. It did not, probably because it was about futuristic baggage handlers. Matthew Perry was – if not officially, then technically – available, and went in the following week to read for David Crane and Marta Kauffman. It turned out that the character of Chandler Bing worked just fine, provided Matthew Perry was the one delivering the lines.

Instead of Hank Azaria or any of the myriad others who auditioned for the role in what was rumoured to be the season's hottest pilot, Matt LeBlanc was cast as Joey. In those early pilot scenes, there wasn't much for Joey to do beyond being handsome and not too bright. LeBlanc was previously best known for a recurring role in the Fox sitcom *Married ... With Children* and its various short-lived spin-offs. Before being cast on *Friends*, he was down to his last eleven dollars. The night before his audition, he took the advice of a fellow actor who suggested going out and getting drunk to get used to the mindset of hanging out with friends. While drinking, LeBlanc took a tumble, and had to apologetically arrive at his audition with a large and obvious scab on his face. The story behind the injury got the creators laughing, set the tone in the room and helped him land the role.

LeBlanc brought a shift to the character originally conceived as the ladies' man of the group. Early on, he began to worry that a character who had little to do beyond hitting on the women around him didn't have much staying power, and he asked if Joey couldn't act as more of a big brother to the three central women. This, combined with a comment during the pilot that he was great at playing the idiot, cemented him deeply into the role of well-meaning dolt, and gave the character its longevity.

In the pilot, after another soft bass sting, Ross – played by David Schwimmer – enters and immediately establishes his character as 'the sad one'. Schwimmer was one of the first actors to be invited to join the *Friends* cast, and one of the last to sign on to the show. About a year before the casting process began, Schwimmer had auditioned for *Couples*, a show written by David Crane and Marta Kauffman. While he didn't get the role, and *Couples* itself went nowhere, he'd lingered in their heads until *Friends* came along. Crane and Kauffman took inspiration from Schwimmer's acting style and wrote Ross with him fully in mind. When the time came to cast the *Friends* pilot, Schwimmer was offered the part with no audition required. There was an obstacle in the way, however, and that was the actor himself. After a disastrous, cut-short run on *Monty*, a Henry Winkler vehicle that lasted just six episodes on the air, Schwimmer had decided to stay away from television. He'd spent many years working hard in the theatre industry and couldn't conflate the collaborative, ensemble process of stage work with the TV industry – where he was expected to say his lines and do as he was told. He insisted to his agent, Leslie Siebert, that he had no interest in television and that he didn't want to see a single script. Siebert sensibly ignored him, insisting he take a look at the *Friends* pilot. Even James Burrows contacted Schwimmer directly, encouraging him to take the role. Eventually, he conceded.

At the time he was cast on *Friends* Schwimmer wasn't well-known for his stage acting – or even at all. In *Entertainment Weekly*'s review of the first few episodes, he was referred to as 'best known as the doomed "4B" on last season's NYPD Blue'. That same reviewer was confused by Ross's role in the group, saying 'it took me two weeks to figure out that he was Monica's brother and not her lover'. The creators of *Friends* might have had clear personalities for each character in mind, but some details weren't so obvious to the audience straight away.

As the opening scenes of the pilot continue, Lisa Kudrow as Phoebe Buffay makes short work of establishing her role as 'the kooky hippy one' – a manic pixie dream girl eleven years before the term was first coined – taking it upon herself to clean up poor, sad Ross's aura. Kudrow had been cast the previous year as Roz Doyle in the pilot of

Frasier, a job which lasted just four days before she was replaced with Peri Gilpin. Thankfully, she landed on her feet with a recurring role as snarky waitress Ursula on *Mad About You*. David Crane's partner, Jeffrey Klarik, was a writer on *Mad About You* and the one to draw Crane's attention to Kudrow, which led to her invitation to read for the role of Phoebe. After auditioning for Crane and Kauffman, Kudrow found herself in the terrifying position of having to audition specifically for James Burrows, the man who had fired her the year before. While Kudrow hadn't worked out as Roz, she was perfect for Phoebe and Burrows had no notes.

The only concern in casting Kudrow was that she wanted to keep her recurring role on *Mad About You*. It was physically possible for her to do both jobs, but did it make sense considering the two shows were both set in the same city, and aired one after the other on the same network? Crane approached Danny Jacobson, co-creator of *Mad About You*, and asked if Phoebe and Ursula could be twin sisters. Eventually, this led to a two-part *Friends* episode that played with the shared universe, with Chandler and Joey visiting 'Riff's' – Ursula's workplace from the Helen Hunt/Paul Reiser sitcom – and meeting Ursula. Hunt and her co-star Leila Kenzle made an appearance in the episode in a brief scene that got plenty of cheers from the live studio audience. The use of crossovers might feel old-hat in the age of sprawling IPs and the Marvel Cinematic Universe, but for its time it was a fresh and exciting way to use this New York based programming block, beyond the realm of sitcom spin-offs.

Finally, the pilot arrives at one of the most iconic character introductions of all time: enter Rachel Green. A rain-soaked Jennifer Aniston sweeps into the coffee shop in a wedding dress so nineties it might as well have been double denim. Timed, of course, just as Ross announces that he 'just wants to be married again'.

It's impossible to imagine Rachel with, say, Courtney Cox in the role, now that Aniston has made it so thoroughly hers. Her casting, however, was almost too much of a gamble for the network. Like Matthew Perry, Aniston was already signed on to another show. Unlike Perry, her show *Muddling Through*, on CBS, had made it past the pilot stage and actually shot a handful of episodes. Aniston had worked with NBC before, having appeared in the dismal *Ferris Bueller* series based loosely on the classic John Hughes film. While that show had been a failure, the network had continued casting Aniston in pilots, trying to find something that would stick. Before *Friends*, there was even an offer floating around for Aniston to join the *Saturday Night Live* cast, alongside Adam Sandler. According to Warren Littlefield, during those dire years of failed pilots he ran into Aniston at a petrol station, and she point-blank asked him if it was ever going to happen for her.

The answer, of course, was yes. She just had to get past CBS first. It was clear that *Muddling Through* was going nowhere, but there was still a contract, and that made casting Aniston as Rachel a massive risk. CBS had kept *Muddling Through* on a shelf for months, but if they decided to pick the show up and order more episodes, *Friends* would have to be reshot with a brand-new Rachel. Aniston begged to be let out of her contract with CBS, and when *Muddling Through* eventually made it to air NBC countered by airing Danielle Steele movies – a guaranteed audience draw – in the same time slot. CBS had no choice but to cancel the show, and the final episode aired just two weeks before *Friends*, complete with Jennifer Aniston, premiered on NBC.

Before the pilot even aired, plenty of people were certain that *Friends* was a hit in the making. One of the most trustworthy opinions was that of James Burrows, who was absolutely sure that this new comedy was going to be a success. So much so that he borrowed the NBC private jet for a weekend and took the six *Friends* not-yet-stars to Las Vegas. He encouraged them to eat, drink and be merry, and enjoy their time in these crowded public spaces. Late in the trip, Burrows explained his motives to the actors. He knew that *Friends* was going to be a hit, that they were about to be catapulted to stardom, and that this might be their last chance to enjoy anonymity. Less than a year later, all six of them were on the cover of *Rolling Stone*.

The 'Must See' marketing paid off. The *Friends* pilot was the fifteenth most-watched show across network television that week. It scored a 14.7 Nielsen rating – meaning it was watched by roughly twenty-two million viewers. For comparison, *Seinfeld*'s audience numbers for the same week were around thirty-two million. The critical response to the first few episodes was surprisingly mixed. While the *LA Times* review of the pilot said that '*Friends* has so many good moves that there's nothing really to dislike', *Variety*'s reviewer thought that the humour was 'less sophisticated than expected from the exec. producers of … *Dream On.*' The *Hartford Courant*'s review was much harsher, calling the pilot 'Anemic and unworthy of its Thursday-night time slot.' That review specifically complained about the line 'I don't know whether I'm hungry or horny' – something Chandler says in response to Joey's monologue comparing women to ice cream and suggesting that Ross 'grab a spoon'. Whether that line has any bearing on the show's worthiness is up for debate, but it was definitely a sign of problems to come with a show that was, and is, very much of its time.

After the pilot, there was a brief dip in viewing figures that had the network concerned. Thursday nights weren't the place for anything less than a hit. Before the season had reached the halfway mark, however, and after weeks of mostly positive reviews, the numbers began to rise. *Friends* went on to average around a 16.9 Nielsen rating for the rest of the season, second only in network comedy to *Seinfeld*'s 20.6. A rearrange of the spring schedule saw the unceremonious end of *Madman of the People*, with *Friends* moving to replace it in that coveted slot between *Seinfeld* and *E.R.*

It was the seventh episode of *Friends* that had the ratings first creeping back up, largely with the help of NBC using Thursdays to their best advantage. In November 1994, the network used the common setting of the sitcoms in the Thursday line up to create a crossover event – the 'Blackout Thursday' stunt – in which a storyline about a citywide power outage ran through three of the four shows. It began at 8 pm with *Mad About You*, and Helen Hunt's character causing the outage during an attempt to steal cable (it's the stories about specific technology that really makes these shows feel firmly of their time). The story continued into *Friends*, with Chandler spending the night trapped in an ATM vestibule with Victoria's Secret model Jill Goodacre, while Rachel meets Paolo the Italian for the first time. *Seinfeld* skipped the blackout, with the 9 pm episode 'The Gymnast' apparently running at full power, despite being marketed as part of the event. Finally, *Madman of the People* concluded the dark night in New York. The stunt was excellent marketing for the block of shows at the time, but now those episodes feel strange in isolation. Watching on a streaming service with no context of the stunt, it feels like the *Friends* episode is supposed to be referencing a bigger historical moment, as if they'd briefly popped back to the famous 1977 blackout. Either that, or it's just an elaborate way to throw a cat at Ross and keep the 'Will they, won't they?' question running a little while longer.

Later in the season, the *Mad About You* crossover led to another big ratings jump. When the show opted to play with the twin sister idea, a B-plot was introduced for Rachel and Monica, sending Rachel to hospital. This was the perfect opportunity to bring in two newly famous actors from the late slot in the Thursday line up – *E.R.* While George Clooney and Noah Wyle couldn't portray their characters from the medical drama, due to the show being set in a different city, the sight of two handsome, famous, fictional doctors in their white coats was enough to get the studio audience screaming, and keep the viewers at home from changing the channel.

The crossover concept might not work so well on a modern rewatch, but the particular set of multi-camera sitcoms that made up Thursday nights shared enough traits that it's easy to think of them as a whole universe. They all took place in a New York recreated on West Coast soundstages, and all used that same camera set-up – multiple cameras forming the fourth wall of a single static set. It was the ideal arrangement for a live studio audience, something *Friends* made the most of. All of those shows used the laughter of their live audiences, but *Friends* was unique in those recordings running for over six hours, double the length of the average, to get the footage that would eventually be cut down to twenty-two minutes. This wasn't due to a lack of professionalism, but a communal sense of perfectionism. Right from the beginning, the creators made the most of having the audience in, testing every laugh and rewriting jokes on the fly. It was one of the strengths of both the ensemble cast and the environment they worked in that everyone cared equally about producing the best possible version of the show.

All of the shows from that Thursday night universe, even *Seinfeld* with its self-imposed distance from marketing stunts, drew constant comparisons. The network was comparing ratings and audience demographics while the critics compared characters and comedy. The differences between *Friends*, centered on optimistic New York twenty-somethings, and *Seinfeld* with its mean-spirited New York thirty-somethings, were in far more than just ratings. *Friends* quickly began to build on continuity, episode to episode. The original plan might have been for a slice-of-life, low-concept show, but there was an appeal to the show becoming a sort-of funny soap opera. Crane and Kauffman created a half-arc show, with a longer, overarching storyline each season taking place alongside individual episode arcs.

In the first season, that thread running through it was Ross pining over Rachel, tangled deftly with the story of his lesbian ex-wife having his baby. Those two arcs were cleverly woven into a series of shorter tales, little twenty-minute narratives neatly wrapped up by the end of an episode. As an example, the fourteenth episode of the season – 'The One with the Candy Hearts', a Valentine's Day-centric episode – managed to show the lingering feeling between Ross and his ex-wife, Chandler briefly reuniting with the iconic Janice, and the three women burning mementoes and meeting firemen; carrying one story forward while keeping an eye on the rest of the characters emotionally. That episode, incidentally, was penned by Bill Lawrence – a man just about to become a big name in American sitcoms.

While, of course, the biggest contributing factor to *Seinfeld*'s greater popularity was its thoroughly established chops against a new contender, audiences at the time often preferred that episodic nature, with no consequences carrying over from week to week. Partly, this was down to catch-up television being less of an option. If missing a single episode of a show made it hard to follow the story, that show was less likely to keep viewers in a time before on-demand services. This was an incredible time for television, with the limits of twenty-two-minute storytelling being pushed and tested on a regular basis. In fact, with *Seinfeld,* those runtimes often came up just a little bit shorter so that the network could sell an extra thirty seconds of ad space around its most popular comedy. The lasting impact of these shows and the way they told stories can't be ignored, even if plenty of moments fall flat.

Friends was somewhat groundbreaking for showing a healthy queer relationship on primetime network television, although the show didn't always do the best job of being inclusive. The first season had a whole episode focused largely on whether or not Chandler 'seems gay'. Worse, the jokes and stereotypes abounded whenever Carol, the lesbian ex-wife and her 'life-partner' Susan appear on screen. Even the label itself – 'lesbian' – for a character who's previously been in a long-term and (the show establishes) sexual relationship with a man – reads as an oversimplification. How any person identifies and labels their queerness is their own choice, but it's difficult not to be cynical and think that in the nineties the choice to use 'lesbian' instead of 'bisexual' was largely down to the writers thinking that lesbians were funnier, with more handy stereotypes. Ross pointing out that his ex and her new partner 'have a lot of books on being a lesbian', and Susan's response of 'You have to take an exam. Otherwise, they don't let you do it.' simply wouldn't be as funny if 'lesbian' was replaced with 'bisexual'.

This dumbing down of queer identities is a long-running issue in the history of network television. Some might claim it's just not the best place to look for social change, but television – especially comedy – is a place where positive ideas can get into people's homes and minds. In 1994 *Ellen*, the first sitcom to (eventually, in a few more years) have an out, gay main character, was airing on ABC. The show had actually just changed its name to *Ellen* from *These Friends of Mine* to avoid being mixed up with a popular new NBC sitcom. The sitcoms of the nineties were showing same-sex weddings years before equal marriage was legalised across America. Plenty of jokes and storylines from the sitcoms of the past don't hold up in modern context, but popular entertainment has always been a place to look for positive sea change.

Change was still a way off, though. That homophobia was still present, and on top of that, sitcoms were still strangely segregated in the early nineties. Shows like *Friends, Mad About You* and *Seinfeld* were overwhelmingly white, with *Friends* only featuring one speaking black role across all of those first twenty-four episodes. Not a named character, but one with all of five lines. People of colour were relegated to their own, separate shows on nights less popular with advertisers, despite all that *The Cosby Show* had done to rejuvenate NBC in the eighties. *Fresh Prince of Bel-Air* was over on Monday nights on NBC, and ABC's *Family Matters* aired on Friday nights – another evening considered unimportant to advertisers. It's easy to say that it was just the nature of the nineties, but it becomes harder and harder to brush away as time goes on. Watching anything from that 1994/1995 'Must See' block now, it's possible to assume that a few decades ago New York was populated almost exclusively by white people. Over the next few years, entire networks would start up that aired predominantly black shows for predominantly black audiences. The main 'big four' networks, however, remained distinctly un-diverse for far too long.

There's a lot of aspects of *Friends* that feel aged now. Those live audiences cheering at cameos lead to rapid googling during a modern watch. Why is the audience excited about the stoned restaurateur? Well, it's Jon Lovitz! That guy from *Saturday Night Live* who did those Yellow Pages ads! The fourth episode of *Friends'* first season, 'The One with George Stephanopoulos', relied largely on the audience knowing that Stephanopoulos was famously attractive, as well as being a senior Democratic advisor. The story works without the knowledge, but the obvious missing context is jarring.

Just as it's strange now to look back on a show released thirty years ago and see now-unfamiliar faces, or much younger versions of familiar ones, it's odd to look back and see now-common tropes being built from the ground up. The idea of 'Will they, won't they?' as a series-long story has been done to death. Of course, X & Y will get together, that's how television works. That predictability isn't necessarily a bad thing. The joy of sitcoms can be in the safety and the familiarity – the 'of course'. It was a groundbreaking hook for *Friends* though. In the background of those short stories – a parent visiting, or Thanksgiving going awry – a bigger story was unfolding between these two crazy kids that couldn't quite work it out. Yet.

Of course, in the cliff-hanger finale episode of the first season, it seemed as if the answer was 'they won't'. There had been plenty of false starts including a poker game that managed to be a masterclass in romantic tension, and a brief reunion between Rachel and her ex-fiancé in the twentieth episode – 'The One with the Evil Orthodontist' – the first episode to feature the iconic 'Rachel' haircut. After getting the birth of Ross's son out of the way in the penultimate episode of the season, that last twenty-two minutes featured a now, and possibly even then, familiar mad dash and missed opportunity at the airport. In the follow-up at arrivals, weeks later in the show and minutes later on screen, it seemed as if Rachel was finally ready to make a go of things with Ross – just as he'd moved on to someone new.

With an audience of over thirty-one million people for the season one finale, NBC clearly had a rising star. While Ross and Rachel's future was uncertain, the future of *Friends* looked bright.

Chapter Two

The One with Tom Selleck and Channel 4

The second season of *Friends* had a lot to live up to. After the first season left Rachel waiting at the airport, disappointment on the horizon, the writers had to find their way to answering 'Will they, won't they?' with 'They will, for now.' Alongside that, the season had new dilemmas to tangle and untangle, an audience to maintain, and the chance that among new conflicts there was more than family, romance or living situations holding the six main characters together. Some of the most relatable stories from that second season, especially to a modern audience, are the dramas around work.

Joey, who spent the first season as a struggling actor, got his big break in the second season of *Friends* – cast as Dr Drake Ramoray in the long-running soap opera *Days of our Lives*. *Days* wasn't filmed in New York, but in Burbank, California – just a couple of miles from the *Friends* soundstage at Warner Brothers Studios. The Joey-as-Drake storyline doesn't hold up to much scrutiny – but then, neither do most storylines in a soap opera, so there's at least a meta element to the lack of logic. Dr Drake Ramoray wasn't the first overlap between *Friends* and *Days of our Lives*. Jennifer Aniston's father – John Aniston – began playing Victor Kiriakis on the show in 1985, remaining in the role until he passed away in 2022. The crossover potential between *Friends* and *Days* was never fully realised, but the use of the soap opera managed to recreate something major happening off-set for all of the main cast of *Friends*. In the summer break between seasons, they all enjoyed a sudden increase in celebrity.

The first season's final episode aired on 18 May 1995. The first episode of the second season aired four months later, on 21 September. In that small gap between seasons came a huge increase in press attention.

Towards the end of the first season, the cast appeared on *The Oprah Winfrey Show* – the American equivalent of getting a royal audience. Even Oprah pointed out the lack of diversity on the show, saying, 'I'd like y'all to get a black friend.' In May, as millions watched Rachel clutching flowers at the airport, the cast appeared on that *Rolling Stone* cover. A shift was taking place in the media. Television was no longer the place where stardom remained second-rate. Nothing showed that quite like those six actors, inexplicably dressed in vintage, fifties-style gear, on a magazine cover with a tagline that read 'No Sex, Bad Job, Hit Show, Go Figure'. By the end of 1995 the cast of *Friends* had featured on the covers of, among others, *Vanity Fair*, *People*, and *Entertainment Weekly*. The public loved *Friends*, and now so did the professionals.

Movie stardom still held appeal, of course. In that summer hiatus many of the cast attempted to make the jump to the big screen, with varying levels of success. David Schwimmer's appearance in *The Pallbearer*, starring opposite Gwyneth Paltrow, is almost forgotten now, but the film did well at the time. Courtney Cox's performance as Gale Weathers in *Scream* – Wes Craven's cult 1996 horror movie – was a roaring and timeless success. The film industry was alluring, and the stars of *Friends* would keep returning to it in memorable and forgettable performances, but in 1995 making that leap wasn't necessary. Thanks to *Friends*, the cast had reached the A-List, and they were changing what it meant to be a star.

While the cast were still new to the world of fame, more established stars were 'queueing on the doorstep' to make an appearance on *Friends*, according to a 1995 *Guardian* review. In the second season, the perfect opportunity presented itself to bring in those big names. Over thirty-two million people watched the opening episode of the season, but the viewing figures didn't hit their peak until twelve episodes in, with an hour-long special episode – 'The One After the Superbowl'. NBC had, in previous years, struggled to maintain viewers in the post-game time slot, and in 1996 the network tried to gain an audience with an impressively star-filled episode of *Friends* – one of its most high-profile series. The network was attempting to achieve the highest grossing day of ad revenue in American history – and it did. Almost fifty-three million people tuned in to watch 'The One After the Superbowl', making it the most-watched episode of the entire series, although the finale came close.

High audience numbers obviously don't mean a perfect episode. This hour of television was never going to show off the best that *Friends* could be. David Crane, speaking to the *Hollywood Reporter*, called it the '*Friends* half-time show.' It was a big batch of funny moments and 'oh my god it's...' cameos, written to draw in new viewers. On that, it delivered.

The episode wasn't written with specific guest stars in mind. As always, the plot came first, in this case a main story revolving around Ross and Marcel – his pet monkey from season one – reuniting. Warren Littlefield, still President of Entertainment, was delighted to see the return of the monkey, but the cast and crew weren't as pleased to be reminded of how rough it is working with a live animal. The B-plots were, as with most of *Friends*, a contest in the writer's room to see who could pitch the funniest idea. Co-writer Jeff Astrof threw the idea of Chandler in a toilet stall wearing nothing but women's underwear into the mix, based on an embarrassing personal experience. Julia Roberts ended up being the one to join the cast and prank the luckless Chandler. She was cast after a series of flirtatious faxes between her and Matthew Perry that included the demand 'Write me a paper on quantum physics and I'll do it.' Perry faxed her the paper the very next day. Roberts also sent Perry a 'Why should I go out with you?' questionnaire. The writers banded together to assist Perry in writing his answers, clearly successful as the pair went on to date for some time.

Brooke Shields, Jean-Claude Van Damme and Chris Isaak filled out the list of big names for the episode, although they weren't the only cameos. Comic actors Dan Castanella and Fred Willard both appeared in minor roles as employees at the San Diego Zoo, and Crane and Kauffman both showed up in the background for a short scene.

Brooke Shields wasn't known for comedy before *Friends*, but Warren Littlefield was so taken with her fearlessness playing Joey's obsessive, delusional stalker that he reached out to her representation; she was soon cast on *Suddenly Susan*, a future neighbour of *Friends* in the NBC schedule. Not everyone was so impressed with Shield's abilities on set, however. Her boyfriend at the time, Andre Agassi, attended the shoot and reportedly went into a jealous rage after watching Shields manically licking Matt LeBlanc's fingers in a scene. Michael Lembeck, the director of the episode, gave the cast a break after the incident, and the three leading women rushed in to care for Shields. Talking to the *Hollywood*

Reporter, he remembers 'She [Brooke Shields] did great because of the support of those three.' Even this early in *Friends*, the bonds between the core ensemble were making for a better show.

Jean-Claude Van Damme, on the other hand, was not so well-loved by the cast or the crew. Arriving to set three hours late, ignoring the showrunners and sending a P.A. out for Cocoa Puffs, he didn't make the best first impression. Warren Littlefield wasn't certain who was more difficult to work with, Van Damme or the monkey. While it would be fair to assume that the Hollywood hunk humped fewer legs than his primate co-star, both Jennifer Aniston and Courtney Cox did have to ask Lembeck if Van Damme could use less tongue in their on-screen clinches. Still, as the hero at the centre of the episode's major conceit – an action movie shot in the streets of New York – Van Damme played himself admirably. As the third point of a love triangle with Rachel and Monica, both Van Damme and the story itself fell flat. A storyline about two women competing for the attention of a man was already a tired idea in the mid-nineties. It felt out of character for a show like *Friends* that made the effort to literally put friendship front and centre. Staff writer Alexa Junge even brought the issue to David Crane's attention. While he did ask Junge to spend the shoot pointing out the most problematic moments to him, the love triangle remained.

More professional in his approach to the show was musician Chris Isaak, appearing as a soft-spoken librarian in a rare romantic storyline for Phoebe. The creators of the show were fans of his music and his hit song 'Wicked Game' would go on to play in the planetarium a few episodes later when Ross and Rachel '… You Know'. Isaak may not have been the strongest actor on set, and Lembeck did say to the *Hollywood Reporter* that his scenes with Lisa Kudrow were 'like working with a salmon', but compared to Van Damme he must have seemed like an angel. Early plans to put Isaak in a wig were vetoed on the basis that the creators wanted the audience to react to his initial entrance. Unfortunately, with this being a time before social media, Isaak's face wasn't particularly well known; there was an awkward lack of cheering from the audience when Isaak made his first appearance on set. The side plot around Isaak's cameo involved Phoebe singing hilariously inappropriate songs for children, and thankfully culminated in a sweet duet of 'Smelly Cat' that allowed the singer to show off his vocal skills for the audience.

52.9 million viewers was a staggering number to hit for a sitcom in its second season, and that Superbowl ratings boost for the hour-long special episode gave the creators room to take a risk in the episode before. In the eleventh episode of the season, 'The One with the Lesbian Wedding', there was a chance of controversy. The nuptials of Carol and Susan formed a backdrop to an episode that still kept the main group at the centre. In particular, Ross was given a chance to demonstrate a softer and more mature side in the episode, after a series of events in the Ross-and-Rachel arc that showed him in a harsh light. Talking his ex-wife out of a case of cold feet, before walking her down the aisle to her new bride, was a sweet bit of closure for their prior relationship. Unfortunately, it also put a straight man at the centre of a queer story.

Jane Sibbet, who played Carol, grew up in a religious household. Her father had become more and more conservative as he aged, and by 1996 he was hosting regular Bible study sessions on Thursday nights to avoid his fellow congregates seeing his daughter playing a lesbian on primetime television. Sibbet was far from the only person on set during 'The One with the Lesbian Wedding' to suffer from homophobic family members. Candace Gingrich, half-sibling of Newt Gingrich, flew in on incredibly short notice to appear as the minister. Candace – known for their work in LGBT activism – had just returned home from a trip on behalf of the Coming Out Project when they received the call asking them to appear on the show. They flew to Los Angeles the next day. The choice to cast someone not only known for the work in queer communities, but directly related to Newt Gingrich – the outwardly homophobic Speaker of the House – gave *Friends* a rare chance for some light political commentary.

In a report from *The Spokesman-Review* at the time, David Crane was quoted saying that the goal 'is not just to push America's buttons. I'm not trying to make people comfortable and I'm not trying to make them uncomfortable. I'm trying to make a point.' The point being that gay people have lives, those lives include weddings, and it should not be an issue to show that on television. *Friends* was a sitcom created to be low-concept, a reflection of normal life. With 'The One with the Lesbian Wedding', the show was bringing a queer story under that umbrella. At a time when network standards and practices required the cameras to cut away before the audience could see the brides kiss, *Friends* was making a powerful statement. This was not a queer-friendly time in America.

Within a year of the episode airing, the 'Defence of Marriage Act' – defining marriage legally as being between one man and one woman – was signed into law. Two local affiliate networks, one in Texas and one in Ohio, refused outright to air the episode due to its 'objectionable content'. NBC brought in over a hundred operators for its temporary complaint line, expecting serious backlash after the episode aired. In the end, they received two phone calls. Change was yet to come from higher levels, but clearly plenty of the viewers were unphased.

The *Friends* episode wasn't the first gay wedding to appear in a major network sitcom. Just a month before 'The One with the Lesbian Wedding', the *Roseanne* episode 'December Bride' aired on ABC. In that episode, again, the cameras swung away before the married couple could actually be seen to kiss on network television. In fact, two men wouldn't be seen kissing on a major network until the year 2000.

Roseanne was a big ratings competitor for NBC's comedy shows. It may not have taken the top ratings spot for the 1995/1996 season, but it was steadily taking away viewers from NBC's Tuesday night 'Must See' comedy block. *Roseanne* is a show probably better known now for controversies other than a gay wedding, and the actions of Roseanne Barr, the eponymous star, have cast a long shadow over its history. Not only was the final season of *Roseanne* distinctly unpopular with the show's audience, but a racist tweet from Roseanne Barr in 2018 led to a revival of the show being cancelled by ABC. At the time of *Friends'* second season though, *Roseanne* was just one of the shows competing with NBC.

While NBC prided itself as a network on the slick, the urbane and the New York of it all, ABC had a reputation for shows more in the family-friendly category. In the autumn of 1995, with *Friends* and *Seinfeld* keeping viewers watching NBC, other networks were pushing themselves into unfamiliar territory. Shows like *Roseanne* and *Ellen* were posing a challenge to the high audience figures NBC were pulling in, but they didn't have the same pull with advertising. 1995 also saw the launch of the WB network, although it didn't pose much competition and would struggle to find its feet until it found the teen market. Networks wanted to pull in the advertising dollar, but they had audiences to retain. ABC began to push shows like *Ellen* in an attempt to get that demographic of young, single adults with a disposable income over from NBC. Audiences might have expected specific types of shows from their chosen networks, but as Ted Havert, President of ABC Entertainment, put it to *The New York Times*: 'My sales department wants shows that appeal to adults.'

This fight over advertisers was what created the challenge of the sweeps period, where television markets would be measured to set advertising rates for the following quarter. Networks made plans to keep their schedules looking marketing friendly, delaying the introduction of less valuable family-orientated shows until after the rates had been set. For Tuesday nights, this put NBC favourites like *Wings*, *Mad About You* and *Third Rock from the Sun* up against big draws like *Roseanne*. On Thursdays, however, NBC remained untouchable. In the 1995/1996 season, all of the shows in the 'Must See' line-up were in the Nielsen ratings top ten.

Meanwhile, in the UK, *Friends* was finding a new audience on Channel 4. As one of a selection of American imports to reach British shores, the show received positive reviews alongside a handful of expected comparisons to *Seinfeld*. The BBC kept *Seinfeld* in a late night, weeknight slot, while Channel 4 ran *Friends, Frasier* and ABC's *Ellen* at primetime on Friday nights. *Seinfeld* was the interesting show that had to be looked for, *Friends* was a gaudy hit plastered all over Channel 4's advertising. A *Guardian* review from 1995 called the first season of *Friends* 'cute enough to make you puke', warning potential viewers attracted to the show by Channel 4's 'near-spotless record of success with import sitcoms' that they may not be able to stomach the 'iconic, adorable' characters. Unsurprisingly, for people familiar with the British style of flattery, it was a positive review, recommending that viewers persist with the show and referring to it as the 'smug, slick antithesis of every current UK sitcom'. In the earliest days of *Friends* on Channel 4, the show aired immediately after *Father Ted*, an iconic and irreverent sitcom about Irish priests. If *Father Ted* was the basis for comparison, *Friends* was indeed the antithesis.

By the end of the second season of *Friends*' run in the UK, the show was a hit. The final episode of the season – 'The One with Barry and Mindy's Wedding' – aired on the 22nd of November, 1996. The following week, an hour-long special episode – 'Friends with Gaby' – aired on Channel 4 as David Schwimmer, Matthew Perry and Matt LeBlanc flew in to be interviewed live on television by Gaby Roslin. The men of *Friends* were quietly self-effacing, with Perry chiming in to grab almost all of the funniest moments. They all seemed bemused by their appeal to the British audience, despite the resounding success they were enjoying in America.

Elsewhere on NBC, new shows were riding the coattails of *Friends*, much as *Friends* had with *Seinfeld* the previous year. New sitcom *The Single Guy* aired between *Friends* and *Seinfeld* on Thursday nights. Critics enjoyed it from the first few episodes, and it held its own in the ratings, reaching number six in the Nielsen rankings for the season. The names Max Mutchnik and David Kohan appeared in the credits of *The Single Guy* as writers and producers. The pair would go on to create *Will & Grace* for NBC just a couple of years later. Around the time of *Friends'* second season, alongside their work on *The Single Guy*, they also co-created *Boston Common*, which briefly took that Thursday Night spot from *The Single Guy* in the spring of 1996. *Boston Common*, with its focus on family and a Boston university setting, didn't quite fit with the other Manhattanites of the programming block. The show still reached eighth place in the Nielsen rankings, but it was never destined for greatness, and is probably most notable now for the use of a very young Zach Galifianakis – star of the *Hangover* trilogy and host of the comedy talk show *Between Two Ferns* – in full stoner mode.

The other new NBC show to fill a gap in the Thursday schedule was *Caroline in the City*. Lea Thompson, best known for her role as Lorraine Bains-McFly in the *Back to the Future* trilogy, played the titular Caroline – a cartoonist going through a series of dating struggles. While not officially another *Cheers* spin-off, the show theoretically existed in that same cinematic universe and had multiple cameos from familiar characters, including Frasier Crane. As with the previous years 'Blackout Thursday' event, the New York setting allowed for the different 'Must See' shows to interact, with both Jonathan, the lead in *The Single Guy* and Chandler from *Friends* popping up in *Caroline*'s first season.

Directed largely by James Burrows in its first season, *Caroline in the City* was well-liked by audiences and critics. Some viewers might have been bored by the 'unlucky in love' stories that seemed to be running rampant through new sitcoms but Carole Horst, writing for *Variety*, reassured the potential audience that the 'snappy, smart dialogue and the empathetic characters transcend the old chestnut of a plot'. Scheduled between *Seinfeld* and ratings winner for the season *E.R.*, *Caroline in the City* successfully held on to those 'Must See' viewers and helped retain the female demographic that were tuning in for the medical drama but tuning out of *Seinfeld*. However, even these shows that were hits at the time – smart, well-written ratings draws that they were – didn't have the staying power that kept *Friends* alive, both then and all these years later.

At the core of *Friends*, and a reason it's still so well-liked, are the show's relationships. In 1996, one particular relationship was the answer to some big questions. What to do after 'The One After the Superbowl'? How could *Friends* follow up on the star-crammed success of its most-watched episode? To answer those questions, the show had to answer the question being asked for the previous twenty-eight episodes: will they?

The answer, of course, was that they will. For a bit. The 'they' in question was Ross and Rachel, whose simmering sexual tension had kept viewers hooked during the show's opening overtures. Whether it was necessary to resolve the tension this early was unclear – after all, *Cheers* kept Sam and Dianne fans on the hook for five seasons. It was a question that David Crane and Marta Kauffman were regularly asking themselves. As they put it, in commentary for the second season: 'How do you sustain it without [the studio audience] throwing shoes at the set?' A handful of 'they won't' teases ran through the earlier episodes of the second season. A fantastic first kiss gets spoiled by a pro/con list, handily keeping the pair apart long enough for Rachel's flirtation with Jean-Claude Van Damme. Then, of course, there was Russ. The episode where Rachel dates a Ross doppelgänger was a remarkable demonstration of David Schwimmer's talents. Carefully made up to look just the tiniest bit different, and with a little bit of television magic applied, Schwimmer perfectly played a caricature of himself. Credited only as 'Snaro' for his work as Russ, David Schwimmer insisted for years that the lookalike was a Croatian friend of his. Watching now, it's impossible to believe anyone but Schwimmer could deliver those mid-sentence 'uh's and bouncing head bobs so convincingly, even if Rachel sees Bob Saget first.

So, after the pro/con list, and Russ, and the Super Bowl: the prom video, a fan-favourite episode of *Friends*. James Burrows returned to direct the episode and take charge of one of the most important moments in the overarching story. Early in the episode, Phoebe insists that Ross mustn't give up hope in his so-far futile attempts to win Rachel's affection. Rachel is, according to Phoebe, his lobster. Way before Jordan Peterson was spouting creative crustacean-based theories about the human condition, *Friends* fans had lobsters and their apparent tendency to mate for life to cling to. Sadly, lobsters are generally only monogamous for about two weeks at a time, and neither do they form social hierarchies similar to those of humans. However, if misunderstandings about the nature of lobsters is the only thing that *Friends* fans and Jordan Peterson fans have in common, that might explain something of the show's success.

As 'The One with the Prom Video' continued, a B-plot revolving around Monica getting a cat provided a way to shoehorn in an old home video. While the episode is understandably cherished among viewers for getting Ross and Rachel together, it unfortunately also ushered in a new and less pleasant running gag for the show – Fat Monica. It would be lovely to think that a nineties sitcom encouraging the audience to point and laugh at a fat person is an artefact of its time, and that it wouldn't happen today. Sadly, that's not the case. More recently, fat suits have been used in sitcoms, such as Fox's *New Girl*, and bigger blockbusters like Marvel's *Avengers*: *Endgame*, as a cheap punchline. Large bodies – whether real or applied by costume and makeup teams – being played for laughs is nothing new, and the joke certainly feels old. Among the other changes made to the eighties' versions of the characters was an impressive false nose worn by Jennifer Aniston, hinting at a nose job in Rachel's past. Alexa Junge, the main writer on the episode, chose to add the detail to give some realness to the good-looking cast's past. This might have been the reason David Schwimmer was sporting an afro wig and moustache that the actor felt made him look like Gabe Kaplan in *Welcome Back, Kotter*; a comparison that eventually made it into the episode's script. One detail that didn't make the final cut was a plan to show an old episode of *All My Children* in the background featuring Gunther as Bryce – a character detail that would be revealed a few episodes later.

In the home movie, Elliot Gould and Christina Pickles made another appearance as the senior Gellers, fulfilling a pre-first season obligation of the *Friends* creators. In the show's earliest days of production, the executives at NBC were concerned that the ensemble of the show was slightly too young, and wanted an older character added to the gang to add some maturity to the show. 'Pat the Cop' lurked around Central Perk and the edges of the early scripts for a while, before Crane and Kauffman begged NBC to reconsider with the promise of regular older guest stars.

Paying off that promise were Gould and Pickles, as well Marlo Thomas and Ron Liebman as Rachel's parents, fulfilling the promise of older characters until it was clear the core six could stand on their own.

The ability *Friends* had to jump from emotional beat to emotional beat by way of big laughs was central to the last few minutes of 'The One with the Prom Video'. Between the nose, the afro and the rustling of polyester prom dresses, a quiet plot twist emerged as the audience got to see the extent of Ross's long-running crush on Rachel. As the gang watches on in the show's present day, the adult Ross slinks to the back of the room as an unwilling participant while in the video a teenage Rachel cries over her lack of prom date. As the younger Ross, in the video, hastily dons a tuxedo only to find himself unneeded at the last minute, an adult Rachel slowly absorbs the depth of his feelings for her. Finally, the audience got what they'd been waiting for. Not the first dramatic kiss in the rain, with all of the problems still swirling around the couple, but a real 'They will'; a resolution of the show's simmering tension to date. The audience cheers, Phoebe proudly reaffirms that 'He's her lobster!' and it seems that the matter of Ross and Rachel is thoroughly settled. At that point, the second season of *Friends* still had ten episodes to go.

While *Friends* was always supposed to be a true ensemble show, Ross and Rachel's underlying romance had provided the bulk of the wider story running through the episodes up to that point. There was a risk, in resolving the relationship before the finale, that the rest of the season might flounder and stagnate without that conflict to hang the comedy on. It was a risk worth taking, however, allowing the rest of the group more time to shine. While Ross and Rachel's storylines shifted from unresolved tension to the troubles of a fledgling relationship – including that romantic planetarium date that the creators had envisioned many months before it ever reached the screen – the rest of the cast stepped to the forefront.

In the second half of the season, the pseudo-romantic relationship between Joey and Chandler played out in a story akin to a break-up, allowing Adam Goldberg to enter for a few episodes as Chandler's temporary roommate, Eddie. The framing of Joey and Chandler's conflicts as fights often overheard between couples – a parting of the ways brought about by an argument about a spoon – explains a lot about the pairing. David Crane used the relationship to gently mock the emotional immaturity present in friendships between heterosexual men, while sneaking in some quietly queer tropes. It worked, delivering genuine emotional moments during the couple's separation, including a 'looking sadly out at the rain' montage set to 'All By Myself' by Eric Carmen; a parody of an earlier scene between Ross and Rachel.

Immediately after the prom video, Tom Selleck joined the cast for the rest of *Friends'* second season in a recurring guest role that would eventually net him an Emmy nomination for 'Outstanding Guest Actor in a Comedy Series'. Your mileage may vary on the gross-factor of Monica's relationship with man old enough to be, and friends with, her father. Selleck, however, had the charisma to get away with it. Best known for his work on *Magnum PI*, he commanded the screen admirably as Dr Richard Burke. After a string of fruitless attempts, Monica was finally able to keep a boyfriend for longer than a single episode. Here was the older cast member the network had wanted in those early days, only appearing after it had been made clear there was no need for one. Richard, however, slotted swiftly into the ensemble comedy. His presence on the show led to an episode that exemplified the complicated relationship the *Friends* writers had with NBC's standards division.

The episode in question wasn't called 'The One with the Condom Conflict', but imagine a world where it could have been. A refreshing aspect of *Friends* was that the women were allowed to be as sexual as the men, and the show rarely judged them for it. In this episode, 'The One Where Dr Ramoray Dies', Monica's history with men became the topic of coffee house conversation, eventually leading to the current *Friends* couples – Monica and Richard, and Ross and Rachel – discussing the number of people they'd slept with. The scene of the episode that raised the most eyebrows is possibly one of the most blatantly sexual of the season outside of 'The One Where Ross and Rachel … You Know'. Rachel and Monica, fresh off the emotional highs of romantic moments with their respective partners, meet in the apartment's shared bathroom to rummage in the drawer and argue over who gets to claim the last … something. While David Schwimmer and Tom Selleck share an awkward moment in the living room, the women in the bathroom struggle with an argument that – according to Standards and Practices – couldn't contain the word 'condom'. The conversation could be shown, but naming the item or even showing an empty wrapper on a bedside table was a step too far.

David Crane would take his weekly calls from the network's standards division in the writer's room; letting the writers in on exactly what they could and couldn't get into the script. It must have been frustrating for the creators to have to negotiate every last 'penis' and 'breast', especially after working at HBO. While *Seinfeld*, in its slightly later time slot, was able to devote an entire episode to the subject of masturbation, admittedly without saying the word, *Friends* writers had to dance around prophylactics. Even when airing in a later time slot, *Friends* was held to a stricter standard than other NBC comedies, with the network pointing to the younger demographic watching the show as the main reason. The writers rose to the challenge admirably, though. The Ross and Rachel 'juice box' moment earned roars of laughter from the studio audience. In episodes like 'The One Where Dr Ramoray Dies', *Friends* managed to develop a careful winking and nudging humour towards the sex lives of the characters, almost quaint on a modern watch.

Nothing dates a show quite like the technology on display, and *Friends* had a few moments that set in firmly in the nineties. Late in the second season Chandler – arguably the most tech-savvy of the group – dramatically announces the stats of his new personal computer. It boasted an impressive 12mb of RAM and a 500mb hard drive; a tiny fraction of the processing power available today. Not only does the new technology in the show serve as the delivery mechanism for that infamous pro/con list, and provide the opportunity for a joke about playing *Doom* (a video game that, famously, can now be run on a microwave, a thermostat and – with a bit of work – a pregnancy test), it also provided Chandler the opportunity to experience some romantic conflict.

In the wild years before Tinder there were chat rooms, for those with a dial-up connection, and there Chandler found himself taking virtual tours of the Guggenheim Museum and chatting in an invented, private shorthand with a woman whose name he didn't know. Throughout the course of the season finale, Matthew Perry leapt brilliantly from playing a man in the giddy throes of a new relationship to a man in conflict without ever moving from his computer. The final revelation – that the married woman he's been chatting with but has never met is in fact his ex-girlfriend Janice – demonstrated what the season did so well. Here Maggie Wheeler, previously a laugh-a-minute distraction in her earlier appearances, got to be the focal point in the final emotional beat of the season. Her 'Oh My God', usually screeched, is instead a quiet and emotional moment before a resounding kiss. Where the first season of *Friends* ended with a cliff-hanger centered on a relationship that the audience had had twenty-four episodes to emotionally invest in, this second season ended with a conflict built up in a single episode.

Almost thirty million people tuned in to watch the final episode of the season and see the characters set up on the chess board for what was to come. There was seemingly no drama left between Ross and Rachel. Jennifer Aniston instead got to portray Rachel's final moments of catharsis after running out on her wedding to kick off the pilot, with a teary and defiant performance of Barry Manilow's 'Copacabana'. Meanwhile, Monica and Richard's relationship ended quietly, without fighting, as the age gap rendered them incompatible. There was enough at the end of the season to be talked about at office water coolers, but the second season finale of *Friends* didn't need the big drama of the first. There was no dash to the airport, and not much of a question mark hanging over the characters. There was absolutely no question mark over the show's future. *Friends* was officially a 'Must See'.

Chapter Three

The One with Bigger Stories

Part of the joy of sitcoms is in watching a story play out in a short space of time. An episode opens, there's a laugh before the credits, conflict is introduced and by the end of the episode most of the stories are neatly tied up. The sign of a particularly good sitcom is the wider story being told, a narrative being carried over the twenty or so episodes of a season while keeping those neater, shorter stories intact. The individual episodes make the audience laugh. The broader stories can keep them coming back.

The third season of *Friends* had the writers building bigger and bigger stories in the background of single, clever episodes. Those episodes don't sit apart from the larger stories, but enhance them as they set up plots further down the line. With at least three more seasons of the show guaranteed thanks to negotiations with the network, the creators of *Friends* were ready to take risks and occasionally introduce wilder ideas into their once low-concept show. There were real highlights early in the third season of *Friends*. In the sixth episode, the character of Janice was still in the forefront. With an expanded role for the first few episodes of the season, Maggie Wheeler got to do more than just spout catchphrases. Unfortunately, while a question from Janice sparked one of the most interesting episodes, she's removed from the rest of the story. Literally sitting front and centre on the Central Perk sofa, Janice proposes a question to the rest of the group: 'Who of the six of you has slept with the six of you?', before modifying it to an 'almost'. The question leads to a single flashback episode – a twenty-minute prequel to the show. It's an episode that today would almost certainly involve a younger cast and exist as a back-door pilot for a possible spin-off. On *Friends*, it was an opportunity to play with chemistry.

Set a year before the pilot episode, 'The One with the Flashback' played with new pairings for the core group. The episode raises a few questions about the timeline of the show, with Phoebe moving out of Monica's apartment and Joey moving into Chandler's, but this was before the days of Twitter threads highlighting continuity errors. It might not make sense for the already well-worn Central Perk to have been a bar only a year before the pilot episode, but it works as a setting; the friends holding beer bottles and pool cues instead of cappuccinos. Jennifer Aniston got to briefly morph back into the earlier version of Rachel as a newly engaged, spoiled, rich girl, and played an unexpected lust for Chandler – at this point a stranger in a bar – hilariously straight. They were the least believable couple of the episode but it was a solid reminder of how far Rachel had come on the show.

Meanwhile, the audience got to see the death throes of Ross and Carol's marriage – although entirely from Ross's perspective. Late in the episode, David Schwimmer resurrects his morose line delivery from the opening scenes of the *Friends* pilot as Ross tells Phoebe that 'Carol's a lesbian'. Phoebe's efforts to comfort Ross led to the two of them intertwined on a pool table, almost doing the deed before the rest of the group interrupts. An important character detail was getting set up there for Ross – he's capable of moving on quickly after heartbreak.

Monica and Joey feel like a weird pairing now with the context of all ten seasons of *Friends*, but in the flashback the sexual tension between them as relative strangers worked. What starts as a sweet flirtation is swiftly ruined by Joey as he rapidly strips down in response to an offer of iced tea. It's just a few minutes in the episode, but originally Monica and Joey were envisioned as a longer arc. In the early days of the show's conception, the creators planned a long-running romance between the two characters, Joey's playboy habits eventually being tempered by Monica's good nature. After noticing Jennifer Aniston and David Schwimmer's natural chemistry on set together, Crane and Kauffman set the Monica and Joey relationship to one side, only to briefly resurrect it here.

The flashback episode was a playground for the writers. With the relationship between Rachel and Ross settled, for now, it was worth seeing what other chemistry could be uncovered in the group. It made sense that, in a group of six people that attractive, other romances could flare up. The most emotional moment of the flashback episode, however, was the furthest away from sex. Chandler comforting (an admittedly towel-clad) Monica as she worries about a lonely future, was the moment of the episode least played for laughs, and the most palpable emotion of the episode, even with no plans yet in place to bring the two together.

Before the flashback episode there was 'The One Where No One's Ready', the second episode of the season. It was another chance for the writers to play with a change in the usual format, this time with a bottle episode taking place in real time. Bottle episodes, in which the action doesn't leave a single set, were fairly common in multi-cam sitcoms. It was an economical way to film, saving budgets for bigger episodes down the line, and on *Friends* episodes with just the main six actors confined to one place, it gave the cast room to work without the noise of background extras or guest stars. 'The One Where No One's Ready' was the only episode of *Friends* to take place in real-time, with Ross counting down the minutes left before a big event.

Just as the writers used the flashback episode to explore potential relationships in the group, the real-time episode was a chance to play with new arguments. The time ticks away as a distracted Monica, still reeling from the end of her break-up with Richard, panics over a voicemail while fights break out among the rest of the group. Ross and Rachel wind each other up almost to breaking point, reaching a sweet conclusion but demonstrating that not everything was perfect for the pair. Meanwhile, Chandler and Joey's fight over an armchair led to an iconic moment for the show – and an injury for Matt LeBlanc. A stunt gone wrong led to LeBlanc dislocating his shoulder, and he had to wear a sling for the following episodes; explained away by a bed-jumping incident. The accident led to filming being paused while he took some time to recover, and the rest of the episode couldn't be shot until he no longer needed the sling. What was meant to be one of the cheapest episodes of the season, and the easiest to film, ended up being one of the most expensive and awkward.

The rest of the fight between Chandler and Joey involved Leblanc making a stunning entrance, apparently dressed in all of the clothes that Chandler owns. The costume designers put a lot of work in for the episode, carefully constructing a giant clothing suit that LeBlanc could quickly put on without interrupting the flow of the real-time episode. The famous 'Could I *be* wearing any more clothes?' question played on an inflection that became Chandler's trademark, despite Matthew Perry avoiding using it as much as possible. The follow-up remark about 'going commando' was new to Crane and Kauffman, but stayed in the script after the rest of the writers insisted that the general public would catch their drift. It's a common saying now but at the time some news outlets assumed that the writers of the show had, in fact, coined a new phrase. The Oxford English Dictionary even credits *Friends* with one of the earliest uses of the term.

'The One Where No One's Ready' received mixed reviews. While bottle episodes would become a regular part of the show, with Kevin Bright asserting that they were some of the best in the series, the real-time concept was never repeated. The episode is remembered as a stand-out from the show now, but at the time it drew heat from critics for using a similar idea to *Seinfeld*'s famous 1992 episode 'The Chinese Restaurant'. A review in the *Guardian* called 'The One Where No One's Ready' a 'shameful Xerox of *Seinfeld*'s masterful Chinese Restaurant episode'. With Monica and George Constanza's respective storylines for the two episodes, a dangling phone cord connected them beyond their similar concepts. Five years separated the air dates, but clearly that wasn't long enough for *Seinfeld* to have left the critic's minds.

In 1996, as the third season of *Friends* began, *Seinfeld* was at the start of what would turn out to be its penultimate season. With Larry David no longer attached and Jerry Seinfeld now running the show solo, *Seinfeld* began to lean more and more towards the absurd. The *New York Times* pointed out that 'this season seems determined to stretch the boundaries of "Seinfeld" lunacy'. The stand-up scenes that previously opened and closed each episode were no longer a part of the show. With Seinfeld now running things on his own, he no longer had the time to write the extra material needed. It hadn't been confirmed yet, but it certainly looked like this ratings leader might be coming to a close. NBC needed *Friends* more than ever to keep Thursday nights a 'Must See'.

Originally, the six actors that made up the *Friends* cast signed on with five-year contracts. In 1996, David Schwimmer was the first of the group to be approached about re-upping his contract, sparking a summer-long salary dispute between the cast, the network and Warner Brothers – the studio that produced the show. For the first season, the actors earned $22,500 per episode. For the second season, that figure was bumped up to $40,000, around $75,000 in today's money. It was a vast amount, but for comparison the *Seinfeld* stars were earning around $150,000 per episode. It was expected that Schwimmer – a man not only raised by a successful divorce lawyer who was more than willing to give out negotiating advice, but also someone who had previously founded an equal-share theatre collective – would ask for a pay rise, but not that he would make an effort to make sure all of his castmates were being paid equally.

Friends was an ensemble show with all six cast members doing an equal share of the work, and they negotiated accordingly. Their initial demand was $100,000 per episode, more than double their current salary. It was a big ask, and Warner Brothers weren't known for giving in to what they saw as excessive contract demands. The cast remained determined, however, especially after executives were caught boasting about the incredible profits expected from the sales of *Friends'* syndication rights. The show was expected to fetch more than $4 million an episode, a figure that would make it one of the most profitable shows in history. Media outlets were getting hold of the notion that all wasn't well with the contract negotiations, and rumours spread that the cast were acting under the leadership of a particularly upset David Schwimmer, who was possibly threatening to leave the show. The actors thoroughly denied that there was any ringleader, or that any of them would be walking away after their fifth year. Matthew Perry, speaking to *Entertainment Weekly* early the following year, claimed 'it was amiable every step of the way', pointing out 'you'd have to be a moron to leave the show'.

Production began on the third season of *Friends* with contracts for the future still unsigned, although a studio executive told the *New York Times* that 'Everything is very close', just a week before the season began airing. After a final five-hour bargaining session that ran late into the night, the group walked away with a new four-year deal. An initial bump to $75,000 per episode took place for the third season, with additional increases planned up to $125,000 per episode – or $236,000 in today's money – for season six. The actors knew their worth and argued accordingly, and in return NBC had another four years of *Friends*, guaranteed to prop up the Thursday night line-up.

Across the evenings, NBC continued to shuffle schedules based on lead-ins and ad revenue during the 1996/1997 season. With *Friends* and *Seinfeld* holding up Thursdays, and a similar Tuesday night schedule tent-poled by *Frasier* and *Mad About You*, at least two nights were set up to boost the ratings on newer shows. *Caroline in the City* moved to Tuesdays for the season, but couldn't quite hold on to the audiences Emmy-winning *Frasier* was pulling in. Other shows, including

NewsRadio and *Just Shoot Me!* aired on the Tuesday night line-up, but nothing new managed impressive numbers in the secondary 'Must See' slot.

One of NBC's biggest decisions was moving *3rd Rock from the Sun*, now in its second year and loved by critics, to Sunday nights in an attempt to compete with strong offerings from other networks. Animated sitcoms were on the rise, with Fox airing *The Simpsons* and *King of the Hill* on Sundays, and elsewhere genre programming dominated on the weekends. CBS's *Touched by an Angel* was consistently in the ratings top ten, ABC had *Lois & Clark* long before superhero stories were everywhere, and Fox was holding on to 9 pm viewers with *The X-Files*. While *3rd Rock* remained popular – and is now something of a cult classic – it never managed to bring in audiences that compared to NBC's weekday primetime slots, and failed to boost the ratings of the shows surrounding it.

On other networks, the sitcom ratings battle continued. There were high hopes at ABC for new series *Spin City* to claim a high spot in the season's rankings. On Tuesday nights, ABC posed the biggest competition to NBC's secondary 'Must See' line-up. *Home Improvement*, the long-running Tim Allen show that was a big part of ABC's family-friendly reputation, held onto audiences that might otherwise have turned to *Frasier* in the same time slot. *Mad About You*, airing against the final season of *Roseanne* on ABC, was still pulling in viewers. While *Roseanne* had been an impressive ratings pull in previous years, the lottery win storyline that formed much of the final season proved unpopular with audiences, who felt the show had departed too far from its blue-collar, working-class roots. *Roseanne* ended the season on a sour note, low in the ratings. It was the 9.30 pm slot on Tuesday that saw ABC's hopes realised. While *Caroline in the City* was failing to retain *Frasier* viewers on NBC, ratings were high at ABC for *Spin City*.

The new sitcom was the first show created by Bill Lawrence. Although *Spin City* was still filmed in the same multi-camera format as most sitcoms, it was a departure from ABC's family-friendly slate. The show took place in a fictionalised version of the New York City mayor's office, and starred Michael J. Fox as the Deputy Mayor Mike Flaherty – a master of political spin. ABC needed a hit with advertisers as well as audiences, and *Spin City* delivered. The show was well-received, and lauded for the producer's decision to shoot in Manhattan rather than recreating New York City on the West Coast. A fresh stable of New York actors, trained on stage more than screen, helped the show stand out against the likes of NBC city sitcoms filmed in L.A. One star of the show, Michael Boatman, played a groundbreaking character for the time: Carter Haywood, a gay black man in charge of 'minority affairs'. Queerness remained a rarity on primetime television, and a queer person of colour whose storyline didn't involve a painful coming-out arc was even rarer. ABC was still better known as the family network, but it was beginning to take risks.

Wednesday nights became another battleground as the new season geared up. For NBC, in another attempt to spread out their comedy programming, the final season of *Wings* propped up the evening. On CBS *The Nanny*, starring Queens queen Fran Drescher, was there to pull in viewers. On ABC, the big draw was *Ellen*. The show, starring and sometimes written by Ellen DeGeneres, had slowly been slipping down the ratings. Producers were frustrated with the titular character showing little to no interest in the trophy dating storylines that populated most sitcoms at the time. In the summer of 1996, with the show about to enter its fourth season, Ellen DeGeneres and the other writers on the show opened negotiations with ABC and its parent company Disney. The creators of the show wanted the main character, Ellen Morgan, to come out of the closet. Before the negotiations started, Disney boss Michael Eisner had suggested that the character should get a puppy, as she showed no interest in dating. The eventual coming-out episode retained the title 'The Puppy Episode' in an attempt to keep rumours from spreading about the contents. Word of the negotiations leaked, however, and by September 1996, as the season was starting, speculation was rife about whether the character or her namesake actor would come out as a lesbian. It wasn't until March the following year that the 'Puppy Episode' script officially got the go-ahead. There was a media frenzy, with Ellen DeGeneres coming out before her character, appearing on the front cover of *Time* magazine with the headline 'Yep, I'm Gay'.

The episode aired on 30 April, 1997. By this point the show had generated enormous amounts of publicity. Right-wing organisations pressured ABC to drop the storyline and even succeeded in convincing some advertisers not to buy time during the episode. Meanwhile GLAAD – The Gay and Lesbian Alliance Against Defamation – organised 'Come Out with Ellen' house parties across the United States.

The LGBTQ advocacy group HRC (The Human Rights Campaign) sent out around 3,000 'Ellen Coming Out House Party' kits that included posters and an *Ellen* trivia game. *Friends* might have broken some queer ground a year earlier in 'The One with the Lesbian Wedding', but an out, queer lead character on a primetime sitcom was something else entirely.

In the UK, almost a year later, 'The Puppy Episode' aired on Channel 4. The British channel was under far less right-wing pressure than its American counterparts, and aired the episode as part of a night of celebration. The channel dedicated an entire evening to LGBTQ-based programming and Ellen DeGeneres flew in to join 'The Party' – a televised celebration for DeGeneres and her family hosted by Graham Norton that aired after the episode itself. DeGeneres herself spoke at the GLAAD awards the following year about being deeply moved by the inclusive efforts of the UK. It stood in stark contrast to ABC who, for *Ellen*'s following season, prefaced every episode with a parental advisory warning. 'The Puppy Episode' was the highest rated episode of *Ellen*'s entire run, watched by around forty-two million viewers on the night it aired.

On Channel 4, although the 'coming out' night was a huge celebration, *Ellen* was never quite able to reach the viewers that *Friends* could. In 1997, as its third season aired, *Friends* was the third most-watched show on Channel 4, with an audience of six million viewers. The only other US sitcom to make it into Channel 4's top twenty that year was *Roseanne*, with 3.8 million viewers. *Friends* was so popular that when Channel 4 opened up a public vote and allowed viewers to create their own schedule – airing the resulting shows on 27 December – *Friends* won the American comedy slot, beating *Cheers*, *Frasier* and *Roseanne*. While *Friends* was a successful export to the UK, English television coming to the states was another matter entirely.

Although American sitcom imports made up a large proportion of British primetime programming, the same couldn't be said for the reverse. The tendency of most British sitcoms to last for short, often only six episode, runs just didn't work with the scheduling styles of American networks. The American television season ran for nine months, requiring shows to produce at least twenty episodes a year (if they weren't abruptly cancelled). This difference in comedy styles and season lengths hinged on numbers.

In the States, sitcom writing was a communal affair, described by *Friends* writer Greg Malins as a group of people sitting around a table, throwing things in. With *Friends* releasing twenty-four episodes a year, the only way to keep the quality consistent was to have a large group of people working on the season. In contrast, British writers tended to work in a much more solitary way, crafting shorter series. British sitcoms that are now considered iconic often had incredibly short runs; *Fawlty Towers* ran for only twelve episodes total across two seasons. British writers tended to leave a party before it lost its sparkle.

There was also a big financial difference, with far fewer well-paid opportunities for British writers. The Writer's Guild of America's most recent strike actions have been, in part, triggered by American writers not wanting to work in a system similar to the British. Adam Chase, another *Friends* writer, pointed out to the *Guardian* in a 1997 interview that 'No way would Jennifer Saunders have stopped writing *Absolutely Fabulous* if British shows got the obscene amounts of money US shows do.' The writers interviewed for that *Guardian* piece pointed out that famous British shows like *Fawlty Towers* and *Ab Fab* are art, whereas for them, television was 'sitting around thinking up jokes and getting paid lots of money'.

In place of direct British imports, American networks went down the remake route. On CBS, *Cosby* began airing in the 1996 season. Along with *Cybill*, a still relatively new show created by Chuck Lorre – who would go on to become a sitcom heavyweight – *Cosby* was an essential tool for CBS in the sitcom ratings fight. This was a time when Bill Cosby was remembered for revitalising NBC's fortunes with *The Cosby Show*, and not for his despicable actions. *Cosby* itself was largely known for being a reworking of the popular British sitcom *One Foot in the Grave*. As with many American adaptations, the tone of the show was significantly lighter than its dark-humoured British counterpart.

On NBC, *Men Behaving Badly* – another remake of a British sitcom – began airing on the Wednesday comedy line-up, eventually moving to follow *Friends* on Thursday nights by the end of the season. Despite taking up some of the most sought-after space in the schedule, the show failed to impress audiences and failed to reach even the top thirty most-watched shows of the season. It was a particular embarrassment for NBC, whose Thursday night line-up the previous year had all been hits. *Men Behaving Badly* was an attempt to bring some of the grime of British sitcoms to American screens. Starring Rob Schneider as Jamie, the American answer to Harry Enfield's Dermot, the show's early episodes had pretty good reviews, with the *New York Times* pointing out that the show 'offers vicarious thrills for everyone'. *Men Behaving Badly* rapidly went downhill, however. The other lead actors, Ron Eldard and Justine Bateman, both elected to leave after the first season. Their representatives told the press that the men simply weren't behaving badly enough. They'd both hoped the show would be more like the 'outrageously crude' series it was based on. The issue with *Men Behaving Badly* wasn't that American audiences couldn't cope with the filth, but that the networks weren't confident enough to deliver it. A familiar name cropped up regularly in the *Men Behaving Badly* credits. James Burrows directed over half of *Men Behaving Badly*'s first season. That same year, he would also return to the *Friends* stage to direct one of the show's most important moments.

Friends had often been criticised for inconsistencies throughout its ten seasons. Ages don't always add up. Characters sometimes meet in flashbacks and then get introduced as strangers years later in the chronology. And sometimes, but not always, there was a wooden post and beam separating the living room and kitchen of Monica's apartment. That last detail belonged almost entirely to James Burrows. Burrows had stepped back from *Friends* after directing the majority of the first season episodes, but the door was left open and he returned for plenty of important episodes. Almost every time he returned; the pillar came with him. This detail of the apartment was put to one side after the first season as it blocked certain camera angles and created awkward shadows. However, Burrows would insist on its return, preferring the added detail in his shots. This did, however, give the makers of the show an excuse to grab the pillar out of storage whenever it might come in handy for a story, or just a joke, like in the episode 'The One with the Giant Poking Device', where Ross eventually runs into the beam. It's an important episode for a few reasons. The return of the 'Burrows Beam' isn't all that notable, but the episode marks the last appearance of that season for Ross's son, Ben. It's often a problem for sitcoms not centered around family life to have a child character without changing the nature of the show. *Friends*, like many sitcoms of the time, dealt with this by simply pretending Ross's child didn't exist for large portions of the show, unfortunately pushing Carol and Susan out to the sidelines as a result.

The main plot of 'The One with the Giant Poking Device' concluded a story that began with the unexpected appearance of Janice in the second season finale. For the first seven episodes of the third season, the relationship between Chandler and Janice ran smoothly. Eight episodes in, the relationship ended with the reveal that Janice was still in love with her ex-husband. Up to this point in the show, Chandler's role had largely been to interrupt a scene with a sarcastic comment. In 'The One with the Giant Poking Device', the audience gets to see him nakedly emotional, wrestling with memories of his parents' divorce and begging his girlfriend not to leave. Throughout the first two seasons of the show, there was a bit of a divide in the characters. Ross, Rachel and Monica got the opportunity for drama and romance, but Chandler, Joey and Phoebe were relegated to being the funny ones on the sidelines. In the third season of *Friends*, all of the characters got the chance to play serious.

Later in the third season, Matt LeBlanc got his turn as Joey fell in love with his co-star Kate, played by Dina Meyer. Their four-episode arc played out as one of the many mid-length stories carried through the season. LeBlanc got to show Joey's softer, more romantic side as the character delightedly learns he's experienced 'The Night' – an evening of communication that opened up his eyes to a whole new world of relationships. It was a story cut short as the woman Joey shares 'The Night' with almost immediately moves across the country. The status quo was rapidly reset as Joey reverted back to type, but *Friends* had shown a whole new side to the character.

Elsewhere in the season, Lisa Kudrow got the chance to show her serious side as Phoebe's brother, Frank Jr, returned to the show. Phoebe's tragic backstory was played as a joke in previous seasons, but got some real weight here as a new relationship formed for the loneliest member of the group. There was a real reckoning moment for Phoebe, who often came across as callous, when she attempted to end the relationship between her brother and his fiancée Alice, played by Debra Jo Rupp. Kudrow adopted the newly protective big sister role seamlessly into Phoebe's character in 'The One with the Hypnosis Tape', with Phoebe eventually bringing the couple back together. Phoebe's newfound need for family life built, in the final episode of the season, towards what could have been a bigger story as she finally got to meet her birth mother. Comedy heavyweight Teri Garr played the older Phoebe in a perfect imitation of the younger character. There was room there for a much longer and more interesting story arc for Phoebe, but casting such a big name in the role of her mother unfortunately pushed the plot to the edges.

The biggest relationship, and biggest story, of *Friends'* third season was Ross and Rachel. The writers of *Friends* knew from when they first brought the couple together that the relationship would eventually have to come to an end. Ross and Rachel as a couple was emotionally satisfying for the audience, but stalled the momentum of the show. Without the tension between them, what else was there to look forward to?

The seeds of doubt were sown into the relationship early on, with Ross repeatedly getting jealous over Rachel's past, but it was in the third season that things came to a head. It began with Rachel, speed-running the parts of adult life she missed as a trophy fiancée, stepping away from serving coffee and making a career change. With the help of the handsome Mark – played by Steven Eckholdt – Rachel landed a job at Bloomingdales and began her dream fashion career. The show was making it clear by this point that Ross wasn't a great boyfriend. His jealous tendencies came to the surface, but there was still room for the audience to sympathise with the character as he opened up about the fear of another relationship ending in the same way as his marriage. It was almost enough to justify his actions, but underneath the jealousy there were levels of possessiveness and a sense of superiority that spelled the beginning of the end for the pair. Ross refuses to take his girlfriend's fashion aspirations seriously. Where before Rachel was 'just a waitress', now her work is 'just a job'. When fighting over whose career is more important, Ross points out that blockbusters like *Jurassic Park* are based on his area of expertise, and the fashion industry hadn't inspired anything on that scale. Perhaps Ross would have been more understanding of Rachel's fashion aspirations after *The Devil Wears Prada* hit the big screen. In the fifteenth episode of the season, 'The One Where Ross and Rachel take a Break', Ross's inability to take Rachel seriously built to an exhausting scene. As Rachel works late, Ross appears at her workplace with a picnic basket, ignoring her repeated requests for him to leave and taking up space where he's not just superfluous but a real irritant, and causes deep feelings of second-hand embarrassment for the audience. It was the catalyst for the real fight later in the episode, in which Rachel suggests taking a break.

While the conflict between Ross and Rachel simmered through the first half of the season, another key character was slowly being built up in the background. From the very first episode of the season, both Joey and Chandler began referring to the 'hot Xerox girl'. As the tension between Ross and Rachel built up, so did mentions of the girl at the copy place with the belly button piercing. Finally, in 'The One Where Ross and Rachel Take a Break', the audience got to meet Chloe. An early manic pixie dream girl, Chloe invites Joey and Chandler out for the night, leading to an educational conversation between the two about threesome etiquette. It's after Rachel suggests taking a break that Ross finds his friends out with Chloe, who's apparently been harbouring a crush on the 'dinosaur guy'. There's a callback near the end of the episode to the previous season's big Ross and Rachel fight as Ross dances with Chloe to U2's 'With or Without You' – the same song Ross requests on the radio after Rachel sees the pro/con list. The episode ended on a rare 'To be continued … ' and over 28 million viewers tuned in the following week to see the resolution.

Both 'The One Where Ross and Rachel Take a Break' and the continuation – 'The One with the Morning After' – saw James Burrows return to *Friends*. The latter episode contains one of *Friends* most iconic quotes: Ross justifying his actions with 'We were on a break!' The outburst became a regular punchline for the show further down the line, but initially it was shouted during one of the most emotionally raw episodes *Friends* had done up to this point. While there were some laughs in the opening scenes as Ross tries to keep Rachel from finding out about his night with Chloe, they were undercut by the fact that even if the relationship could survive, it wouldn't be on an honest foundation. As it is, Ross fails and the laughs stop as the pair talk things through, while the rest of the group serve as a proxy for the viewers. Trapped in Monica's bedroom and forced to eavesdrop on their friends' break up, the characters channel the audience's fears. Phoebe asks 'They're going to make it through this, aren't they?', just as viewers at home might. Chandler's answer of 'c'mon, it's Ross and Rachel', is a brief reassurance. Surely, nothing could split the lobsters up for good. It was a short-lived hope for the audiences as the relationship came to an end. The final one-two punch of dialogue, Ross's 'this can't be it', and Rachel's 'then how come it is?' closed the episode as the actors stood frozen with nothing left to say. It was a visceral, heart-wrenching scene, especially for a sitcom. Being this raw and emotional on a comedy show wasn't popular in the mid-nineties. The fallout of the break-up lingered through the rest of the series as the group dynamics rearranged around Ross and Rachel.

As with the previous season, Ross and Rachel changing their relationship status led to bigger stories for the rest of the group. Alongside Phoebe's family revelations and Joey's pining, Monica got to flourish in a new relationship while struggling with a career low. While working her unhappy diner job, dressed in a cheap wig and padded bra, Monica meets Pete Becker, a fictional tech-millionaire. In 1997, the writers were drawing inspiration from Bill Gates, but now Pete feels like a harbinger of Elon Musks to come. It was difficult to cast the role, needing someone handsome enough for the audience to root for, but not so stunning that viewers wouldn't understand why Monica rejects him. Jon Favreau, who had previously come close to playing Chandler, was eventually cast as Pete. Fresh off his role in the 1996 comedy hit *Swingers*, which he also wrote the screenplay for, Favreau chafed against early versions of Pete and insisted on putting his own spin on the character. While the writers originally envisioned the character as a shy nerd that Monica could eventually warm to, Favreau wanted to play it cooler. Eventually, the writers went his way, adding the Ultimate Fighting Champion subplot that both ended Pete and Monica's relationship and gave Favreau the chance to play someone impressive.

Big names like Jon Favreau were becoming more and more commonplace on *Friends*. Isabella Rossellini's appearance early in the season was a solid pay-off to an episode-long joke about a 'freebie list' of celebrities that Ross was allowed to sleep with. Although Rossellini wasn't on Ross's final list, having been bumped for Winona Ryder (who would eventually show up on *Friends* playing an old friend of Rachel's), David Schwimmer still got to do an excellent job with Ross's crash and burn flirtation. Some cameos were less obvious to the audience, such as David Arquette – Courtney Cox's at-the-time boyfriend – appearing as Malcolm, a brief love interest for Phoebe who was unfortunately obsessed with her twin sister. Ben Stiller is a comedy giant now, but 1997 wasn't too long after his directorial debut and appearance in *The Cable Guy*. His appearance in 'The One with the Screamer' as Tommy – a date of Rachel's who couldn't control his temper – was a get, but not a big one.

Two of the biggest names to appear in the credits for *Friends*' third season were Billy Crystal and Robin Williams. Their cameo, a short pre-credits argument between the hastily invented Tomas and Tim, was completely unplanned and never a part of the episode script. The pair happened to be working on a nearby set filming *Father's Day*, a film that would sadly go on to be a total flop critically and commercially. Crystal and Williams wandered on to the *Friends* set during a work day and writers immediately asked if they'd be willing to appear on the show. They appeared in the opening spot that same day, and ad-libbed their entire salacious conversation. The episode ended up airing the day before the cinematic release of *Father's Day*, and probably played a part in the film succeeding at the box office over its initial weekend (though things would quickly go downhill); it finished only behind *The Fifth Element* in ticket sales.

Just as *Friends* boosted the *Father's Day* sales, it was also becoming a launchpad to success on NBC. As well as providing a boost to new shows on the Thursday night schedule, *Friends* became a career catalyst from some of its guest stars. NBC was boosting new shows by interspersing them between *Friends*, *Seinfeld* and *E.R.* during the 1996/1997 season. The most anticipated show of the season came about thanks, in part, to *Friends*. After her appearance on 'The One After the Superbowl', Brooke Shields was tapped to front a sitcom of her own. Although it struggled to get off the ground, with everything but the most basic building blocks of the plot, and Shields herself scrapped after the pilot tested poorly, NBC had high hopes for *Suddenly Susan*.

The slot between *Seinfeld* and *E.R.*, as the *New York Times* put it, was 'where NBC could probably produce hit ratings for yodelling concerts'. The initial concept of *Suddenly Susan* shared some DNA with *Friends*. The show focused on the titular Susan, played by Shields, navigating single life after leaving her fiancé at the altar. *Susan* didn't get quite the same burst of positive media attention that *Friends* received in its first season, with a lot of reviewers quick to point out just how much the show borrowed from the tropes of other sitcoms. However, that time slot definitely gave the show some breathing room to find an audience, and almost definitely contributed to it beating even *Friends* in the ratings for the season.

While NBC cemented its reputation for shiny, white New York sitcoms with its Thursday line-up, competing networks tried different tactics. In the 1996/1997 season, two of NBC's most prominent shows with black casts – *Fresh Prince of Bel Air* and *In The House* – had been replaced in the Monday night schedule by predominantly white shows. At the time, *Friends* was still under fire for its overwhelming whiteness. Gregory Malins, a member of the *Friends* writer's room, acknowledged the issue in a 1997 interview, insisting that they were working on it. A regular speaking role for a black actor wouldn't happen on *Friends* for quite some time.

Meanwhile, the fledgling networks The WB and UPN (established in 1995) were becoming known for showing plenty of comedies with predominantly black casts. A *New York Times* piece on the two networks bore the headline 'Two Upstart Networks Courting Black Viewers'. Words like 'Uppity' have long been used to put people of colour down, and while the use of 'Upstart' may not have been referring to anything other than the comparative newness of the networks, it has unpleasant connotations. Both networks were experiencing some success with a mixture of new programming like *The Jamie Foxx Show* and *Malcolm and Eddie*, and shows cancelled by other networks such as *Moesha* and *Sister Sister*. This trend towards programming for a non-white audience lasted longer at UPN than it did at The WB. In searching for new growth areas, executives at The WB attempted to distinguish themselves by shifting their target audience. Speaking to the *New York Times*, Jamie Kellner – head of The WB – said 'We've sort of been lumped in with what the other guys [UPN] did, but we're balancing ourselves out.'

There was a whole market that had so far been mostly ignored by primetime network television: teenagers. The teen market had largely been watching similar programming to their parents, but younger-skewing shows like *Friends* were becoming a hit among the demographic. While NBC had a dedicated programming slot for teens, it was on Saturday mornings – far from primetime. In that season, The WB began moving more towards shows for teens, with some that could appeal to broader families. On Monday nights The WB began pushing two new shows aimed at the teen market. First, at 8 pm, *7th Heaven*, a family-friendly drama that would go on to be the longest running show on the network. Second, at 9 pm, *Buffy the Vampire Slayer*, now an iconic part of television history. These weren't sitcoms, but the shows held their own against the comedy dominating other networks. Both shows helped cement the reputation of The WB as a teen-friendly network, even as the schedule got whitewashed.

All of the networks had a challenge in common as the season drew to a close: May Sweeps, in which networks competed for audiences and advertisers. Season finales were approaching for most shows, and with sweeps in session gimmicks, cliff-hangers and cameos were everywhere. ABC saw success with Ellen coming out of the closet, but they also planned a bigger experiment. At the beginning of May the network aired a 3D week, with nine of their sitcoms squeezing in brief moments of three-dimensional special effects. It wasn't a high point for the use of the technology. The brief special segments in the shows were generally irrelevant to the plots, with *Home Improvement*'s Tim Allen just throwing tools at the camera. ABC used anaglyph 3D technology, relying on a red/blue colour shift. The glasses required were available through a promotional tie-in with a fast-food chain, and without them the special effects were fuzzy and unwatchable.

Meanwhile, on NBC, *3rd Rock from the Sun* used a similar gimmick, but with different technology. Network executives on both sides said that there was no imitation, just two concurrent ideas. The *3rd Rock* episode came out ahead, viewed much more favourably by critics. The technology NBC used relied on the 'Pulfrich Effect' rather than anaglyph. It was a technique that required constantly moving cameras while filming the episode and that, as well as the huge, surreal set pieces, made it one of the most expensive sitcom episodes ever produced. A big part of the marketing push for the episode – 'A Nightmare on Dick Street' – was the fact that it remained totally watchable even without special glasses. The eyewear needed to view the 3D effect was, as with ABC, made available via promotional tie-in, and the different technologies meant that the same pair of glasses couldn't be used for both *3rd Rock* and ABC's 3D programming block. The use of these three-dimensional effects in sitcoms wasn't a new idea, for either network. Back in 1988, plans were made for a 3D episode of the hit sitcom *Moonlighting*. Coca-Cola was due to sponsor the episode, and planned to air a 3D ad in the commercial break. Unfortunately, the writers' strike of 1988 prematurely ended production of *Moonlighting*'s fourth season. The special episode was never produced, and Coca Cola were left with millions of 3D glasses, eventually using them for a Superbowl advert.

Elsewhere, and airing in the traditional two dimensions, *Friends* ended its third season with another cliff-hanger. While Ross and Rachel's relationship had ended to keep up the show's narrative momentum, the tension between the pair was still enough to keep viewers hooked. Almost nineteen million people watched the beach-house finale, as

Ross agonised over the choice between Rachel and his new girlfriend, Bonnie. Critics at the time complained of a staleness to sweeps season, and season finales like this one were bemoaned for cliff-hangers no one wanted to hang on to. 'The One at the Beach' introduced Phoebe's mother, built further on the chemistry between Chandler and Monica, gave viewers a memorable view of Joey with sandcastle breasts and gave viewers a hint that Ross and Rachel had more to come. It was a cliff-hanger, but an inevitable one. It was also far from the most gimmicky or cameo-filled episode of television to air during the usually stunt-filled Sweeps season. That balance, and ability to step back and just focus on the characters, might be why *Friends* remains so loved.

Chapter Four

The One Where Seinfeld Ends

Clip shows are rarely an enjoyable episode of a sitcom. At best, clip shows were a handy recap for potential new viewers before streaming made playing catch-up convenient. At worst, the clip show is a low-budget filler episode – a break for the writer's room. Somewhere in the middle lies 'The One with the Invitation', the twenty-first episode of *Friends'* fourth season. It was an easy shortcut, rebuilding the audience's emotional investment in Ross and Rachel with a series of clips summing up the relationship so far as the show built up to a big London season finale. The clips should be enough to make the one plot point of the episode – Rachel deciding not to attend Ross's wedding – bittersweet. They have the opposite effect, reminding the audience that the majority of the relationship was a series of fights and misunderstandings. 'The One with the Invitation' is consistently considered one of *Friends'* worst episodes. It was a smudge on a season of television that also had some of the very best the show had to offer.

A quick Ross and Rachel refresher was necessary after the bulk of the fourth season of *Friends* focused on anything but the two of them. The beach house cliff-hanger from the previous season was handled in the space of a single episode, Ross and Rachel imploding again as 'We were on a break!' gets cemented as a punchline. After the rest of the group overhear Ross screaming those famous five words the break-up played out for the second time, in comedic miniature rather than the intense emotional scenes from the previous season. It was clear that nothing had changed, no one had grown and the relationship remained as unworkable as it ever was.

With Ross and Rachel over to one side, the season had space to play with different dynamics. Joey and Chandler weren't new ground for conflict after their romantically-coded break-up in the second season, but in the fourth season a woman coming between them dominated a handful of episodes. Matt LeBlanc hit the ground running in the fourth season, with early episodes giving him a chance to play the vulnerable comedy that Joey does best. The burglary of the not-couple's shared apartment left them bereft of furniture beyond a patio table and a rowing boat, and Joey follows up by considering purchasing encyclopaedias from a persuasive salesman – played by Penn Jilette – in an attempt to keep up with his friends intellectually. In 'The One with the Ballroom Dancing', Joey played dancing partner to Mr Treeger, the building superintendent played by the sadly departed Mike Hagerty. The episode saw Joey unexpectedly delighted by both his and Treeger's newfound skills, leading to a small sad moment at the end as Treeger heads off to dance with a 'real woman'.

In the fifth episode of the season, Paget Brewster joined the show as Kathy, Joey's new girlfriend and the object of Chandler's inadvertent affections. Something new was at play as first Joey, then Chandler, both entered into their first serious romances of the show. While Monica, in the background of 'The One with Joey's New Girlfriend', called Rachel and Ross out on their continuing antagonism and forced them into an uneasy friendship for the bulk of the season, a new love triangle formed. Over the next few episodes, as Rachel completes the *New York Times* crossword for the first time and Ross becomes the butt of the joke while exploring his love of music, Matthew Perry plays quiet tension with Brewster as the pair orbit each other, eventually reaching their breaking point with a kiss that had the audience cheering.

Things came to a head at Thanksgiving in the eighth episode of the season: 'The One with the Box'. This episode introduced *Die Hard* as a running punchline between the men in the group, even as Chandler gets literally separated from the action by spending the episode shut in a large wooden crate as atonement for kissing Kathy. While Chandler is locked away, the rest of the group gather around the television for the Macy's Thanksgiving Day Parade – directed that year by regular *Friends* director Gary Halvorson. Thanksgiving episodes tended to be bottle-ish on *Friends*, an excuse to keep all of the cast gathered in a single location. They were a challenge for the writers but a necessity for a season building to such a big budget finale, and in 'The One with the Box' there was solid pay-off to the restrictions. Matthew Perry, despite spending the episode out of sight, still managed to deliver one of the best gags of the show as he waves goodbye to Kathy with a single finger through his lone airhole. Joey frees Chandler from the box and gives his friend his blessing to pursue his ex-girlfriend, but the real reconciliation is between the two men. In commentary for the episode, Kevin Bright described Joey and Chandler as a pair you look at 'as a couple'. While Chandler and Kathy reunite off screen, it was important to see him and Joey reconnecting. Above everything, the writers knew to put their relationship first.

Writing television often requires dealing with real-life restrictions and events. The actors starring in *Friends* had plenty going on outside of the show, and their life events needed to be accommodated into the show. So, for the fourth season, with Lisa Kudrow expecting a baby, the writers had to find a way to bring a very real bump into the story. Some shows have been known to hide visible pregnancies, covering actors with loose clothing, directing them to hold bowling balls in front of their stomachs or carefully shooting them from the waist up. These techniques had worked in the previous television season for the *Seinfeld* creators during Julia Louis Dreyfuss's pregnancy, but the *Friends* writers chose to take Kudrow's pregnancy as a challenge.

With Phoebe being the most 'out-there' of the group, the writers had the opportunity to get creative with her pregnancy. This was a character that consistently remained a step outside of reality, and was due a big emotional storyline after her brief stories during the previous season. The idea of Phoebe acting as a surrogate for her brother and his wife was immediately escalated with the suggestion of multiple births. Higher and higher numbers were kicked around the writer's room before they settled on triplets as the option closest to realistic. With the pieces of Phoebe's pregnancy in place, the stage was set for an episode often touted as one of *Friends*' very best: 'The One with the Embryos'.

The writers of *Friends* knew that some of the very best stories came out of getting the core group alone in a room together. With Phoebe's implantation storyline as the central emotional beat of the episode, the writers looked for a reason to get the rest of the group in one place. A conflict over Joey and Chandler's pet chick and duck set the group up for the big quiz. Episode writer and co-producer Seth Kurland once watched a group of friends, known as the 'Pad O' Guys', host a game show based on trivia about each other in their living room. Kurland claims the original idea for the apartment-based game show didn't come from him, but it was his idea to go the extra step with Ross's handmade game board.

The quiz was an excellent way to deliver new trivia about the characters without heavy-handed exposition, and writers threw in facts from their own lives as answers to the quiz questions. Monica's inability to eat Tic Tacs in odd numbers came from writer Jill Condon's father, while the name on Chandler's *TV Guide* – 'Miss Chanandler Bong' – originated in a story from Kurland's childhood about a nickname based on a misprinted fan club newsletter. Marta Kauffman, in commentary for the episode, remembers being the 'only human to laugh' at a question about the *TV Guide* falling into the 'literature' category. Multiple variations on the title for Chandler's father's drag show were pitched before the writers finally settled on 'Viva Las Gaygas', something which David Crane describes as not being his proudest moment.

The stakes got higher and higher as the episode progressed until finally the iconic purple-walled apartment was on the line. The final, lightning-round question that loses Rachel and Monica the contest is one the show consistently didn't bother answering: 'What is Chandler Bing's job?' The writers had created what David Crane liked to call schmuck bait – stakes raised so high that the foreshadowed ending could never actually happen. Of course, Monica and Rachel could never actually give up their apartment to Joey and Chandler. The studio audience's reaction to the girls losing the contest is both loud and lengthy. The rest of the episode has the viewer on tenterhooks, waiting to see how they'll get out of the proposed swap. The big twist of the episode is that they don't. Condon called it 'anti-schmuck bait', pulling the rug out from under the viewers and subverting that audience expectation that a sitcom episode ends with the status quo intact. Even as Chandler majestically rides into the apartment on the famous white porcelain dog, the audience expects things to be undone.

While the contest takes place, Phoebe spends a chunk of the episode away from the core group in some of the most emotional scenes. Jill Condon had the idea of Phoebe taking the time to give the embryos a pep talk in a speech that David Crane recognised as one of the most special parts of the episode, even giving Condon extra time to rework it into something perfect. It's a scene that Lisa Kudrow shines in. She's alone on screen, making an impassioned plea to a petri dish. In the final beats of the episode, as the rest of the group gets into a screaming match over the lost bet, Phoebe makes the announcement that the implantation has worked, and she's pregnant. Giovanni Ribisi as Frank Jr. throws a fist in the air and screams 'my sister's going to have my baby', as the friends celebrate, all conflict temporarily forgotten. It's a big end to the episode as the audience realises that Phoebe will indeed give birth to her brother's kid, and the rest will really trade apartments. The final shot, of Chandler and the duck perched on the yellow leather sofa as he celebrates his new living arrangement, hit the point home. *Friends* wasn't afraid to change. Kevin Bright described 'The One with the Embryos' as the catalyst that rejuvenated season four. Sitcoms, by a fourth season, can risk stagnating if they don't shake things up, and *Friends* proved it was ready to try something different. 'The One with the Embryos' is still a favourite among fans now, and landed at number 21 in *TV Guide*'s list of 'Top 100 Episodes of All-Time', the only episode of *Friends* to make it into the list.

With the show finding new energy, it was time to introduce new relationships. In the following episode, 'The One with Rachel's Crush', Chandler's budding relationship with Kathy came to an end. In its place came a new relationship for Rachel; her first since the break-up with Ross. An off-screen romance contributed to the casting as Tate Donovan joined the show to play Joshua, Rachel's new personal shopping client. Donovan and Jennifer Aniston had been dating for some time before he began his guest role on the show, and he was almost a part of the family having spent plenty of time on set and at live-tapings watching his girlfriend perform. Unfortunately, what the creators of the show didn't know was that when Donovan was offered the role, he and Aniston were in the midst of a break up. Having decided to keep the news quiet, Donovan agreed to the five-episode arc under the mistaken belief that working with his ex-girlfriend would somehow make the break up easier, a decision he came to regret. Speaking to Brian Baumgartner of *The Office* on his podcast *Off the Beat*, Donovan recalled that 'it was very difficult to work and be in a comedic scene with somebody you were breaking up with'. That might explain the total lack of chemistry between the two actors. Aniston did, at least, get the opportunity for bigger comedy moments as Rachel pines, takes flirting advice from Joey – in a scene that introduced the famous chat-up line 'How you doin'?' to the world – and eventually dons a cheerleading uniform to impress the reluctant Joshua.

While the relationship between Rachel and Joshua clearly wasn't written to last, it was a great chance to demonstrate how far Rachel had come since the first season of the show. In multiple moments, she experiences what, for some, would be total humiliation. For Rachel, they were just events to be shrugged off. On a date gone wrong, off screen, Rachel inadvertently flashes not just her new boyfriend but his parents and a waiter. Season one Rachel might have recounted this as a story of colossal embarrassment. For season four Rachel, it's a shrug and a 'well, I've got nice boobs'. A couple of episodes later, when Rachel answers the door to Joshua while wearing a wedding dress and announcing 'I do', a misunderstanding not helped by her earlier panicked attempts at commitment in response to Ross's engagement, Joshua understandably runs for the hills. Instead of lamenting the final nail in the coffin of her relationship, Rachel calmly accepts that she's 'never seeing him again'. Where, in *Friends*' fourth season, Ross often lapsed back into immaturity, even resurrecting a childhood 'not swearing' gesture that provided the writers a handy way to add a 'fuck you' to the script without actually saying it, Rachel grew up and became someone capable of calm acceptance when faced with the comically tragic.

Only an episode after the introduction of Joshua came 'The One with Joey's Dirty Day'. It's an episode that carefully juggles its three plots, giving them all equal weight. While Joey heads to a film shoot desperate for a shower, before coming face to face with Charlton Heston while clad only in a towel, the girls attempt to get Chandler over his recent break up by getting him out of his sweatpants and into a strip club. The scene in which the girls discussed how much they'd enjoyed the dancers' performances, and waxed lyrical over the women they'd consider being with, was the closest *Friends* had come to queerness since brief Carol and Susan moments in the previous season.

Meanwhile, Rachel's dire pursuit of Joshua leads to her setting Ross up on a date with her boss's niece, Emily, and Helen Baxendale – already well-known in England for her role on *Cold Feet* – joined the *Friends* cast for the latter half of the fourth season. The whirlwind date between Ross and Emily began with a bedraggled Baxendale berating the group, and ended with the pair at a bed and breakfast in Vermont. It was a micro version of the pair's eventual relationship, as they took risks and rushed forward at a reckless pace. Most importantly, it set up a new dynamic between Ross and Rachel. The two of them had spent the first half of the season bickering after they almost got back together, but once Emily came on to the scene, they both genuinely attempted to embrace the other moving on. If 'The One with the Embryos' was the episode that breathed new life into the season, then this arc was that rejuvenation in action. The characters were growing up, along with the show, and the audience had a new romance to enjoy. Admittedly, as with Rachel and Joshua, that romance was severely lacking in chemistry, and in this case served largely to deliver the cast to England for the season finale.

While *Friends* was building new relationships, elsewhere on NBC some things were coming to an end. Partway through the 1997/1998 season, NBC entered into negotiations with Warner Brothers for the rights to continue airing *E.R.* There was much more at stake there than just a single show. Around October every year, Warren Littlefield would visit Jerry Seinfeld and inform him that the network wanted another season of *Seinfeld*. Often, as a reward for the show's success, Seinfeld and his writing staff would be invited to take the company jet to New York for an all-expenses-paid 'research trip'. In 1997, however, something was different. Jerry Seinfeld didn't want to make a tenth season of *Seinfeld*, no matter how much money, how many jets or free sneakers from Nike were on the table. With the highest-rated sitcom on the Thursday 'Must See' line-up coming to an end, and NBC's relationship with the National Football League still up in the air, the network needed to act swiftly to make sure it didn't lose another ratings leader. *E.R.* had been consistently landing at the top of the Nielsen ratings since it began in 1994 and its preceding, post-*Seinfeld* time slot had been a launchpad to success for multiple sitcoms; including, of course, *Friends*. *Seinfeld* even mocked its own power as a hitmaker in the first episode of the ninth season – 'The Butter Shave' – in which Jerry gets frustrated with a fellow comedian constantly riding his coattails by ensuring he always followed Seinfeld's successful act.

Despite Jerry Seinfeld receiving offers of over $100 million to make a tenth season, he opted to end the show on the high note it had been hitting for years and left NBC needing *E.R.* more than ever. In 1997, Warner Brothers were producing the majority of NBC's Thursday night line-up, and wanted to maintain a decent relationship with the network even as they looked for the best deal possible for *E.R.*, a show that was making NBC around $200 million a year in profit. The final figures for the new, three-year deal had NBC paying around $13 million an episode for the hospital drama, making it the most expensive television series ever produced. In the current era of prestige genre television, that figure has obviously been overtaken many times over since the deal was made.

As the final season of *Seinfeld* was airing, rumours and speculation circulated around the finale, due to air on 14 May 1998. The first half of the episode acted as a fake-out, doing what the viewers expected with Jerry receiving a pilot deal from NBC and agreeing to move to California with George. The convoluted story featured faux TV-execs discussing Seinfeld's pitch for 'a show about nothing', calling it perfect 'water-cooler television'. At this point in TV history, it was shows like *Seinfeld* and *Friends* that had office workers gathering around water coolers – or coffee machines – to discuss the events of last night's television. In the decades to come, it was prestige dramas and streaming hits that would dominate cultural and office conversations, but in the late nineties sitcoms still held sway.

Larry David returned to write the *Seinfeld* finale, freeing Seinfeld himself to create stand-up sequences that bracketed the episode – the first to feature since the seventh season. The episode saw the core four celebrating Jerry's success on a private jet to Paris before air trouble lands them in Massachusetts, just in time for them to scathingly commentate a car-robbery and find themselves in court having violated a new 'Good Samaritan' law. The Massachusetts set itself, a generic town square arranged around a central gazebo, might seem familiar. It was an often-used piece of Warner Brothers scenery, and would become a regular fixture on screens a couple of years later in *Gilmore Girls*, another of The WB's teen dramas.

As the *Seinfeld* gang found themselves on trial, a parade of previous guests came through the courtroom to give evidence of the group's callous disregard for their fellow humans. Among the cameos were Larry Thomas as the infamous 'Soup Nazi' Yev Kessem, Jane Leeves – at this time best known for her role as Daphne Moon on *Frasier* – as 'The Virgin' Marla from 'The Contest', and Teri Hatcher who, after her guest appearance in the 1993 *Seinfeld* episode 'The Implant', had risen to fame playing Lois Lane on ABC's *Lois & Clark: The New Adventures of Superman*. The evidence sequence served as a greatest hits of the core character's most awful moments, with clips from previous episodes delivering punchline after punchline. Despite this, NBC also opted to air an hour-long clip show and retrospective of the series before the episode itself. Where *Friends* used its season four clip show to hammer home the emotional impact of the finale to come, here *Seinfeld* used its nostalgia tour to remind viewers again and again that this was a nothing show about terrible people.

'The Finale' was the fourth most-watched series finale in American television history, after *M*A*S*H*, *Cheers* and *The Fugitive*. Cable network TV Land even opted not to air any programming against the episode, instead displaying a handwritten note that said 'We're TV Fans so … we're watching the last episode of Seinfeld.' Although the finale was watched by over seventy million people, the critical response was less than enthusiastic. At the time, *Entertainment Weekly* described the episode as 'like taking your doctoral exam in Seinology – and about as funny'. A recent *Vanity Fair* article recalled that 'the next day, even shock jocks on the radio were complaining about it'. The pall of the finale hanging over *Seinfeld* became a running pop-culture joke, with even the creators and stars of the show acknowledging its failure to stick the landing. While Larry David has continued to defend the episode, Jerry Seinfeld has since spoken of his reservations about it. The difference of views between the two even came up as a joke on David's HBO show *Curb Your Enthusiasm*.

The *Seinfeld* finale ended with a rehash of a conversation from the pilot about the correct height of shirt buttons, and the show still lives on today as a beloved piece of pop-culture. The end of a show can make or break its long-term perception, but *Seinfeld* survived the embarrassment of a weak ending. The finale failed to redeem the characters, punishing them instead for nine years of callous behaviour for which they'd already experienced the consequences, and despite (or because of) that, *Seinfeld* remains a cult classic. The legacy of *Seinfeld*, and its ability to generate millions of dollars' worth of profit for NBC, would hang over Thursday nights for a long time to come.

One of the last sitcoms to receive the post-*Seinfeld*, pre-*E.R.* boost was *Veronica's Closet*. With *Friends* running smoothly and successfully, its creators found themselves caught up in the idea of creating an entire slate of shows. *Veronica's Closet* was the first of these new shows from the Bright/Kauffman/Crane partnership. Starring Kirstie Alley as the titular Veronica 'Ronnie' Chase, a woman with a slick public persona and disastrous private life, the show was one of many new offerings in 1997 that put women at the forefront. The premise of the show, which was created specifically for Alley, was Veronica coping with imminent divorce while publicly running a lingerie business and selling romance to its customers.

Before *Veronica's Closet* Alley was best known for her role as Rebecca in *Cheers*, and this was her first major television appearance since the hit sitcom ended in 1993. Despite Alley receiving a promise from Crane and Kauffman that her new role would be more than just a rehash of Rebecca, critics were quick to jump on the similarities between the characters. *Friends* owed its success to the freshness of the storylines and characters, and Crane and Kauffman were attempting to recreate that magic with *Veronica's Closet*, while letting Kirstie Alley explore new ground. Speaking to the *Los Angeles Times*, Crane pointed out that while trying to make something new, 'a lot of shows go wrong by doing something 180 degrees different from what they did before'. Whether due to the familiarity of Alley's performance, the spark of darker humour in the show compared to some of its Thursday counterparts, or the show's schedule placement, the first season of *Veronica's Closet* was a huge success. The *New York Times* admitted that while any show airing at that particular time would become an instant hit as during that half-hour 'an evil wizard takes control of your television', that article also called the show 'the one consistently funny new comedy of the season'. *Veronica's Closet* reached third in the Nielsen rankings for the 1997/1998 season, and maintained its audience even after moving to the post-*Friends* slot to replace the abruptly cancelled fellow-newbie *Union Square*. It seemed to everybody that Bright/Kauffman/Crane had another hit on their hands. Whether they wanted it was another matter.

Replacing *Veronica's Closet* in the post *Seinfeld* slot was the still relatively new show *Just Shoot Me*. The show's first season had been just a short run of six episodes in March 1997. Originally renewed for thirteen episodes as the season began, *Just Shoot Me* originally took the post-*Frasier* slot on Tuesday nights, even overtaking *Frasier* in the ratings to become the twelfth most-watched series of the season. Just two episodes into *Just Shoot Me*'s second season, that thirteen-episode renewal became a full series order, and the show got a boost when it moved to Thursdays. Although it never had a consistent time slot in the schedule, *Just Shoot Me* – set at the office of a fictional fashion magazine inspired by the likes of *Vogue* – was a consistent hit, and eventually became a Tuesday night mainstay.

On Mondays, however, NBC was still looking for a winner. Since the end of *The Fresh Prince of Bel-Air* in 1995, NBC's Mondays had been suffering an identity crisis. With other black-led sitcoms like *In The House* cancelled only to immediately be snapped up by other networks, and teen-friendly *Blossom* recently finished, in 1997 NBC was looking to create another night of hit comedy. For that season the network created a line-up of 'time slot hits' – shows that got their starting success thanks to *Friends* and *Seinfeld*. The programming block included *Suddenly Susan* and *Caroline in the City*, and the network made much of this set of female-driven shows. Unfortunately, none of them were hitting the mark with audiences or critics. Other networks were working to prevent NBC from getting yet another foothold in primetime programming, and both CBS and Fox were providing big competition on Monday nights. Both *Cosby* and *Everybody Loves Raymond* were bringing viewers to CBS in the first half of that Monday block. In the second hour, between 9 and 10 pm, Fox was airing a new legal dramedy – *Ally McBeal*. Another cult classic of the nineties, *Ally McBeal* held a sway with female audiences that at this point neither *Caroline* nor *Susan* could manage.

The biggest network competition for NBC came, in 1997, from ABC. The only sitcom not on NBC to reach the Nielsen top ten for the season was ABC's *Home Improvement*, which aired on Tuesday nights directly against *Frasier*. The latter was claiming plenty of Emmy wins but it wasn't getting the audiences that the Tim Allen vehicle could gather. On Wednesday nights it was new ABC show *Dharma and Greg* – an 'opposites attract' sitcom from Chuck Lorre – that provided the ratings challenge. Very few of the many new sitcoms launched during the 1997/1998 season survived for a particularly long time. *Dharma & Greg*, with its eventual five seasons, would become one of the longest-running sitcoms to come out of the season. The only other major new show to come out that season was *Dawson's Creek*, a new teen drama on The WB.

NBC's Wednesday nights, originally envisioned to be another night of comedy to match Tuesdays and Thursdays, became a mess of repeats and schedule-shifting short-lived shows as the network threw things at the wall to see what stuck. *3rd Rock from the Sun* remained the only constant through the season. Wednesdays also saw ABC's biggest rating drop of the season with *Ellen*. After the previous season's controversial 'Puppy Episode', the network had pushed the show back to a much later space in the schedule as well as adding in those parental advisory warnings. The message was clear – queerness on network television was still tolerated, not celebrated. The show still managed some stand-out episodes in its final season, especially 'Emma' – in which Emma Thompson appeared as a fictionalised version of herself grappling with her own queerness. *Ellen* may have fallen behind in ratings but it was still loved by many. Al Gore, the Vice President at the time, even praised the show publicly for allowing Americans the opportunity to 'look at sexual orientation in a more open light', while the *New York Times* praised the show for 'genuine comedy and social commentary'. Where *Seinfeld*'s ending was very much a choice by the creators to go out on a high, the cancellation of *Ellen* in May 1998 came as a shock to many, not least of DeGeneres herself. While it was a sad end to a television show that had paved the way for queer stories, later reports of DeGeneres treating writers on her next sitcom *The Ellen Show* 'like shit' (according to a former writer's assistant) cast a larger pall over her sitcom history.

By the late nineties, there was a constant cycle of commissions and cancellations across network television. This cycle was indicative of a larger fear, and holding onto viewers was more important than ever to networks as the end of the decade loomed. Premium cable networks were continuously growing, bringing in more money to spend on even bigger talent. In 1997, *Oz* premiered on the HBO cable network, sparking the beginning of an era of prestige cable dramas. The standard broadcast networks weren't just competing with each other, but with everything paid-for television had to offer.

In the UK, a similar problem was emerging. While *Friends* was a broadcast success in America, it was about to land on a premium channel in England. For the first three seasons of *Friends*, the terrestrial Channel 4 exclusively held the airing rights. During the 1997 summer hiatus, it was Channel 4 who approached the producers of *Friends* with the idea to film an episode in England. Despite that, it was new digital channel Sky1 who claimed the first opportunity to air the fourth season. Unfortunately, Channel 4 only owned the terrestrial rights to *Friends*, having paid around £80 million for the show alongside *E.R.* back in 1995. This allowed Sky1 to get in, buy the satellite rights for the fourth season and with them the right to run the show before anyone else in the UK. Sky1 paid around £8 million for a set of shows that would, in 1998, set them up with a Thursday night line-up very similar to NBC's own. *Friends*, *Veronica's Closet*, *Suddenly Susan* and *Seinfeld* aired in a two-hour sitcom block followed immediately by *E.R.* BBC2, at this time, had a far cheaper deal for the terrestrial rights to *Seinfeld*, but due to first-run complications along with the fact that the Beeb was rarely considered the place to go for American programming, they were running at least two seasons behind at the time. For British viewers, Sky was the place to see American hits first.

Channel 4 might have been the ones to suggest a transatlantic *Friends* episode, but it was the profit brought in by fantastic British VHS sales that convinced Warner Brothers, who would be footing the bill for the trip, to go ahead. Alongside the cast and creators, a full complement of writers and crew would have to travel from LA to London to pull the episode together. It was an expensive prospect, not just financially but in regards to the stories *Friends* was telling. The London trip was the impetus for the Ross and Emily storyline, with the rushed wedding forcing almost all of the group to travel abroad. It was expensive in what the arc did and didn't do for the show. It was invigorating to see Ross and Rachel in new relationships, but forcing a relationship to move so quickly was dangerously close to schmuck bait. The audience were bright enough to understand that a character like Emily couldn't last on the show without drastically changing the dynamic. There was also the offscreen issue that Helen Baxendale was pregnant and didn't want to continue on the show after the fourth season. The best-case scenario would be the relationship predictably coming to a dramatic end. The worst would have been giving Emily the Susan, Carol and Ben treatment, pushing her to the background of the show. An off-screen, unseen spouse worked on *Frasier*, but for *Friends* it would have been a step too far.

Financially, getting all of those people to London was a huge challenge, and assistance came from an unlikely source. Richard Branson, the British billionaire, is founder of (among other things) Virgin Media and the airline, Virgin Atlantic. His Virgin group also, at one point, owned the infamous London gay club Heaven. In the late nineties, Branson was also a huge *Friends* fan. When he caught wind of the approaching London-set episodes, Branson approached producer Kevin Bright with an offer: seventy-five first-class airline tickets in exchange for a small cameo (and, admittedly, a lot of advertising). The resulting appearance wasn't the strongest part of the episode. Filmed outside the Tower of London, Branson appeared as a tourist-tat-touting vendor, convincing Joey to buy a ridiculous Union Jack hat. Huge crowds of British *Friends* fans were gathered just out of shot, which might have contributed to Branson's nerves. The minute-long scene took far longer to shoot. Richard Branson has been many things across the years, but professional actor has never been one of them.

The other non-actor to appear in a brief cameo in 'The One with Ross's Wedding' was Sarah Ferguson, the Duchess of York, who briefly turned up outside Westminster to compliment Joey's hat. In the British broadcast of the episode, Joey's attempt to chat up Ferguson with the line 'So, I hear you're single now', didn't make the final cut. The *Friends* creators wanted to cram some royalty into the London episodes and apparently Sarah Ferguson, although technically no longer part of the royal family, was 'available'.

Plenty of big names from British comedy also joined the cast for 'The One with Ross's Wedding'. When Phoebe attempted to contact the Walthams and warn them of Rachel's imminent arrival, it was June Whitfield who answered the phone as the stern housekeeper. Lisa Kudrow was heavily pregnant and unable to fly when the London episodes were being filmed, and actually gave birth on the day that the finale aired, but she was still padded when playing Phoebe to maintain the illusion of triplets. As a result of Kudrow's pregnancy, the writers had the challenge of not just keeping her character involved in the action, but organising two separate shoots for the finale as Kudrow remained in LA. All of Phoebe's scenes with Rachel and the transatlantic phone call were recorded on the usual *Friends* soundstage. The other half of the phone call was recorded with Megan Mullaly – who would go on to become an NBC regular on a new sitcom the following year – playing the part. However, Whitfield became available during the London shoot and sadly, Mullaly's role was cut. Instead, the conversation was filmed again, against a recording of Phoebe's part, for the benefit of the live British audience.

Alongside June Whitfield, another star of the BBC sitcom *Absolutely Fabulous* appeared in 'The One with Ross's Wedding'. Jennifer Saunders created and starred in the classic British comedy after rising to fame in the long-running sketch show *French and Saunders*. On *Friends*, Saunders played Emily's disinterested stepmother, but the cameo wasn't her first American sitcom appearance. In 1996 Saunders appeared as her Ab Fab character Edina Monsoon alongside Joanna Lumley as Patsy Stone in the *Roseanne* episode 'Satan Darling'. In commentary on the episode, the *Friends* creators described Jennifer Saunders' performance as 'just hysterical'. It was a close-lipped and permanently tipsy bit of acting that Saunders based partly on Joan Collins.

Alongside Saunders, the second half of the hour-long finale introduced Emily's father Stephen Waltham, played by Tom Conti. The theatre veteran delivered possibly one of the best lines of the episode during an altercation with Elliot Gould as Jack Geller: 'I could kill you with my thumb, you know', delivered in a stage whisper as he walked off screen. Gould and Christina Pickles both returned as the senior Gellers, but Gould found himself in trouble with Marta Kauffman after letting slip to the media that Rachel was going to turn up at some point during the wedding.

Elsewhere in the episode, as Rachel desperately tried to get to England, Jane Carr appeared as an unhelpful but incredibly British ticket agent. Carr, an English-born but America-based actor, has turned up as a Mary Poppins-accented actor in many American sitcoms over the years. At the time she appeared on *Friends*, she had already guest-starred on plenty of NBC's staple shows including *Wings, Caroline in the City* and *Mad About You*.

When Rachel finally made it on to her flight, the writers having worked hard to stall the character to time her arrival for the best dramatic moment, she met an exasperated Hugh Laurie – whose character appeared in the credits as 'Gentleman on the Plane'. Laurie – well known now for playing a grumpy doctor on the Fox medical drama *House* and known at the time for his long-running comedy partnership with Stephen Fry – had also recently appeared in the live action adaptation of *101 Dalmatians*, bringing him to wider American attention. His character calmly explained to Rachel that she was, in fact, a terrible person for flying to London to interrupt her ex's wedding, while *Friends* writer Greg Malins feigned sleep in the background, one of the many *Friends* writers who appeared in brief cameos during the episode.

'The One with Ross's Wedding' received a mixed response. One UK reviewer called it one of *Friends*' worst episodes to date, thanks largely to the unfunny cameos, while American outlet *Entertainment Weekly* gave the episode an A rating, calling it a 'near perfect finale'. Despite Channel 4 not being the first to air the episode, they did claim the rights to run a special preview – 'The One Where Johnny Makes Friends' – in which Johnny Vaughn attempted to interview the cast while being kept entirely in the dark about the contents of the episode. The interview special was, unsurprisingly, not very well-liked; *The Guardian* described it as 'one for the hardcore fans only'. Critics might not have loved the fourth season finale, but fans were delighted to watch on both sides of the Atlantic. Around twenty million viewers in the States meant the episode landed third in the Nielsen ratings for the week, and around 6.5 million viewers watched the episode when it finally aired on Channel 4, making it the highest-rated show for the channel that week.

The decision to film not just the location scenes but the bulk of the episode in London gave many British fans their first and only opportunity to see the show recorded live. The location scenes were filmed first before the cast and crew began the arduous process of studio shoots at Fountain Studios in London. Kevin Bright directed the finale, as he did many of the show's most important episodes. The double episode was filmed on three consecutive nights for audiences of around 500 people. The creators of the show were concerned, despite the popularity of *Friends* in the UK, that audiences might not get all of the jokes. Those fears were unfounded, and later Marta Kauffman described the crowds as one of the best audiences they'd ever had.

As was often the case with *Friends*, jokes and dialogue were being reworked and rewritten as filming went on, based on audience reactions. The writers' room kept working late into the night in the hotel rooms of The Marriot – also used as a location in the episode. The importance of the episode, combined with Bright's perfectionism, meant the studio shoots ran well into the early hours of the morning. The final scene of the wedding ceremony was being filmed hours after the wrap party had been and gone. Time was so tight that Matt LeBlanc performed only a single take of his long walk down the aisle while on the phone to Phoebe, gamely holding up his end of the conversation against a recording filmed the week before.

The biggest, loudest and most dramatic audience reaction of the entire shoot came late in the episode. Ross enters Chandler's hotel room to proudly announce 'I'm getting married today' to a still-in-bed Chandler. After he leaves, Monica's head appears from beneath the covers. The writers' room had been bandying about the idea of Monica and Chandler together for some time and, as the audience screamed with joy for minutes at the reveal, they knew they'd made the right choice.

Ross and Rachel's relationship still consumed the final minutes of the episode. Ross's 'take thee Rachel' formed a colossal cliff-hanger, one of Crane's favourite episode endings they'd ever done, but it wasn't the most important romantic shift of the finale. Rachel's realisation that she still loved Ross and her decision to interrupt the wedding would have undone much of the maturity and growth the audience had seen over the previous season if it wasn't for her final realisation that Ross had truly moved on. Ross's mistake wasn't a reassurance that the character's would reunite, and it didn't need to be. The real shocking twist of the episode was Monica and Chandler pairing up, another example of the show finding new ground to tread and staying fresh by taking the weirder route. The idea of the two characters together had cropped up before, especially in the previous season, but this wasn't the realisation of a long-running story arc. It was a huge turn for the show that felt much more exciting than the mutual pining of Ross and Rachel. *Friends* took a risk in going to London and a risk in almost marrying off Ross. Chandler and Monica pairing up, although the episode implied it was temporary, was a risk too, but it was the kind of risk the show needed to take. This was a chance for the show to reset its relationships again. It was a bigger version of the 'wow, they actually did that' moment earlier in the season when the apartment switch happened. Other sitcoms struggled with falling into staleness and clip shows. It had looked like *Friends* was at risk of doing the same, but not after this finale.

Chapter Five

The One with a New Schedule

It's scary to fall in love with a new show in the modern streaming era. This is a time when anything getting a second season, no matter how popular, is far from guaranteed. Network television hasn't gone away, but in the last few years more and more people have turned to the on-demand giants for watercooler-worthy entertainment. Factors like release-day binges of full season drops hold huge amounts of power over whether or not a show is considered worthy of renewal for a second or third season. It's a singularly contemporary complaint. Except, really, it isn't. Networks were abruptly cancelling shows with avid fan bases when Netflix was still just a postal DVD-rental service. Making those decisions based on ratings and potential advertising sales has always been a part of the television landscape.

By 1998 and the beginning of the fifth season of *Friends*, the number of sitcoms on NBC – the network that considered itself the best home for comedy programming – had begun to fall. Choices of what to keep or what to cancel were largely based on cash, not critical acclaim. It was a rare show that could survive those cut-throat choices for more than a few years. *Seinfeld* was one, the creators choosing to end it on their own terms. *Frasier*, running partly on the power of its predecessor, was another. Of course, there was also *Friends*. With the average network sitcom running for around twenty-four episodes a season, reaching a fifth season generally meant that a show got to celebrate a milestone episode. For *Friends*, that episode was simply called 'The One Hundredth'.

A storyline that began as a creative way for Lisa Kudrow to be visibly pregnant on screen culminated in the 100th episode of *Friends*, after the birth of her actual child. It was just three episodes into a season that had picked up where the preceding finale left off, with the bulk of the cast in London as Ross fumbled his way through his disastrous wedding. After an episode focused on Phoebe's jealousy about not being part of the London trip – her envy shared by Kudrow herself – culminated in the promise of a trip to Atlantic city that was swiftly interrupted by the onset of labour, *Friends* was set up for a big event episode to celebrate the rare milestone. The bulk of the episode took place in the hospital. It was a rarity for an episode to concentrate all of the characters in a single location without using the apartment sets, but the choice paid off as the friends sort-of helped Phoebe, but largely got distracted by their own stories.

The central joke of the episode was that Phoebe's otherwise completely normal doctor had an overwhelming adoration for 'The Fonz' – Arthur Fonzarelli, the iconic *Happy Days* character played by Henry Winkler. *Happy Days* hit dips in popularity during the show's eleven-year run, and an episode from the show's fifth season (just a few before that 100 mark) involved Fonzie jumping over a shark on water skis. Thanks to that episode, the phrase 'jumping the shark' entered the lexicon when American radio personality Jon Hein made a reference to it, using it as a shorthand for shows that had lost what made them great and now resorted to cheap publicity stunts to draw in viewers. Thankfully, no sharks were harmed in the making of *Friends*' 'The One Hundredth'. While it was an event episode, it was an expected one. There was no big gimmick to grab headlines, just the cast doing what they did best in an unusual setting. Initially, David Crane and Marta Kauffman were unsure about the running Fonz joke, but the writers' room convinced them to keep it in, and the deadpan delivery of lines like 'Fonzie dated triplets once', from character actor Sam Anderson brightened up the episode.

While Phoebe suffered through her contractions, a B-plot paralleled her pain as Joey struggled through the agony of kidney stones. The writers needed to give the rest of the group something to do, and putting Joey and Ross in a storyline that rhymed with Phoebe's provided a great comic offset. According to Crane and Kauffman, those scenes with Iqbal Theba as the doctor were some of the hardest to shoot; his ridiculous, repeated delivery of the phrase 'kidney stones' had the actors cracking up long enough to slow down the night's filming.

The laughs were needed in the episode. *Friends* was, above all, a comedy, but within 'The One Hundredth' was a deep emotional payoff for a storyline carried over from the previous season. This was the kind of thing *Friends* thrived on, earning quiet, sad contemplation from the audience in exchange for a few laughs. As in the season four episode

'The One with the Embryos', it was Phoebe at the centre, giving a sweet speech to the newborn triplets that echoed her earlier impassioned pleas to that season four petri dish. Real babies, at certain points covered in grape jelly, were cast to play the triplets. Strict restrictions around filming infants meant they could only be filmed for a few minutes at a time, away from the noise and chaos of the main studio. While the reaction shots of the babies are real, including an unexpected and perfectly timed high-five from one of the infants, the main tear-filled speech was delivered by Lisa Kudrow to an armful of dolls for the sake of the live audience. It didn't detract from her performance, a rare and much-needed vulnerable moment for Phoebe that managed not to be mawkish.

Both Giovanni Ribisi and Debra Jo Rupp reprised their roles as Phoebe's brother and sister-in-law for 'The One Hundredth'. The latter was only able to appear for the final few minutes due to her role as a series regular on *That '70s Show*, Fox's nostalgic new sitcom. Ribisi's career was taking off too, and this episode marked the last time the whole family would appear on screen together, unfortunately giving the writers one less way to tell good emotional stories about Phoebe.

While Phoebe laboured and Joey passed stones, the rest of the episode was given over to Chandler and Monica's burgeoning relationship. So far, the characters themselves – and the show itself – had been hammering home that this pairing was temporary, just a fling. That had been the original plan in the writers' room. However, the audience's warm response to the clear chemistry between the two kept them together far longer than anyone had expected. In 'The One Hundredth', their relationship was cemented for the first time as something real, more than a passing fancy, as Rachel's actions forced a conversation about commitment between the pair. It was a golden, if malleable, rule of sitcoms that the status quo should be re-established, a bit, at the end of most episodes. Altering the dynamic of the group by pairing Monica and Chandler was a risky move, and right at the beginning of the season the Ross and Rachel relationship had been up in the air and beginning to bore the audience. By resolving the Ross and Rachel issue in the season's second episode with an almost-fourth-wall-breaking acknowledgement of how ridiculous things had become between them, the status quo was reset just enough to be upended by Chandler and Monica. The longevity of *Friends* owes a lot to the willingness of the writers' room to take a risk and break or bend that golden rule.

Friends wasn't the first sitcom to reach the 100-episode mark, and it certainly wouldn't be the last. Not every show, however, made a point of celebrating the milestone, and those that did rarely went the 'event episode' route. *Seinfeld* reached 100 episodes in 1995, celebrating the occasion with an hour-long clip show marking highlights from previous seasons. *The Nanny*, on CBS, saved any nod to the 100th until the episode's end credits, presenting a celebration cake as star of the show Fran Drescher thanked the viewers. In 1996, *Mad About You* also went down the clip show route, with a 99th episode consisting mostly of flashbacks. In 1997, a year before *Friends* reached the big number, *Frasier* went for the event episode with a storyline about Frasier Crane celebrating his 1,000th radio broadcast. As with *Friends*, *Frasier* was filmed almost entirely in a studio in Los Angeles, but for 'The 1000th Show', the episode was filmed on location in its Seattle setting for the first and only time.

Having moved to Tuesday nights as part of the satellite 'Must See' line-up in 1994, *Frasier* had spent four years shoring up a second evening of essential sitcom entertainment. In 1998, with *Friends* airing its 100th episode and *Seinfeld* gone for good, *Frasier* made a triumphant return to Thursdays for its sixth season, taking the *Seinfeld* 9 pm slot. As in previous years, those Thursday 'Must See' shows dominated primetime ratings for the '98/99 season. *E.R.* still claimed the number one spot, with *Friends* taking second place. *Frasier* didn't quite match the success of *Seinfeld*, but being the third most popular show of the season was still a step-up from its Tuesday night success. *Veronica's Closet*, now in its second season, was no longer quite as beloved by critics as it had been the previous year, but still managed success in the ratings thanks to its post-*Frasier* time slot. David Crane, Marta Kauffman and Kevin Bright's production company was, by 1998, creating three quarters of the Thursday sitcom line-up. NBC continued using Thursdays to launch new shows, and *Jesse* – the latest show from Bright/Kauffman/Crane – benefited greatly from airing between *Friends* and *Frasier*. *Seinfeld* going off the air had changed Thursdays for good, but *Frasier* was holding its own.

NBC's sitcom scheduling across the rest of the week had suffered in the previous couple of years, and while Thursday's sitcoms were still dominating the ratings, other networks had begun to pose a challenge to NBC on other nights with popular sitcoms of their own. Moving

Frasier to Thursdays made sense – with *Seinfeld* off the air and *Frasier* a consistent, Emmy-winning success NBC wanted another sure-fire hit to keep Thursdays as essential viewing – but it left the rest of the week looking bare. The schedule was full of sitcoms, but the need to tune in to NBC any night but Thursday had faded for audiences, and inconsistency across the schedule was doing more harm than good. The creators of *3rd Rock from the Sun* have long cited the show constantly being moved around the schedule as the reason it struggled to climb in the ratings. Moving shows around during a season to different times and even days hinted at desperation. It was as if finding the specific spot that would get *Mad About You* viewers tuning-in in droves was the only thing needed to keep NBC as the dominant network.

In part, NBC's struggles were down to a decline in the sheer quantity of available shows. Quality was an issue as well, but where in previous years the network had been able to throw a vast number of shows at the schedule in the hope that at least a few could go the distance, by 1998 that volume of sitcoms simply wasn't available to the network. Warren Littlefield had worked hard during his time as President of Entertainment to build a reputation for NBC as the place for new comedy – the place to which pitching writers should come first. By 1998 that reputation had faded, thanks to the network's failure to let new shows build audiences at their own pace. In the autumn of 1998, NBC's ratings were down by more than 20 per cent. Warren Littlefield had been replaced by Scott Sassa, with Don Ohlmeyer still acting as an overseer.

The hopes were that Ohlmeyer's guidance could see the kind of comeback that had taken place at the beginning of the decade, but the odds were stacked against NBC largely thanks to the network's own actions. After the prior year's off-air drama over *E.R.*'s future on the network, NBC had begun a new negotiation tactic in the hopes that the future would never again be so precarious. Unfortunately, the tactic backfired. The network began insisting on an ownership stake in new programming, rather than just the rights to air it. The studios that supplied those shows largely refused, creating a stand-off and effectively a boycott of the network. It wasn't a death knell for NBC, but it certainly wasn't a good sign.

NBC had, in the previous three years, not found a new *Friends*, and certainly not a new *Seinfeld*. There's a common problem, and not just on television. Something – a new sitcom or book or film – garners huge amounts of success because it's new, it's different and unexpected. *Friends* was such a thing, the twenty-something hangout comedy a refreshing change after endless family-centric sitcoms. The key to *Friends'* early success was in its difference. The problem arises when attempts to recreate that success focus on the style, trying to do the same thing again and ending up with a poor imitation, rather than finding something new. In 1997, NBC's schedule boasted eighteen sitcoms, a record at the time, and nine of those were brand new. Few of those shows, however, were doing anything new, exciting or different. Instead, they largely attempted to focus on urban city life and wit that couldn't be reproduced. By 1998 and the fifth season of *Friends*, multiple NBC sitcoms focused on a single (but not for long) woman, with some kind of job, living in or near New York, with a colourful cast of side characters. Despite Brook Shields (*Suddenly Susan*), Kirstie Alley (*Veronica's Closet*) and Christina Applegate (*Jesse*) taking the lead in these shows, the rinse and repeat approach was failing NBC. Monday nights had become a 'Must See for Women', with a line-up of largely female-driven shows. *Mad About You* had been a prevailing hit in previous years, but its ratings had dwindled after becoming part of that Monday night line-up. The show was in its final season and its ending was approaching with little to no fanfare. NBC was losing relevance and dragging once-hit shows down with it. The network's only saving grace was that so far, none of the others had risen to prominence in its place.

Once again, the only sitcom not on NBC to reach the ratings top ten for the 1998/1999 season was *Home Improvement*. Unfortunately for ABC, this was the show's final season. The end of *Home Improvement*, after eight seasons, signified a change in the land of network sitcoms. It was one of the last family-focused sitcoms on the air – in multiple ways. Not only were sitcoms themselves no longer centered on family units, but networks were no longer looking to attract families as viewers. Advertisers were pushing for narrower slices of demographics, and shows no longer needed to appeal to a broad range of tastes the way they did in 1991 when *Home Improvement* began. The fall of the domestic sitcom coincided with the rise of multiple television sets in households. With no need to gather as a group in front of a single screen in most homes, there was no need to create shows that would appeal to an entire family. *Home Improvement* ended entirely on the creator's terms – much like *Seinfeld* – with Allen ready to down tools and move on. This was a rarity by the end of the nineties, with abrupt cancellation the usual way to end a show. It was unlikely though, that ABC would want something similar as a replacement.

CBS carried an exception to the decline of the domestic with *Everybody Loves Raymond*, at this point in its third season, but much of *Raymond*'s success was down to shifting the focus away from family and keeping it on the main character. It was a domestic comedy, but one pitched entirely at grown-ups. Children and teens in a family unit would have their own screens, and find their own shows. Possibly the most successful sitcom to maintain that broad family appeal was the one created to be the antithesis of domestic comedies – in 1998 *The Simpsons*, on Fox, had been running for ten years and showed no signs of stopping. At the current time of writing, the show is in its thirty-fourth season.

1998 saw the beginning of two new animated sitcoms on Fox. *Futurama*, the futuristic comedy from the brains behind *The Simpsons*, never posed a major ratings threat but managed to build a solid audience and went on to become a cult-classic, recently rebooted. *Family Guy* didn't manage incredible ratings in its first season either, but it marked a shift in the animated world that had long been taking place across sitcoms: from domestic comedy, to anything but, to a family show that held little appeal for kids, all in a short space of time. *Family Guy* was met with a solid critical response in both America and the UK, becoming an unexpected hit for a network that had long been invested in animated comedy.

The sheer volume of new shows in 1998 wasn't as impressive as previous seasons, but there were still plenty of new sitcoms making their debut. The end of *Seinfeld* had left more than just a gap in the schedule – there was a push from all of the networks to find the next big thing and plenty of *Seinfeld*-seasoned writers with pilots to produce. While the end of *Cheers* in 1993 had led to the creation of *Frasier* and an expansion of the world in which it took place, *Seinfeld* wasn't quite so spin-off worthy. Instead, new projects by members of the show's team began to crop up the next season. One such show demonstrates the huge difference between critical appreciation and ratings success.

It's Like, You Know... began on ABC in the spring of 1999 as a mid-season replacement. Created by Peter Mehlman, who had previously served as a producer and prolific writer for *Seinfeld* during the bulk of its nine-year run, and with Andy Ackerman – another key part of the *Seinfeld* machine – in the director's chair for the first episode, the short first season of *It's Like, You Know...* exceeded critical expectations. There was an air of uneasy anticipation around the show before its release – the title was off-putting and with so much talent inherited from *Seinfeld* there were fears of a dull carbon-copy – but the show managed to make a successful impression. *It's Like, You Know...* was about the culture clash between the East and West coasts, focusing on New Yorker Arthur – played by Chris Eigeman – as he moved to California to write a book about the difficulties of living in Los Angeles.

This was Eigeman's first time in a leading role on network television, but he almost had the opportunity six years earlier. In 1992, Eigemann played Arnold Rimmer in the pilot for an American remake of the cult British series *Red Dwarf*. The show was never picked up, a better fate than many American adaptations of British shows received. In *It's Like, You Know...*, Eigeman's ability to deliver dry, sardonic wit was perfect for a show written to appeal to fans of *Seinfeld*. The biggest criticism of the show was that the inclusion of Jennifer Grey – almost a decade on from her starring role in *Dirty Dancing* – just didn't work. Grey was playing a fictionalised version of herself, calling herself 'the wacky next-door neighbour', and constantly referencing her history of cosmetic surgery. It was a joke that could have worked as a one-off, but instead was dragged out through the first series.

Still, *It's Like, You Know...* was well liked, with Caryn Janes in the *New York Times* referring to it as 'one of the few new series to deserve a long life'. Sadly, the ratings didn't agree, and the show didn't survive to finish its second season. *It's Like, You Know...* came off the air in January 2000, with seven episodes left unaired. The cancellation was, of course, down to ratings, but the competition wasn't coming from other, better sitcoms. Instead, the fledgling show struggled to impress against a new challenger to sitcoms and dramas – reality TV was about to rise.

On NBC, despite the studio boycotts, the network had two new shows that they hoped would land with a splash in 1998. The first, and the most highly anticipated, was *Encore! Encore!* – a new vehicle for Nathan Lane. Lane was a huge star of both stage and screen at the time, and he was no stranger to sitcoms – he'd even received an Emmy nomination in 1995 for a guest appearance on *Frasier*. *Encore! Encore!* was a show set up to succeed. David Angell, Peter Casey and David Lee were masterminding the project, and it was their names being attached that had people excited. There was an assumption that Lane wouldn't consider being a part of anything that wasn't at least decent, and a firm belief among critics and potential audiences that anything from the team behind *Frasier* must be brilliantly written.

The eventual version of *Encore! Encore!* that made it to air had Lane playing a womanising opera singer forced into early retirement and exiled to his family vineyard. The early episodes received fair reviews, with the *New York Times* praising Lane for his 'talent for creating flamboyant, theatrical characters'. Even in those early reviews, however, there were hints of struggles to come for NBC's biggest bet of the season, as upcoming plots were gently criticised for being too predictable. The issue for the network was, of course, the ratings. *Encore! Encore!* was the show that NBC envisioned keeping viewers tuning in on Tuesday nights after the *Frasier* move. Unfortunately, it failed. Given a chance, it could have been a slow-burn hit, but the network wasn't willing to wait, putting *Encore!* on hiatus after just three episodes. (The show originally had a thirteen-episode order.) In December, the remaining episodes began airing on Wednesday nights and still failed to pull in viewers. Only eleven of those thirteen episodes made it to air, and the show was cancelled mid-season.

While those first reviews had been good, it turned out that difficulties had surrounded *Encore! Encore!* from its first inception. Television is, by nature, created by committee, with networks and big stars often getting as much say in a story as the writers themselves. Ann Flett-Giordano and Chuck Ranberg – two key writers on the show – originally had something Broadway-themed in mind for the Lane vehicle. Nathan Lane himself wanted to play a chef. The writers and the star came close to calling things quits, citing irreconcilable differences, but the network had spent far too much to lose Nathan Lane. The opera-singer-no-more turned vintner and lothario was a compromise that pleased no one. The *New York Observer* turned out to be quite prescient when a review of the early episodes promised 'the recollection of [*Encore! Encore!*]'s awfulness will give you untold delight for years to come'. When *Encore! Encore!* is remembered at all, it is as a failure, not a forgotten gem. The show became shorthand for bad television. In much the same way that a camel is a horse designed by committee, so *Encore! Encore!* became far less than the sum of its parts due to the overwhelming amount of creative involvement.

One of the other new NBC comedies that began in 1998 was a much nicer success story. In 1997, David Kohan and Max Mutchnik – who, as well as their work on *Boston Common*, had previously served as staff writers on *Dream On* – were developing an ensemble comedy about a group of three couples. Around the same time Warren Littlefield – not yet replaced – was looking for a new relationship comedy to replace *Mad About You*. Littlefield took an interest in the project but wanted the focus of the show to be on just one of the couples – the gay man and straight woman living together. The pair duly set off to write the pilot for what would eventually become an NBC mainstay: *Will & Grace*.

Times were slowly changing for queerness in comedy. *Ellen* might have been cancelled the previous year, but it had opened the door for queer stories on television. The latest version of 'acceptably gay' to become trendy on screen formed the central idea of *Will & Grace* – the gay man/straight woman partnership. Kohan and Mutchnik were aware of this, including the box office figures for films like recent hit *My Best Friend's Wedding* to Littlefield as they pitched their script. In April 1998, Jennifer Aniston starred with Paul Rudd – future *Friends* cast member – in *The Object of My Affection*, a rom-com with a similar plot. The relationship between the titular Will and Grace was the safe way to be gay on television.

A selling point of the show was that Will Truman, the handsome gay lead, was as far from a homosexual stereotype as you could get. Of course, the show wasn't exactly progressive. Sean Hayes joined the cast as Jack McFarland – the most stereotypical caricature of a gay man imaginable, complete with jazz hands and a deep Cher obsession – to keep the show funny. There's nothing wrong with camp, but there's an awkward feeling in the early episodes of *Will & Grace* that the audience was laughing at the characters, not with them. Progress was still at a snail's pace. Eric McCormack, as Will, was allowed to play gay opposite Debra Messing's Grace, provided he demonstrated little in the way of his own sexuality. Sighing over George Clooney was acceptable, but kissing another man on screen would remain a step too far for some time to come. *Will & Grace* would eventually become not just a hit for NBC, but a groundbreaking queer comedy. In 1998, however, the show wasn't quite doing the work or getting the ratings.

NBC had put plenty into the show. *Will & Grace* was one of the few times that the network's tactic of demanding ownership stakes in new programming had succeeded, and with the series belonging in part to the network, it had to do well. Eventually, the complicated relationship between *Will & Grace*, the network and the production arm of NBC – NBC studios – would come back to bite the network, but at the time that ownership meant that the show had more of a chance to build an audience.

James Burrows got involved with *Will & Grace* early, first reading the script in November of 1997 and eventually coming in to direct the pilot. It was his attachment to the project, and therefore the opportunity to work with American sitcom's most iconic director, that convinced Debra Messing to take on the role of Grace. Burrows would go on to direct every single episode of the series, from the pilot right through to the final season of the revival in 2020.

The first eight episodes of *Will & Grace* aired on Monday nights. NBC were still attempting to find shows that could hold up the flagging line-ups on Mondays and Tuesdays, but by the November sweeps period it was clear that Mondays weren't working for *Will & Grace*, and the show was struggling with declining ratings week to week. One issue was the competition. In the same time slot, CBS had *Becker*, a new series starring Ted Danson and produced by Andy Ackerman. The big names on *Becker* helped pull in ratings that *Will & Grace* just couldn't compete with. NBC tried Tuesdays next. With no *Frasier* and the crashing failure of *Encore! Encore!*, there was hope that *Will & Grace* could revive the flagging secondary 'Must See' evening. It didn't do the trick, but the show had at least started finding its feet among critics. Eventually, *Will & Grace* moved to Thursday nights for the final five episodes of its first season. It was too little, too late – but unlike other shows with poor ratings, NBC was willing to give *Will & Grace* a few more chances. If the network hadn't had that ownership interest, it's likely that the show would have been cancelled before the end of the first season. As it was, the Thursday night slot would eventually make the show a hit.

In 1998, NBC had more to worry about than just the other networks and their line-ups. The competition from premium cable was continuing to grow. Not only were audiences divided with their separate screens in different rooms, but choice fatigue was becoming a real issue as viewers were confronted with more and more options. HBO, in particular, built on the success of *Oz* the previous year and 1998 and 1999 saw the launches of what would become two of the channel's most iconic shows. In the summer of 1998, the world met Carrie Bradshaw for the first time when *Sex and the City* made its debut – and just like that, the world of female-driven television was never the same. Later, in January

1999 Tony Soprano began visiting a therapist, and *The Sopranos* reset the idea of what a good drama could be. Against these big hitters, sitcoms struggled as networks looked for more ways to compete.

The WB slowly became a success story as it focused more and more on the teen market – now a popular demographic for advertisers. The other small network competing against 'The Big Four' – The UPN – was struggling without its own unique selling point. Network president Dean Valentine claimed that network television still had an important role in uniting a divided country, but viewers were more separated than ever. The idea of families gathering to watch a shared, beloved show had simply become unrealistic. Streaming has since been the big television game-changer. Now, entire seasons of shows drop at once, or they air weekly but appear on the app as soon as the clock strikes midnight and release day begins. Without a schedule, there's little to encourage people to gather around and watch a new show together. As with the risk of sudden cancellation, it's not a brand-new issue linked solely to the current world of television, but a constant state of shifting tides in how we consume media.

In the United Kingdom, back in 1999, a different kind of fatigue was emerging. There was excitement in the UK over new imports from the States. The Sopranos was a hit, ABC's new Aaron Sorkin comedy *Sportsnight* – which had failed to make waves in America – was finding an audience, and Fox's animated comedies were proving popular. Old favourites, however, were beginning to suffer. For the second year in a row Channel 4 only had the terrestrial air rights to *Friends*, with Sky1 still airing the show first, just a few weeks after episodes went out in the States. While not needing to wait months to find out what Rachel and Ross were up to after *Friends* aired on NBC was a bonus for those who could afford premium television in the UK, it meant a certain weariness by the time *Friends* reached terrestrial screens. By the time the show returned to Channel 4 for its fifth season, *The Guardian* was asking 'can we really be bothered?' Throughout *Friends'* fifth season, the show was somehow wearily received and ubiquitous at the same time. Gone were the glowing reviews and anticipation the show had received in earlier seasons. Now, *Friends* was simply there, a constant cultural point of reference as female relationships were regularly compared to Rachel and Monica, while sarcastic men of any kind were Chandlers.

The finale of the fifth season was described in *The Guardian* as a 'feeble climax'. The show was clearly losing its 'Must See' cache in the

UK, with viewers tuning in more out of habit than anything else. Five years and over 100 episodes was a long time for a series to last on US television, and with British sitcoms tending towards far shorter runs, the critic's fatigue wasn't so surprising. Channel 4 continued to air a block of American hits on Friday nights, but it wasn't quite the sitcom star line-up of previous years, now consisting of just *Friends*, *South Park* and *Frasier*. It wouldn't be long before the channel started making much more of home-grown comedy.

There's often an issue with shows that last for the long haul, especially sitcoms. It can happen slowly enough to be almost unnoticeable, but eventually characters start to become shallow parodies of themselves. The writers become so used to writing a particular character in a certain way that there's no room for anything else. This was clearly a risk going into the fifth season of *Friends*, but it was one that the writers managed to sidestep by sticking to what always worked best for the show and subverting expectations. The 'take thee Rachel' cliff-hanger from the previous season was wrapped up in the first two episodes of season five when the characters acknowledged what the audience already knew – that Rachel's feelings for Ross were ridiculous and unsustainable. Tension between them remained as the show spent a few episodes writing off Helen Baxendale, but the focus was on the importance of their relationship as friends, not their romantic history.

Ross was the character that, in the fifth season, fell deepest into parody. His second divorce and subsequent sabbatical from work dropped the character into a pit of life struggles that brought out some of David Schwimmer's best comedy acting. It's hard to imagine the Ross of season one playing the fastidious roommate, sadly standing in a bathroom doorway with talcum-powder coated legs and a balled-up pair of leather trousers, performing apartment window mimes for his friends or intensely screaming 'PIVOT!' while wrestling with a new sofa. All of this was there in the fifth season. Moving the character from romantic lead to butt of the joke gave Ross room to be more funny than irritating. David Schwimmer even gamely stripped naked in a scene which only appeared in the DVD release, drinking tea in the buff with Ugly Naked Guy.

With Ross and Rachel off the table, the show instead turned to the budding romance between Monica and Chandler. Thanks to that positive audience response and the joy the writers found in scenes between the two, Monica and Chandler quietly became the foundational relationship of *Friends*. In the eighth episode of the fifth season, Chandler and Monica became the emotional throughline in a Thanksgiving episode made up of flashbacks to holidays of the past. 'The One with All the Thanksgivings' was a difficult episode to make. A chaotic mix of costumes and the special effects needed to show Phoebe losing limbs in her past lives meant much more of the episode than usual was shot without an audience. Callbacks to Rachel and Monica's teen years allowed for both great and terrible costume choices. The fat suit on Courtney Cox was bad enough, but the implication in the story that both her weight loss and future career choice centered around the words of an adolescent crush is painful. However, the raids on the Warner Brothers costume house and local thrift shops led to incredible matching *Miami Vice* suits for Ross and chandler. The essential takeaway of the episode was that, despite some awful Flock of Seagulls hair, questionable fashion choices, turkey headwear and a severed toe, there was real love between Chandler and Monica.

Things came to a head between Chandler and Monica at the midpoint of the season – 'The One Where Everybody Finds Out'. It's an episode regularly considered to be one of *Friends*' very best, and thankfully the last to feature Ugly Naked Guy – one of the show's worst jokes. At this point in the season, the creators of the show were committed to Chandler and Monica, and wanted to see the relationship get serious. They needed to bring the relationship out into the open, and in 'The One Where Everybody Finds Out', a game of chicken begins between Chandler, Monica, Rachel and Phoebe, with the stakes building higher and higher until Chandler finally admits that he's in love with Monica. Even on its own, without all the build-up, the episode was still a demonstration of how far Chandler had emotionally matured, previously the commitment-phobe of the group. Consistently, *Friends* was better for allowing its characters to grow and change.

The final sting of the episode was Ross, the last to know, catching sight of Chandler and Monica in the act as he stood in his new apartment. That final credits tag was almost the opening of the following episode, but stayed in 'The One Where Everybody Finds Out' as a way to keep all six of the group in the action. This was an episode that showed what *Friends* did best – keeping the action tight between the core six characters, building up the tension and still finding a way to pull the rug out from under the audience with that declaration of love. *Friends* remained anti-schmuck bait.

That ability to keep the audience on their toes, even after five seasons, was key to the success of the season finale. In a two-part episode set in Las Vegas, the final minutes saw Chandler and Monica in the waiting room of a wedding chapel, on the verge of a last-minute marriage. For most shows, that event on its own would be enough of a cliff-hanger to keep the anticipation high for the next season, but *Friends* had more confidence. After almost an entire season of platonic friendship between Ross and Rachel, the finale ended with the pair bursting through the chapel doors in an incredible state of inebriation, apparently joyfully married. Many shows fell into the trap of parodying themselves, but *Friends* did it well. Ross and Rachel as a cliff-hanger was overdone. It had happened every season so far and there was no need to bring the two together again. What could be more ridiculous than a drunken Vegas wedding? Chandler and Monica provided the emotional hook for the audience, still poised on the edge of nuptials, but it was Ross and Rachel that closed the season, and this time the writers knew just how silly that was.

Chapter Six

The One with All the Changes

When people criticise television of the past, there's a handy excuse that's often touted: 'It was of its time'. Television isn't created in a vacuum. Any show, of any genre, can't help but be influenced by the time and place it's created. Neither is television consumed in a vacuum. Different influences can affect viewing experiences years or decades after a show was created. Even humour that was commonplace thirty years ago wasn't necessarily funny, or even acceptable. Just as television influences viewers, so do viewers form their opinions based on their own cultural influences. Calling something 'of its time' is a handy get-out-of-jail-free card. It's an excuse to enjoy a joke that really isn't funny anymore. A lack of diversity, punchlines that punch down, lazy stereotypes – these are things that get handwaved as just being part of nineties comedy. Not acceptable now, but apparently funny enough then.

There are, however, elements of humour that lingered for far longer than they should. Even as the show transitioned into a new millennium, *Friends* still had its faults. *Friends* wasn't, and isn't, unique in encouraging an audience to point and laugh at a fat body. Neither is it the only show to have opted for a fat suit over casting a fat actor. In previous seasons of *Friends*, 'Fat Monica' had been a punchline in flashbacks. It was humour that asked the audience to imagine the impossible: 'What if Courtney Cox actually looked like that?'

In the sixth season of *Friends*, that question was taken a step further as the show asked 'What if Monica still looked like that?' The fifteenth episode of the season, an hour-long episode called 'The One That Could Have Been', imagined an alternate history for the group. Each character got a different 'What if?' scenario. What if Joey was still on *Days of our Lives*? What if Ross was married to Carol? What if Chandler was a writer? The big question: what if Monica was still fat? The answer the show provided to that question was unpleasant, to say the least. Imagining Monica as a plus-sized adult, the show fell back on lazy and tired stereotypes. Monica was almost never depicted without food in her hand, and not because of her career as a chef. The re-envisioned opening credits showed Monica tilting the famous sofa on its side due to her weight. The credits sting for part one of 'The One That Could Have Been' consisted of Monica dancing, while eating a bagel, getting out of breath and needing to rest before the end of the song.

Possibly the worst part was the changes made to Monica's character to go along with her fatness. Monica in her usual form on *Friends* was consistently confident in so many areas of her life, including her sexuality. 'Fat Monica', on the other hand, was still in possession of both her virginity and an inability to even broach the topic of sex verbally. The implication that fatness means being less open to sex or confident about engaging in it may not have been intentional, but it's present nonetheless. In *What We Don't Talk About When We Talk About Fat*, Aubrey Gordon, writing on fat suit narratives, points out that these stories (often contrived by thin people) make the assumption that 'becoming thin is a life accomplishment and the only way to start living a real, full, human life'. It was an attitude evident in the episode, with Monica's life found lacking without thinness. At least until Chandler saved the day with his penis.

In commentary for the episode, Marta Kauffman mentioned how much she loved that plus-sized Monica was a 'happy heavy woman', as if plus-sized women are not usually joyous. Sadly, on television, that's often the truth, and not just back in the days of *Friends*. Fat women were, and are, rarely depicted as comfortable and confident in their own skin. When they are, it's often a punchline, inviting an audience to laugh at someone who doesn't fit the beauty standard and somehow likes themself anyway. Concluding 'The One That Could Have Been' by bringing Chandler and Monica together was sweet in the contest of *Friends'* sixth season, but the journey there was heavy with lazy humour.

The alternate-reality was a solid opportunity for the *Friends* writers to try something different. With the hour-long runtime and the need to do something special for the sweeps period, there was a chance for the show to be inventive and send itself up. The idea of a parallel universe in which Rachel never grew up resulted in fantastic work from both the costume department and Jennifer Aniston, bedecked in Rachel's zebra-print leggings. A role-reversal between Joey and Chandler was an entertaining twist on their friendship. Lisa Kudrow was incredible as the chain-smoking, stockbroker version of Phoebe screaming threats into a mobile phone. It was a completely different take on the character with just enough lingering kookiness (and kinkiness) in the background. The Ross storyline was a more painful watch. A version of Carol that never came out was played for laughs right up to Ross being pushed out of a threesome. The truth of a queer person unable to live as they'd like was an uncomfortable reality lingering in the background.

'The One That Could Have Been' is considered one of *Friends'* funniest episodes and regularly appears in best-of lists. It's unfortunate that so much of the humour came from an unkind place. The Ross and Carol storyline did, however, birth a funny coincidence. Their son Ben appeared briefly in the episode, played for the first time by Cole Sprouse. The show's creators worried in the episode commentary that viewers in the future might not understand what these *Archie* comics are – the ones that Chandler's so desperate to write for. At the time of writing, Cole Sprouse has recently completed seven seasons starring as Jughead in *Riverdale*, the surreal teen drama based on the *Archie* comics.

In the sixth season of *Friends*, Ross almost experienced his own teen drama when he began dating a college student. *Friends* often had the luxury of not sticking too closely to strict continuity. Twenty or so episodes spreading out across nine months meant viewers weren't so detail-oriented week to week, and binge watching to catch up wasn't yet an option. That meant that while some episodes would drive straight into the next one, even picking up the dialogue where it left off, entire storylines could also be forgotten or abandoned by the wayside. The nature of Ross's employment towards the end of the fifth season was vague. In the sixth season, he appeared to go from sabbatical to full-time university professor in only a matter of weeks, and the process happened entirely off-screen. There was a single episode where Ross was a guest lecturer, putting on an excruciating British accent. Then there was very little mention of his job until the final third of the season, beginning with the episode 'The One Where Ross Dates a Student'.

Said student was 20 years old, so not quite a teenager. Still, there's an unpleasant power imbalance there that went unacknowledged in the show. The age of Ross's student girlfriend Elizabeth was a constant source of humour for the group, but there was no real interrogation of the relationship. Instead, there was gross, thigh-rubbing glee from

Joey about 20-year-old women. The idea that Ross, after inadvertently marrying Rachel at the end of the previous season and briefly falling in love with her again at the beginning of this one, is glad to have a casual relationship without looking towards the future, doesn't sit well with the clingy, jealous persona that had become part of his character. In the Elizabeth storyline, he went as far as to follow his new young girlfriend to Florida for Spring Break in the hope of keeping other men's hands off her.

The relationship was short-lived, ending in the season finale when Ross eventually came to terms with how ridiculously poorly matched they were, but it almost lasted another season. An early plan for the season six finale had Elizabeth announcing that she was pregnant. The plan was to carry the storyline through the seventh season, only to reveal at the end that Ross wasn't the father. The writers thankfully dropped the story, not wanting to spend a season building an emotional relationship doomed to end. While Alexandra Holden as Elizabeth was fun to watch on screen, the baby storyline would have pushed *Friends* too far into soap opera. The writers also already had another pregnancy in mind for a future season; if the show made it that far.

The Elizabeth relationship might not have been one of the best choices the writers made, but it did lead to one of the very best celebrity cameos on *Friends*. Bruce Willis, star of *Die Hard*, *Pulp Fiction* and *The Sixth Sense* (among others), already had a decent amount of sitcom experience after spending five years as the lead in *Moonlighting*. His appearance in a three-episode arc on *Friends* as Elizabeth's father, and briefly Rachel's boyfriend, won him an Emmy award for 'Outstanding Guest Actor in a Comedy Series'. Willis being on the show was, as with Julia Roberts a few years before, down to Matthew Perry. Willis wasn't faxing questionnaires or demanding papers on quantum physics, but he did co-star with Perry in *The Whole Nine Yards*. Bruce Willis wasn't so sure that the movie, a comedy gangster story directed by Johnathan Lynn, would be a success. Perry bet Willis that the film would be a hit, and if Willis lost, he would have to do a guest spot on *Friends*. *The Whole Nine Yards* went on to become the No. 1 film in America for three weeks straight, and Willis agreed to appear in the show's sixth season. His three-episode story provided a decent ratings boost in the late sweeps season and served as a fantastic reminder that, when he wanted to, he could be hilariously charming – especially when serenading himself in the mirror

Rhea Perlman, John Ratzenberger and Ted Danson behind the bar in *Cheers* – the sitcom that made Thursdays a must. (*Album/Alamy Stock Photo*)

A bedraggled Rachel holds court in her wedding dress in the *Friends* pilot. (*Photo 12/ Warner Bros Television/Alamy Stock Photo*)

Left: The cast of *Friends* in their inexplicable vintage gear for Rolling Stone – 1995. (*Alamy Stock Photo*)

Below: The *Seinfeld* cast celebrate the show's first (and only) Emmy for 'Outstanding Comedy Series' in 1993. (*PHOTO link/Alamy Stock Photo*)

Above: Ross and Rachel kiss for the first time in the season two episode 'The One Where Ross Finds Out'. (*Photo 12/ Warner Bros Television/Alamy Stock Photo*)

Right: Peri Gilpin, David Hyde Pierce, Jane Leeves, John Mahoney, Moose the dog and Kelsey Grammer in *Frasier* – the hit sitcom that preceded *Friends* by a year. (*Pictorial Press Ltd/Alamy Stock Photo*)

Above: Robin Williams and Billy Crystal make a surprise appearance in the third season episode – 'The One with the Ultimate Fighting Champion'. (*PictureLux/The Hollywood Archive/Alamy Stock Photo*)

Left: Isabella Rossellini takes offence at Ross's list in 'The One with Frank Jr.' (*PictureLux/ The Hollywood Archive/Alamy Stock Photo*)

Right: John Lithgow, Jane Curtin, Joseph Gordon-Levitt, Kristen Johnston and French Stewart in *3rd Rock from the Sun*. (*Everett Collection Inc/Alamy Stock Photo*)

Below: The group watch on as Chandler reunites with Kathy in the fourth season's Thanksgiving episode – 'The One with Chandler in a Box'. (*Photo 12/Alamy Stock Photo*)

Joey, Chandler, Rachel and Monica face trivia questions from Ross in season four's 'The One with the Embryos'. (*Photo 12/Alamy Stock Photo*)

The cast of *Friends* arrive at Heathrow airport to begin filming 'The One with Ross's Wedding'. (*David Parker/Alamy Stock Photo*)

Jennifer Saunders and Tom Conti appear as Emily's parents in 'The One with Ross's Wedding'. (*Photo 12/Alamy Stock Photo*)

Royalty (or close enough) appears on *Friends* as Sarah Ferguson makes friends with Joey in 'The One with Ross's Wedding'. (*Photo 12/Alamy Stock Photo*)

Above: Warren Littlefield and John Wells join the cast of *ER* to celebrate the show's 100th episode in 1998. (*Associated Press/Alamy Stock Photo*)

Left: The only thing she can't have is dairy. Reese Witherspoon makes a guest appearance as Rachel's sister Jill in the season six episode 'The One Where Chandler Can't Cry'. (*Landmark Media/Alamy Stock Photo*)

Right: Regis Philbin in a promotional image for *Who Wants to Be a Millionaire*, the ABC hit that caused a brief resurgence in game shows. (*ZUMA Press, Inc./Alamy Stock Photo*)

WHO WANTS TO BE A MILLIONAIRE-The program with popular host, Regis Philbin, will become a regular part of the network's primetime lineup beginning on "ABC's Super Tuesday," JANUARY 11, 2000 (8:00-9:00 p.m., ET) on the ABC Television Network. "Millionaire" will then air in hour-line installments on Tuesday, Thursday (9:00-10:00 p.m.) and Sunday nights(9:00-10:00 p.m.). PHOTO SUPPLIED BY ABC/GLOBE PHOTOS,INC K17101JDE

Below: Ross tried to get theological in the season seven episode 'The One with the Holiday Armadillo'. (*PictureLux/The Hollywood Archive/Alamy Stock Photo*)

Sean Penn guest stars, dressed as the solar system, in 'The One with the Halloween Party' – the sixth episode of season eight. (*Photo 12/Warner Bros Television/Alamy Stock Photo*)

The cast of *Friends* at the 2002 Emmy awards, celebrating their win for 'Outstanding Comedy Series'. (*Featureflash Archive/Alamy Stock Photo*)

John Lovitz returns, appearing in *Friends* for the second time in the season nine episode 'The One with the Blind Dates'. (*Photo 12/Warner Bros Television/Alamy Stock Photo*)

Freddy Prinze Jr. poses on set with David Schwimmer and Jennifer Aniston while filming the 200th episode – 'The One with the Male Nanny'. (*Warner Bros Television/AJ Pics/Alamy Stock Photo*)

Above: Hank Azaria and Paul Rudd get into a less-than-impressive fight in 'The One with the Male Nanny'. (*Warner Bros Television/Maximum Film/Alamy Stock Photo*)

Left: Fans of *Friends* gather in Times Square to watch the finale on the Jumbotron screen. (*Abaca Press/Alamy Stock Photo*)

After the end of *Friends*, Matthew Perry guest stars on Scrubs the following season in 'My Unicorn'. (*Album/Alamy Stock Photo*)

James Burrows and Jennifer Aniston on stage at 'The Academy of Television Arts & Sciences Presents An Evening Honoring James Burrows' in 2013. (*Associated Press/Alamy Stock Photo*)

Warren Littlefield and Jay Sandrich attend 'The Academy of Television Arts & Sciences Presents An Evening Honoring James Burrows' in 2013. (*Associated Press/Alamy Stock Photo*)

Matt LeBlanc appears on a panel discussing *Episodes* with Kathleen Rose Perkins, Mircea Monroe, David Crane and Jeffrey Klarik in 2014. (*Associated Press/Alamy Stock Photo*)

Thousands of people queue for the Central Perk pop-up cafe created to celebrate the 20th anniversary of *Friends*. (*Abaca Press/Alamy Stock Photo*)

One of the most successful sitcom revivals to date – Bob Greenblatt, Eric Garcetti, David Kohan, Max Mutchnik, Eric McCormack, Debra Messing, Megan Mullally, Sean Hayes and James Burrows at a ribbon cutting ceremony to celebrate the *Will & Grace* 2017 revival. (*ZUMA Press, Inc./Alamy Stock Photo*)

Above: Marta Kauffman and David Crane accept the Heritage Award at the 34th annual Television Critics Association awards in 2018. (*Associated Press/Alamy Stock Photo*)

Left: Poster for the HBO Max *Friends: The Reunion* special, eventually released in 2021. (*Album/Alamy Stock Photo*)

with a falsetto rendition of 'Love Machine'. Bruce Willis also opted out of keeping his pay cheque for himself, instead donating it across five charities: The American Foundation for AIDS Research, AIDS Project Los Angeles, the Elizabeth Glaser Pediatric AIDS Foundation, the Rape Treatment Center, and UCLA Unicamp for underprivileged children.

After the second season episode 'The One After the Superbowl' drew criticism for relying too hard on guest stars, *Friends* learned to be more creative in using big names for a ratings boost. During the February sweeps period – just after 'The One That Could Have Been' – Reese Witherspoon appeared in a couple of episodes as Jill, Rachel's spoiled younger sister. Witherspoon hadn't yet bent and snapped her way into viewers hearts with her performance as Elle Woods in *Legally Blonde*, and was best known during *Friends'* sixth season for the 1999 movies *Cruel Intentions* and *Election*. While her appearance might not have got the same levels of audience excitement as Bruce Willis, it was enough to gain a few extra million viewers for *Friends*.

The storyline itself, Jill coming to town after losing the financial support of her father and briefly attempting to date Ross, was a clever way to keep the underlying tension of Ross and Rachel alive. After the disastrous drunken nuptials that ended the previous season, and Ross's clumsy attempts to avoid a third divorce, any hope for a future between the two seemed utterly dead. Rachel admitted that a promise of 'someday' existed for the two of them, at least if Ross avoided dating Jill, allowed a hint of the relationship that had sustained *Friends* through its early season to stay alive.

Witherspoon was hilarious in the episode, playing the brat and dramatically announcing that 'The only thing I can't have is dairy', before storming out after Rachel asks her to stay away from Ross. Jennifer Aniston and Reese Witherspoon would go on to work together again, and recreate that moment online, at a very different point in their careers. Twenty years later, in 2019, the pair began co-starring in *The Morning Show*, an Apple TV+ drama centered around a breakfast news programme. Aside from the first and last episodes, 'The One with Rachel's Sister' was the most viewed episode of *Friends'* sixth season, thanks in large part to Reese Witherspoon's appearance.

Reaching high ranks in Nielsen ratings, especially during sweeps week, wasn't a new challenge for NBC. In the previous years of sitcom's golden age, the network had consistently been top of the ratings. The top ten shows of the television season had, for the last few years, consisted largely of sitcoms. There'd be some American football and a couple of dramas in there too, especially *E.R.* – still NBC's biggest ratings draw. However, in the 1999/2000 season, one of the other networks presented a challenge with a new genre. In August 1999, ABC premiered the American version of *Who Wants to Be a Millionaire*, hosted by Regis Philbin, as a fortnight-long daily special event. *Millionaire* was such a success that ABC aired a second two-week event in November, before eventually commissioning a regular series beginning in January 2000. The show aired three nights a week and consistently brought in close to thirty million viewers a night. It was a dramatic change, with the quiz show beating *E.R.*, *Friends* and *Frasier* in ratings for the season and making ABC the top-rated network.

Other networks swiftly reacted to the changing tides, commissioning their own game shows to compete now that ABC had revived the genre. For NBC, the show in question was *Twenty-One*, a revival of a popular show from the fifties. There were risks involved, both in programming a game show on a network best known for comedy and drama, and in reviving a show whose original run had ended in controversy.

Game-show fixing was common in the fifties, and *Twenty-One* was one of the most infamous examples. In 1956, both audiences and sponsors had grown tired of the game's long-running champion Herbert Stempel, and the producers of *Twenty-One* instructed Stempel to throw the game in favour of challenger Charles Van Doren. Stempel attempted to bring the rigging to the public's attention, but had little luck until 1958 when the CBS game show *Dotto* was quickly cancelled after a contestant found and released evidence of the producers cheating. A grand jury was convened to investigate game-show fixing, and after multiple prior contestants testified; it was revealed that *Twenty-One* had been rigged by producers from the start. The ratings rapidly fell, and the show was abruptly cancelled in October 1958, just one casualty in the storm of fifties quiz-show scandals. In 1994 the movie *Quiz Show*, starring *Friends* guest-star Hank Azaria, recounted the scandal. Despite that, NBC executives were confident that the scandal would have little effect on the revival of the show, being all but forgotten by younger viewers and possibly boosting its notoriety among older generations.

Simply scheduling a game show wasn't enough to challenge ABC and *Millionaire*, but that didn't stop the networks trying. Producers, writers and directors of scripted comedies and dramas began to worry as ABC dominated the ratings. Cancellations ran rampant across networks who were more unforgiving of ratings slumps than ever, and the uptick in relatively cheap-to-produce game shows left creatives worried that there was a lot less of the pie left for them. Commissioning new shows became even more of a challenge. Judd Apatow, at the time a well-respected comedy writer and executive producer of the new, critically acclaimed *Freaks and Geeks*, said in the *New York Times* that 'with the quiz shows it just makes you wonder how much time will be available for writers now', after having a new show rejected by NBC. ABC's scripted offering lessened, but the shows that remained got a helpful ratings boost from *Millionaire*, as *Dharma and Greg* climbed the ratings in its third season.

May sweeps presented the biggest competition between NBC and ABC as the television season drew to a close. The final, two-part episode of *Friends*' sixth season drew around thirty million viewers to NBC on 18 May, but the final episodes of *Spin City*'s fourth season – the last to feature Michael J. Fox – got thirty-two million viewers a week later, a final boost to ABC's year of success.

In general, far fewer new comedies made any headway into the ratings compared to previous years, However, the Fox network made one appearance in the Nielsen top thirty with new family sitcom *Malcolm in the Middle*. It's a series notable now as a career breakthrough for Bryan Cranston, best known for his incredible work as Walter White on *Breaking Bad*. At the time, *Malcolm in the Middle* presented a marked difference to the shows it was competing against with its single-cam set up. This method of filming – largely on locations instead of sets, no live audience and single cameras used for shots instead of the multi-cam method of filming a scene from multiple angles at once – wasn't new to comedy television, but it was a real rarity in sitcoms and helped boost *Malcolm in the Middle*'s popularity with its fresh, energetic take on family comedy.

NBC's focus might have begun to shift away from comedy, but Thursday nights remained a draw. *Friends* and *Frasier* were still mainstays, but other comedies were struggling to pull in the ratings of sitcoms past, even with big shows as lead-ins. The lack of consistency in the schedule remained an issue, as anything that looked capable of drawing viewers was swiftly moved to other slots in an attempt to recreate the 'Must See' magic. Workplace sitcom *Just Shoot Me* couldn't get audiences to Tuesdays the way *Frasier* had in the past, although the show still managed a respectable average of eleven million viewers despite being in the same time slot as *Who Wants to Be a Millionaire*. *Will & Grace*, now in its second season, had moved back to Tuesdays, and its ratings sank as a result. *Suddenly Susan* and *Veronica's Closet* were both struggling to bring viewers in on Monday nights. Both shows were put on hiatus and cancelled by the end of 1999. On Thursdays, *Jesse*, the Christina Applegate sitcom now in its second season, was expected to maintain high ratings thanks to its *Friends* lead-in. While the show was highly rated, and far from hated by critics, it failed to deliver the numbers NBC expected, losing almost 20 per cent of the *Friends* audience. This was enough for the network to cancel another of the Bright/Kauffman/Crane shows.

New shows sometimes only lasted a few episodes if they couldn't deliver. *The Mike O'Malley Show* was panned thoroughly by critics and came off the air after only two episodes. One show that almost made it to the finish line of the season was *Stark Raving Mad*, airing after *Frasier* on Thursday nights. The sitcom starred Tony Shalhoub, well-known at the time after a six-year stint as cab driver Antonio Scarpacci in *Wings*, as well as starring roles in cult classic *Big Night* – in which he performed opposite Stanley Tucci – and *The Siege* with Denzel Washington and Bruce Willis. Alongside Shalhoub, *Stark Raving Mad* featured Neil Patrick Harris, still incredibly famous for his time on *Doogie Howser, M.D.*

Stark Raving Mad could have been a recipe for success, with Shalhoub playing a horror novelist obsessed with practical jokes, and Harris as his phobia-filled, obsessive-compulsive editor. Despite that, the show was cancelled in April 2000 with five episodes left unaired. The show's inability to hold onto the full *Frasier* audience or compete with *Who Wants to Be a Millionaire* led to its inevitable fate. NBC didn't want anything less than a top sitcom, and the definition of 'top' was getting narrower.

With new sitcoms seeming to be a continually riskier bet, NBC's focus that season switched to hour-long dramas. *E.R.* had been a consistent hit for the network, and NBC was ready to try to replicate its power. In previous years the success of shows like *Cheers* and *Seinfeld* had NBC putting all of their eggs in the sitcom basket. By the beginning of the season, the number of sitcoms on the network had dropped from eighteen the previous year to ten. By the end of the season, there were only eight left. Some of this was down to the studio boycott the previous year giving NBC less new material to work with. There was also a sense, however, that audience preferences were shifting. Five new dramas began airing on NBC in September 1999. Of those shows, three were new and original ideas, one was a remake of a British television series and one was a spin-off of an existing NBC drama.

The spin-off – *Law and Order: Special Victims Unit* – is, at the time of writing, the longest-running live-action scripted American primetime series, currently in its twenty-fourth season. The original series – *Law and Order* – holds second place. The original title of *Special Victims Unit* was *Sex Crimes*. It's possible that the series might not have survived so long without that title change. A spin-off in little more than name only, *SVU* was the brainchild of *Law and Order* creator Dick Wolf, and shared only a single character with the original series. Wolf was unhappy with *SVU*'s original 9 pm time slot on a Monday night, wanting a later airing for the show focused far more on adult content than its counterpart. After the first nine episodes, *Law & Order: Special Victims Unit* moved to Fridays at 10 pm and began to grow in ratings. In the show's first season it was far from challenging the likes of *E.R.* in the ratings, but it was more than successful enough for NBC.

Not all of the network's new dramas were success stories. The original show in that Friday night slot was *Cold Feet*, an American version of the British comedy-drama series of the same name. It followed the same structure as the original – following three couples at different stages of their relationships – but moved the action to Seattle. NBC originally commissioned thirteen episodes of the American *Cold Feet*. Only eight were filmed in the end, and only four of those made it to air. *Cold Feet* managed the lowest ratings ever for a Friday night show on NBC. Cross-continental remakes are rarely success stories, and while its British counterpart went out on a high, *Cold Feet* proved to be a dismal failure in America.

Two of the new original dramas on NBC came from John Wells, executive producer of *E.R.* One of them, *Third Watch* – a crime drama centered on the lives of police officers, paramedics and firefighters in a fictional New York City precinct – resurrected an idea that had been tried before. In 1990, Dick Wolf's *H.E.L.P.*, starring Wesley Snipes, attempted to tell a story about the three branches of emergency services. Unfortunately, *H.E.L.P.* was cancelled after only six episodes. *Third*

Watch, on the other hand, proved successful enough in its original Sunday-night time slot to move to Monday nights at 10 pm partway through the season, and even held its own in the ratings against Monday night football on ABC. The show would go on to run for six seasons – not quite as impressive as *SVU* but a good run during a time of rapid cancellations.

The second new drama to be executive-produced by John Wells was *The West Wing*. This was, quite possibly, NBC's most ambitious show for quite some time. Set in a fictitious version of The White House and featuring Martin Sheen as the president and Rob Lowe as his communications aide, *The West Wing* would go on to last for seven seasons and remains one of the most essential shows of the era. Created by Aaron Sorkin, best known at the time for *Sportsnight*, *The West Wing* was critically acclaimed and appreciated by audiences from the start. A huge part of its legacy is the 'walk-and-talk', a filming technique in which a Steadicam leads two people up a hallway, for example, as they converse. Aaron Sorkin didn't invent the 'walk-and-talk', but he certainly popularised it. It was a refreshing break at the time from the common quick cuts used to liven things up, and the technique has since become a mainstay of television that saves necessary-but-long expositional dialogue sequences from becoming static and dull. Sorkin went as far as to nod to the technique in *West Wing* dialogue as characters walk and talk before admitting they were each following the other, and he parodied the idea during a guest appearance on *30 Rock* years later, walking and talking with Tina Fey through the halls of a fictionalised NBC. *The West Wing* was a standout of the new season, and it looked like audiences were taking more of an interest in dramas during water-cooler conversations. The rise of dramas also meant more and more workplace-based shows – an indication of things to come in sitcoms.

The fifth new drama in the NBC schedule was the network's first primetime foray into the teen market. While The WB had already had great success in targeting teenagers, and Fox had long been finding success with teen soap *Beverly Hills 90210*, for NBC in 1999 *Freaks and Geeks* was the network's first real attempt at appealing directly to teen audiences. The show was created by Paul Feig and executive-produced by Judd Apatow. Feig, previously a stand-up comic with a handful of television roles including a teacher in the first season of *Sabrina the Teenage Witch*, wrote the initial pilot as a criticism of the teenagers and children he was seeing on television. The smart, fast-talking and precocious teens of fictional high schools were so removed from his own experience that he wanted to create something realistic; a show representative of the freaks and the geeks that made up his own teenage experiences.

Paul Feig passed that original pilot script to Apatow, who was an old friend from Feig's time as a stand-up. Apatow, at that point under an overall contract with DreamWorks, sold the script to the studio, who went on to sell it to NBC. *Freaks and Geeks* was set in 1980 and followed the life of Lindsay Weir, a previously good girl opting out of academics in favour of hanging out with the high school 'freaks' – a loose assortment of implied stoners devoted to Led Zeppelin and Rush – and her younger brother Sam, a *Monty Python*-quoting, *Star Wars*-obsessed geek.

Freaks served as a launchpad for a number of household name actors. Linda Cardellini starred as Alison, and would go on to a long-running role in *E.R.* as well as playing Velma in the live-action *Scooby-Doo* and starring in myriad other movies and television shows. Both James Franco and Seth Rogen – who played Daniel Desario and Ken Miller respectively – went on to have long acting careers, co-starring again in Judd Apatow-produced stoner comedy *Pineapple Express*. Jason Segel appeared as Nick Andapolis and went on to become a sitcom staple, appearing for nine years as Marshall in *How I Met Your Mother*. The series also featured a handful of well-known faces in minor roles including Rashida Jones, who made a single appearance as Karen Scarfolli and would go on to star in two hit NBC sitcoms: *The Office* – executive-produced by Paul Feig – and *Parks and Recreation*.

The early episodes of *Freaks and Geeks* struggled to gain decent ratings, but the reviews were fantastic. NBC remained optimistic about the show, moving it from a consistently unpopular Sunday evening time slot to Monday nights as a replacement for *Veronica's Closet* and *Suddenly Susan*. That move, in January 2000, came before DreamWorks had any answer from NBC as to whether they should continue producing the show for the rest of the season. Garth Ancier, the latest President of Entertainment for NBC, insisted publicly that he would be happy with a surprisingly minimal audience share, and claimed to the *New York Times* that 'the show's chances of returning next season are better than even money'. Behind the scenes, however, Ancier was voicing concerns that the show was just too realistic. He claimed to enjoy the characters but wanted them to have 'less depressing lives'. This became something that Paul Feig would struggle with throughout his career – network notes looking to add some television shine to characters he'd written as the antithesis of just that. *Freaks and Geeks* didn't change its tone and, despite the network's promises, didn't survive the season. The show ran for eighteen episodes but three of them remained unaired by NBC, eventually making it onto the Fox Family cable network later in 2000.

Despite, or because of, the short-lived nature of *Freaks and Geeks*, the show became a cult classic and is still loved today. There's a dissonance in the abrupt cancellations of both *Freaks and Geeks* and *Stark Raving Mad*, both launched and cancelled in the same year and by the same network. One was a show about high-school misfits featuring a cast of mostly unknowns and humour derived from organic realistic situations; many of the plots in *Freaks and Geeks* came from Paul Feig and Judd Apatow's own recollections of their disastrous high-school experiences. The other was a sitcom – something NBC was best known for – in a prime slot, starring two well-known actors. The latter show has been almost completely forgotten, a blip in the landscape of television history. The former is still lamented today as being over too soon.

A key factor in *Freaks and Geeks* surviving the tests of time to become a classic is nostalgia. In the case of *Freaks*, not just nostalgia for the late nineties television era, but a misty-eyed view of the early eighties when the show took place. The show wasn't just relatable for the teenagers watching it, but that slightly older generation that came of age during that era of *Star Wars* obsession for the geeks and Led Zeppelin obsession for the freaks.

It was that same nostalgic appeal that had *That '70s Show* pulling in so many viewers for the Fox network. *That '70s Show* began its second season just as *Friends* was airing its sixth. The year before, it ranked only fifty-fourth in the overall ratings but was a hit with specific demographics, ranked sixth for teenagers and twelfth for the 18 to 34 age range. The show appealed by avoiding constant tongue-in-cheek references to the news and politics of the seventies, and by staying away from exaggerated costumes and haircuts. As with *Freaks and Geeks*, *That '70s Show* was a launchpad for several young actors including Topher Grace, Mila Kunis and Ashton Kutcher (whose role of Michael Kelso almost went to James Franco). The show was created by Mark Brazill, who shared the duty of overseeing it with Terry and Bonnie

Turner – the couple and writing partners who were also supervising *3rd Rock from the Sun* at the time. Brazil attributed *That '70s Show*'s success to their realistic writing, telling stories true of their own teen years. The same kind of nostalgia was the selling point for *Freaks and Geeks*, but where Fox could afford to take risks and let *That '70s Show* find its audience, NBC had spent too long at the top to try.

It's that same nostalgia that now fuels a modern love for this golden age of sitcoms. The appeal of *Friends, Seinfeld* and others to contemporary audiences lies in the almost time-capsule nature of the shows. *That '70s Show* and *Freaks and Geeks* serve as dual-nostalgia, reminding the viewer not just of the seventies and eighties, but of the television era they aired in.

In 2023, *That '70s Show* got the reboot/sequel treatment with *That '90s Show*. Debra Jo Rupp and Kurtwood Smith reprised their roles as Kitty and Red, and most of the original cast made returns in a cameo-heavy first season. The reboot lacked much of the original's charm, but Netflix opted to renew it for a second season a month after its original release. *That '90s Show* is a clear attempt to play on nostalgia for both the nineties themselves, and *That '70s Show*'s role in that era of television. Whether it survives on Netflix beyond a second season is yet to be seen.

Early cancellation was never something a creator wanted for a show, but the sitcoms that lasted the long haul faced their own challenge of not going stale. While it looked like the writers had dodged that bullet in *Friends'* fifth season, in the sixth the cracks were beginning to show, with fewer long-running storylines to hold the show together. For *Friends* to last, big changes were the best way to keep the audience engaged. The relationship between Monica and Chandler was the real backbone of the sixth season, providing a catalyst for shifting living arrangements and the set-up for some of the season's most memorable moments. The first episode picked up exactly where the previous season left off – Chandler and Monica looking stunned in a wedding chapel having been beaten to the altar by a very drunk Ross and Rachel. The pair faced the question of marriage as they walked through the casino and eventually travelled back to New York. The marriage plot could easily have been hand-waved away with Chandler's commitment-phobia, but instead a gentler and more thoughtful tact was taken as both characters admitted they weren't quite ready to take the plunge. Instead, the episode ended with them choosing to live together. In the break between seasons Courtney

Cox married her fiancé David Arquette, and the first episode of season six was dedicated 'to Courtney and David, who did get married', with all of the actors' names in the credits receiving the suffix '-Arquette'.

Up until the sixth season of *Friends*, the roommate arrangements had been a safe, consistent part of the show. Rachel and Monica were there, Chandler and Joey were there, Ross was separate but close and Phoebe, appropriately, stood a little further apart. Shifting the gears in Chandler and Monica's relationship allowed for a reset among the rest of the characters. Phoebe presented an obstacle by claiming an off-screen, never-mentioned roommate. Rachel temporarily considered living with Ross, forcing the issue of the unresolved end to their marriage to a head and once again closing the door (for now) on the threat of romance between them. Eventually, Rachel and Phoebe moved in together, allowing the audience into Phoebe's living space for the first time in a few seasons. The need to fill a room in Joey's apartment allowed for the introduction of a new character, and supermodel Elle Macpherson joined the cast as Janine for a three-episode arc.

Both the change in living situations and growth of the characters allowed for an excellent twenty minutes of comedy in 'The One Where Ross Got High', an episode often ranked among the funniest. The ninth episode of the season, this was the traditional Thanksgiving episode. The holiday was often an excuse to force the characters into a single space for the bulk of an episode. 'The One Where Ross Got High' isn't quite a bottle episode, but it's close, and the episode took advantage of the addition of Jack and Judy Geller to divide the action into four plots instead of the usual three.

The main focus of the episode was Chandler's attempts to get on Jack and Judy's good side – after it's revealed that they have a long-held dislike of Chandler thanks to Ross using his friend to cover up some college-age marijuana usage – before he and Monica reveal that they're dating and living together. The rest of the episode was divided between Phoebe's unexpected lust for Jack, Ross and Joey's expected lust for Janine and her dancer friends, and Chandler's surprising lust for cooking magazines that led to Rachel's appalling mistake with the trifle.

When it's revealed that the pages of the magazine are stuck together – causing Rachel to put a layer of Shepherd's Pie into the traditional English Trifle – Ross responds 'Chandler!', implying that Chandler might have enjoyed the magazine a bit too much. This was an improvisation from

David Schwimmer – the writers wouldn't have bothered trying to get that joke past NBC's standards and practices department. In fact, the entire storyline about Ross smoking weed at university had to be run by standards and practices. It was permitted only as drug use wasn't actually depicted, and clearly only took place in the past.

Rachel's decision to take part in the actual preparation of the meal by making dessert was a choice by the creators to demonstrate her character growth – it's something that the Rachel of season one would never have opted to do. The end result was, of course, disastrous, but it was a testament to the camaraderie built in the group over five-and-a-bit seasons of the show that they all attempted to ignore her mistake and eat the meat-filled trifle. Just as Rachel would never have prepared dessert in season one, the group rallying around her, albeit for selfish reasons in Ross and Joey's case, feels like something earned after years of watching these friendships grow.

The episode came to a head as the chaos of the four storylines escalated into a series of rapid-fire revelations from the group: Monica reveals that Ross was the one smoking pot all those years ago, Ross announces that Chandler and Monica are living together, Phoebe loves Jaques Cousteau and Joey wants to leave. There was an incredible moment of stillness on stage after the revelations, before Christina Pickles as Judy took a rare moment front and centre to put the group back together. *Friends* was at its best when it gave equal weight to the silly and the serious, and Monica's parents accepting her relationship with Chandler provided a perfect underlay to the chaos.

The sixth season suffered for any long-term romantic relationships other than Monica and Chandler, but with the roles established for so long there was space to keep exploring different connections within the group. Joey's fling with his roommate Janine was short-lived, but it did provide a backdrop to a new part of Ross and Monica's sibling history. In the tenth episode of the season, 'The One with the Routine', Janine invited Joey, Ross and Monica to join her as background dancers for a pre-recorded segment of *Dick Clark's New Year's Rockin' Eve*. The long-running annual television event has been on the air since 1972, and it's easy to imagine Ross and Monica growing up watching the infamous Times Square Ball Drop every year. While most dives into Ross and Monica's past focused on their romantic relationships, or the antagonistic aspects of their sibling one, 'The One with the Routine' allowed them to be unapologetically goofy as they shared in the excitement and eventually performed an old, obviously well-rehearsed high school dance routine.

Elsewhere in the season the living situation changes, more permanent than the apartment switch in the fourth season, allowed the show to delve deeper into those relationships between characters. Rachel and Phoebe had, in the previous season, fantastic comedic chemistry as they worked to reveal Chandler and Monica's secret relationship. In the sixth season, they were allowed to settle into domestic almost-bliss. Early in the season they contrasted their personalities in 'The One Where Phoebe Runs'. Later, in an episode heavily laden with product placement for Pottery Barn which fails to land for a British viewer, Phoebe's sensibilities around home decor were explored in a surprisingly kind way. Yes, she was lied to, but the show itself didn't go quite as hard on making fun of her 'kooky' tendencies compared to other episodes.

While Phoebe rarely had a plot of her own to carry her through the season, she was regularly posed as a foil to other characters. In the early episodes, she became Ross's judgemental confidant as he navigated the aftermath of the Vegas wedding. There were regular moments throughout the season that appeared to be a test of chemistry between Phoebe and Joey as they quietly flirted. Admittedly, after the fire in Phoebe's apartment, it was Rachel who found herself living with Joey, although it would take another couple of seasons before the writers considered pairing Rachel and Joey off. Phoebe's rare solo storylines across the sixth season were often B-plots. One stood out as her sister Ursula made a return, using Phoebe's name to perform in pornographic films like *Bouffay the Vampire Layer*. *Buffy the Vampire Slayer* had only been on the air for two years at this point, but it was clearly present enough in the public consciousness to warrant a fictional porn parody. Towards the end of the season, still playing the sidekick, Phoebe was the one by Chandler's side as he chose an engagement ring for Monica.

Chandler's proposal to Monica was something Crane and Kauffman had in mind from the very beginning of the sixth season. They always knew they were building to it, even if they weren't certain of how to get there. After the almost-wedding of the previous season's finale was interrupted by Ross and Rachel, there was room across the sixth season to let Chandler's choice to commit grow naturally. Possibly the biggest change that prevented *Friends* stagnating was, after five seasons, to end one with absolutely no reference to the relationship between Ross and Rachel. In fact, there was no cliff-hanger at all.

The proposal began building in the pre-finale episodes as Monica took a risk by booking a beautiful wedding venue with a two-year waiting list. The resulting panic when Chandler received a call from that venue reassured the audience – the status quo was still in place and Chandler wasn't ready to move the relationship forward. At least, until the final sting of the episode, when Chandler admits to Phoebe that he's visited the venue and intends to propose. The following episode – in which Chandler shopped for an engagement ring – let the writers spend more time playing with the dynamic between Chandler and Phoebe, this time with both of them being honest rather than performing clumsy attempts at faux seduction. The comic build-up to a tiara-clad, musket wielding Phoebe trapped in the security system of a jewellery store gives the viewers a break as the tension builds to one of the most important questions asked on the series, almost as essential as 'How you doin?'

The hour-long finale, 'The One with the Proposal', brought Tom Selleck back to *Friends*. Originally, the writers had plans for a cliff-hanger ending more in line with previous seasons, this time with Chandler and Richard both down on one knee and Monica forced to choose. Instead, they opted for a clearer finish. Choosing to avoid ambiguity in the episode's final moments was due in part to the fact that this could have been not just the season finale, but the end of the show all together. At the time the episode was coming together, contract disputes were still taking place between the cast and the network, and the creators had to allow for the fact that this could have been the end of *Friends*. Of course, in the end, their fears were unfounded.

The build towards a compelling finale wasn't without struggle. Tom Selleck was only willing to come back to the show after seeing a draft of the script – he had strong feelings about Richard not being too antagonistic. In the end, Richard ends up providing Chandler with almost paternal advice, echoing their brief friendship from season two. Even with the continuation of *Friends* in doubt, season six needed a finale that would drive forward the show's future. The trickiest part was creating believable jeopardy despite an almost foregone conclusion. There had to be a slim possibility that things wouldn't work out. It helped that with Ross and Rachel, the show had form for not always taking the easiest, most obvious or most romantic option.

Although the two halves of the finale ran together in a single hour, each half had its own B-plot. The Elizabeth relationship was handily taken off the board in the first part, ending with an exterior shot of Ross on the receiving end of a handful of water balloons. This was the last exterior shot to be used in the show. Also, Joey acquired a boat, a story that the writers had no idea what to do with and eventually went nowhere. Adding to the challenge of creating the hour-long episode, which gave room to tell the story more fully but made it harder to maintain the sense of event throughout the hour, was David Schwimmer's schedule. He was unavailable to film the second part of the episode, having already left for the season to film *Band of Brothers*. The writers considered ignoring his absence, eventually acknowledging it in the final group celebration after the proposal with a joke about his multiple marriages.

It was a struggle to find a compelling but cliff-hanger-free ending. The duelling proposals would have been too funny, and instead the relationship jeopardy was maintained right up to the final minutes, as Joey tells Chandler that Monica's too confused and had left to stay with her parents. As Chandler entered the candle-lit apartment and the audience saw Monica ready to propose herself, the cheers lasted almost as long as they did in season four when Monica was revealed in Chandler's bed. In lieu of one last joke over the credits, the episode ended with no dialogue, just the couple dancing to *Wonderful Tonight* by Eric Clapton. David Crane said in commentary for the episode: 'Thank god we didn't do the comedy scene; it wouldn't have been good enough.' *Friends* had accomplished something rare in sitcoms. The show had changed its focus, and compelled the audience to return for the next season without a heavy-handed cliff-hanger.

Chapter Seven

The One Where Everybody Ages

For different generations, a milestone like turning 30 can mean a lot of different things. By the year 2000, as *Friends* was entering its seventh season, the show had celebrated many important sitcom milestones. There had been the 100th episode, the awkward clip show, and the big trip somewhere else. Making it to a seventh season was a huge deal at a time of network cancel-culture. It's the milestones celebrated within the show, however, that keep it ringing true with audiences today. *Friends* was such an essential hit for NBC because it appealed to that important range for advertisers – 18- to 34-year-olds. In the late nineties and early noughties these were the consumers with the most disposable income and the likeliest to spend heavily. The ages of the main *Friends* characters reflected the audience the networks most wanted to attract, and that made a set of thirtieth birthdays an ideal set-piece for an extra-long episode of the show.

In the fourteenth episode of *Friends'* seventh season, 'The One Where They All Turn Thirty', Rachel's birthday provided a framing device to explore how each of the group felt about reaching a milestone age. The episode carried a running thread of regrets as the group bemoaned the end of their twenties. Joey cries to God on both his and Chandler's birthdays, clearly in the bargaining stage of grief. Courtney Cox was hilarious as 'drunk Monica', attempting to feign sobriety at her fancy surprise party. Ross embraced the traditional mid-life crisis with a shiny red sports car, and Phoebe attempted to complete a list of accomplishments with the help of a space hopper. By the end of the episode, Monica has revealed her drunken state and Ross has realised that his purchase has made him old before his time. Bringing Phoebe's twin sister Ursula back to the show led to Phoebe discovering that she was actually celebrating her 31st birthday, with a list of things still undone. In a surprisingly tender moment, she shared a passionate kiss with Joey as he helped her through the new emotional challenge. There was no romance to the scene, although it could have easily been a jumping-off point for the two of them if the writers had chosen to go in that direction. Instead, the show embraced the depth of their friendship as Joey attempted to calm Phoebe's turmoil at having misplaced a year of her life by delivering on her wish to experience 'the perfect kiss'.

For Rachel, on the other hand, there was an end to romance. Realising that her life plan for the next ten years, including marriage and children, required her to already be in a relationship with her future husband, she chose to break up with her younger and less mature boyfriend. There was, as with Ross's relationship in the previous season of *Friends*, very little interrogation of the situation between Rachel and Eddie Cahill's character Tag. There was a double standard in the depiction of the two relationships, both with the age-gaps and the dubious power imbalances. Rachel's relationship with her younger employee was hand-waved away with comments about his attractiveness. While it appeared consensual, if Ross had used similar justifications for his relationship with Elizabeth, it could have come off as leeringly creepy. Both relationships ended due to Ross and Rachel looking towards the future, even as the show required them to stay single or away from serious relationships for a while longer.

Across *Friends'* seventh season, there was a distinct lack of romance for anyone but Monica and Chandler. Phoebe briefly reunited with David, played by Hank Azaria, one of her only near-serious relationships on the show. Joey briefly dated a woman named Erin, played by *Sex and the City* star Kristin Davis, after attempting to use Rachel to break up with her. It was only an episode-long romance, but one that cemented the new status quo as Rachel took on the roommate role. Ross and Joey found themselves in a love triangle for an episode as both attempted to date a woman named Kristen – played by Gabrielle Union just a year after she starred as a high school cheerleader in classic teen movie *Bring It On*. Kristen was a rare speaking role for a black woman, at a time when *Friends* was still being criticised for its lack of diversity. The needs of the narrative in the show consistently affected how viable relationships could really be on *Friends*, and that left Chandler and Monica very much carrying the emotional load for the seventh season. The characters were all growing up, but there were very few relationships to grow into.

The stories of turning 30 on *Friends* were consistent with cultural attitudes of the time. An often-cited aspect of *Friends'* success while it was airing was how relatable the characters were. The networks' and advertisers' target audience would have been experiencing the same doubts as Rachel and the rest of the group. The modern viewers with whom *Friends* remains so popular might experience turning 30 a little differently. It's unlikely, in this day and age, that every woman in a group of friends shares the long-term goal of marriage and children. This was true at the time *Friends* was airing as well, but that wasn't a reality commonly shown on mainstream television. *Friends* might have owed its success to being part of a new generation of sitcoms that stepped away from television centered on family life, but it still had to keep those ideas of family as a goal for the characters. Now, after years of economic crises, younger generations watching *Friends* might find the idea of 30 as a terrifying age to be ridiculous, as children, big weddings and stable housing become less attainable goals. Nonetheless, *Friends* keeps appealing to new generations, even as the characters grow less relatable.

Friends had so much clout and appeal at the time of its seventh season that it had become the cornerstone of NBC's fight to remain relevant in the ratings. *Frasier* was the older (admittedly only by a year but with the history of *Cheers* behind it) and more mature of NBC's two biggest hit sitcoms, but *Friends* was the Thursday night draw. In the 2000/2001 season, *Frasier* returned to Tuesday nights and *Friends* became the focal point of Thursday ratings. In that season, the Thursday launchpad was in limited use. Where, in previous years, both *Friends* and *Frasier* had been used to bump up the ratings of new shows, now only *Friends* had the honour.

The coveted post-*Friends* slot went to new sitcom *Cursed*, later renamed *The Weber Show*. Adam Chase, previously a member of the *Friends* writers' room, served as an executive producer on the Steven Weber vehicle. The original idea of *Cursed* was that Weber's character had been cursed by an ex-girlfriend to constantly suffer from bad luck. *Cursed* struggled to build an audience in the first half of the season, despite the *Friends* lead-in. Rather than getting cancelled, possibly thanks to NBC Studio's involvement in the show's production, *Cursed* was paused in February to allow for special sweeps programming. It returned as *The Weber Show*, reworked into a more traditional sitcom with the name changed to reflect its leading man. The changes didn't help, and possibly hindered the show. It didn't survive the year.

Will & Grace had far more success in its new Thursday slot. It was a move to Thursdays that had built the show's audience in its first season, and returning to the 'Must See' line-up gave *Will & Grace* another boost, moving it up to the top twenty in Nielsen ratings for the year. Despite its shifting position in the schedule over the previous year's *Just Shoot Me*, at this point in its fifth season, rounded out Thursday nights and continued to enjoy a steady audience; although it never proved a real threat to bigger ratings heavyweights.

In previous seasons other networks would avoid the risk of fighting NBC for ratings on Thursday nights, especially during sweeps. After ABC's success with *Millionaire*, however, networks were more willing to challenge the hallowed block of 'Must See' programming. Over the summer before the season began, CBS had an immense ratings success with the first ever season of *Survivor* – a groundbreaking bit of reality television that would go on to run for over forty seasons. *Survivor* was the first reality show to become a major ratings hit on a primetime network, and the finale of that first season was watched by over fifty million people. The show was such a hit that CBS decided to launch a second season, set in the Australian outback, in February 2000. It aired at 8 pm on Thursday nights – directly opposing *Friends*. CBS also opted to move the new, highly-rated crime drama *CSI: Crime Scene Investigation* from Friday nights to Thursdays at 9 pm, and add another new crime drama to Friday nights. *The Fugitive* – based on the movie based on the television show of the same name – was less of a success story than *CSI* and deservedly faded into obscurity almost as soon as the season was over.

Survivor was by far the biggest challenge to Thursday nights that NBC had faced in a long time. The network countered during February sweeps with 'Super-Sized Thursdays', extending four weeks' worth of *Friends* episodes to fill a forty-minute time slot instead of the usual thirty. *Cursed* conveniently came off the air for the month, and for the first two weeks the rest of that *Friends* hour was taken up with a set of specially created sketches from *Saturday Night Live*. The first two super-sized *Friends* episodes, 'The One Where Rosita Dies' and the aforementioned 'The One Where They All Turn Thirty', were neither written nor shot specifically to fill the longer runtime. The decision to release extra-long episodes had come from Jeff Zucker, the new President of Entertainment at NBC, fairly late. Often, the producers of *Friends* would struggle to cut an episode down to the standard twenty-two-minute length, and they were grateful that for once they could actually use some of the excess material. For the third week of the sweep's month, the extended *Friends* episode was followed by an outtake special hosted by Conan O'Brien in a rare primetime appearance for the late-night host. For the final Thursday of the month, both *Will & Grace* and *Just Shoot Me* also aired 'super-sized' episodes to fill the programming block.

Other networks backed down from the struggle between NBC and CBS entirely. The WB even pulled popular new teen drama *Gilmore Girls* off the air for February, rather than confusing viewers by moving it to a time slot other than Thursday nights. While the extra-long *Friends* episodes did well in the ratings, they struggled against *Survivor*, just as the show would for the rest of the season. The success of *Survivor* continued a trend that had begun the previous season. Both comedy and drama were struggling to compete against game shows and reality television. Fox even found success in a time slot contest with NBC's *The West Wing* as younger viewers headed to the network to watch reality dating show *Temptation Island*.

CBS was challenging NBC with comedies as well as the network's Monday sitcom line-up continued to draw viewers. Popular family sitcom *Everybody Loves Raymond* was in its fifth season and landed in the ratings as the fifth most popular primetime show of the year, and Ted Danson vehicle *Becker* was a consistent success. However, CBS had its fair share of failures too. New and highly anticipated sitcom *Bette*, starring Bette Midler as a fictionalised version of herself, only lasted until the spring as the early hype of big celebrities doing guest appearances on the show rapidly died down.

Unlike CBS, ABC failed to leverage their big ratings hit into success for their other shows. *Who Wants to Be a Millionaire* was still huge, one of the most-watched shows of the season. The programmes next to it on the schedule, however, were less successful. *Spin City* – now without Michael J. Fox – had far fewer viewers compared to previous years. *Dharma & Greg* was the show most likely to benefit from a *Millionaire* lead-in, airing at 9 pm on Tuesday nights. Unfortunately, it couldn't compete against *Frasier* in the same time slot and fell sharply in the ratings. New shows *What about Joan* and *The Geena Davis Show* were poised with their name-dropping titles to hold onto those *Millionaire* viewers, but neither show quite delivered on comedy or ratings.

While game-shows and reality television were growing as a threat, *Friends* remained one of the dominant comedies, and those super-sized episodes really showed why. It's unfortunate that the episode preceding February wasn't included in the promotion. 'The One Where They're Up All Night', the twelfth episode of the season, was a rare four plot episode instead of the usual three as the characters struggled through a night of insomnia. It was an episode that could have comfortably benefited from an extra ten minutes to tell the wider set of stories, even the simple ones like Phoebe's frustration with an unquiet smoke detector. The last of the super-sized episodes, 'The One with the Truth About London', cast an interesting light on the early hours of Chandler and Monica's relationship as their wedding planning – the only real story arc to run through the entire season – continued. The B-plot of Rachel teaching practical jokes to Ross's son Ben was a nice chance for the child character to be more than just a mute toddler.

The super-sized episodes, both planned and unplanned, were also an opportunity for small and large cameos. The first of the four, 'The One Where Rosita Dies', was an extended cut rather than planned as a longer episode. The extension allowed more time for the episode's c-plot as Phoebe, the character once again side-lined to a solo story, took on a job in telesales. Jason Alexander, best known for his nine years as George Constanza in Seinfeld, appeared as the suicidal office worker on the other end of the phone. It was a strangely sad story for a comedy, but in Kudrow's hands it worked surprisingly well; especially played against the loss of Joey's Chair and Monica's loss of her childhood things.

The biggest guest star, however, appeared in the third of the extended episodes. 'The One with Joey's New Brain' was written with the longer runtime in mind. The *Friends* writers wanted to get Joey back on *Days of our Lives* and enlisted Susan Sarandon for the story. It was often difficult to get big guest stars willing to appear on *Friends*, and Sarandon was a huge get. Both her then-husband Tim Robbins and her children were big fans of the show, and she was willing to appear provided her soap-opera star character got to wear 'A really big wig', as she told *US Weekly*. In the side plots, Ross practised bagpipes – a skill Schwimmer insisted on learning for the storyline – and Phoebe and Rachel fought over a fairy tale for the new digital age, while in the main story Joey's character Dr Drake Ramoray received a brain transplant. Sarandon owned every scene she was in, as both the soap actress and fictional *Days of Our Lives* character, dramatically slapping her fictional (on the soap) daughter – played by Sarandon's actual daughter Eva Amurri.

Friends wasn't alone in bringing in big names, especially for sweeps episodes. On the same night that Susan Sarandon appeared on *Friends*, both Ellen DeGeneres and Leslie Jordan appeared in the *Will & Grace* episode 'My Uncle the Car', the latter in a role that became a string of guest appearances as the incredibly camp Beverly Leslie. Jordan was a last-minute addition to the episode, taking on a role originally written to bring back Joan Collins after her cameo on the show in the previous season, but he went on to be one of the most enduring and endearing parts of the show.

Will & Grace was growing a steady audience after the move back to Thursday nights, and was also growing in critical acclaim; the show won three Emmy awards in September 2000. In fact, while NBC was struggling overall in the ratings, the network was doing incredibly well with awards. That same night that *Will & Grace* got its big wins, *The West Wing* steam-rollered *The Sopranos* – touted as the biggest awards contender of the year – to win an impressive five Emmys.

The success of *Will & Grace*, specifically, marked a shift in queer acceptance. The early seasons of the show were considered to be a pioneering bit of television, even as it did little to dispel stereotypes of gay men. More shows with queer characters were growing, including cable network Showtime's *Queer as Folk*, a rare American adaptation of a popular British series – this time one created by Russel T. Davies – that actually succeeded, going on to run for five seasons. In the spring of 2001 CBS launched a new sitcom called *Some of My Best Friends*, a short-lived and ultimately unsuccessful show starring Jason Bateman (a straight actor) as the gay main character. A review in the *New York Times* called *Some of My Best Friends* 'shameless in its use of hoary stereotypes'. The queer shows being made weren't necessarily good, but shows with gay leads being commissioned was definitely a sign of progress. Things had moved far past the need for extra helplines in case of customer complaints over queer stories.

Two people of the same sex sharing a kiss had gone from something that cameras had to cut away from, to a marketing gimmick. *Friends*, in the last sweeps period of the season, unfortunately employed the 'Lesbian Ratings Stunt' (as named by the website TV Tropes) during the season seven episode 'The One with Rachel's Big Kiss'. Winona Ryder guest starred in the episode as an old sorority sister of Rachel's. Initially in the episode, her character Melissa denied any memory of a drunken kiss with Rachel in their shared youth. Phoebe is cynical, insisting that Rachel would never do anything quite so 'wild' – it was a sign of how far things still had to come that this would be considered a particularly wild act. At the end of the episode, Jennifer Aniston and Winona Ryder kissed on screen, before Melissa confessed her undying love for Rachel and got in a taxi never to be seen again. Afterwards, Phoebe kissed Rachel to 'see what all the fuss is about'.

The news that Jennifer Aniston would kiss both a female guest star and a co-star was leaked to the press in the weeks leading up to the episode airing. Where in previous years, the kiss might have led to complaints, a parental guidance warning at the head of the episode – a step taken with an episode of Roseanne featuring two women kissing back in 1994 – or threats to pull advertising, with this the response from the public and the press was a weary sigh at the blatant ratings stunt. It didn't help that the moment between Aniston and Ryder stood in sharp contrast to two women kissing on another network. Just a few months before, in *Buffy the Vampire Slayer* on The WB, lesbian couple Willow and Tara shared their first on-screen kiss, although the couple had been dating on the show for over a year. It was a small moment of emotional support in an episode far more notable for the death of Joyce Summers, and couldn't have been any further from the Winona Ryder ratings grab.

Where *Friends* really dropped the ball on depicting queerness was in bringing Chandler's father to the screen. The character had long been the butt of jokes on the show. Chandler's father was described as a gay man at first, then the host of that all-male burlesque show named in 'The One with the Embryos', but wasn't truly introduced on the show until the penultimate episode of *Friends*' seventh season: 'The One with Chandler's Dad'. The character was depicted and described as a drag queen – Helena Handbasket – hosting a Vegas show, and was then shown living full-time as a woman. The actor portraying the character, however, was a cisgender woman: Kathleen Turner. An earlier plan involved casting a variety of queer icons to play the part, with Liza Minelli and Cher considered for the role, but said icons turned the show down, stating they were uncomfortable with the character. The *Friends* writers spent a long time discussing whether to show Chandler's father at all, and felt it was natural to cast a woman as the character was a well-known female impersonator.

The role was pitched to Kathleen Turner as a chance to play the first woman playing a man playing a woman. There was laziness there, conflating gay men, drag queens and trans women under a single umbrella. It's not that there's no such thing as overlap between those categories, but that they are still distinct and separate identities. Casting a cis woman to play either a male drag queen or a trans woman was a poor choice, and refusing to acknowledge that the character was trans while showing her clearly living her life as a woman led to a three-episode run of painful misgendering.

Kathleen Turner saw the role as groundbreaking at the time, but has admitted since that it didn't age well. Marta Kauffman has also acknowledged in recent years that the character was handled badly. On *The Conversation* – a BBC World Service programme – Kauffman mentioned that the character was very much written as a trans woman, even though she was constantly referred to as a father and as a 'he'. Kauffman explained that 'pronouns were not yet something that I understood'. Kathleen Turner, when appearing on *Watch What Happens Live* with Andy Cohen, said that she wouldn't take on that role now 'because there would be real people able to do it'. Of course, those people were just as real in 2001, but they weren't being offered roles on primetime television.

The mishandling of a trans character dates *Friends* far more than a storyline about a voicemail tape or the use of a clunky old phone. Chandler's unease and inability to form a relationship with his trans parent was resolved quickly, but persisted in the form of lazy punchlines about a woman with a penis. In earlier seasons, *Friends* was a driving, if problematic, force in the depiction of queer people. In the last episodes of the seventh season, it was unpleasantly lazy. 'The One with Chandler's Dad' wasn't helped by a B-plot in which Joey tried wearing feminine underwear for the first time, before rapidly reaching a point where his masculinity felt under threat. *Friends* often did well at playing with stereotypes, but the show was at its worst when it fell back into the status quo.

The seventh season of *Friends* had plenty of positives alongside the negative. In the tenth episode of the season, 'The One with the Holiday Armadillo', the writers used the traditional festive episode to expand on Ross's Jewish background. In earlier seasons, *Friends* hadn't engaged much with Ross, Monica and Rachel's faith and cultural upbringing.

In 'Holiday Armadillo' faith was briefly taken more seriously as Ross tried to teach his son about Hanukkah, fighting against the ubiquitousness of Father Christmas. Taken seriously is probably an overstatement considering Ross eventually resorts to donning a large – intricately detailed thanks to the incredible work of the *Friends* costume department – armadillo costume to teach his son about the history of Hanukkah. Not only did the episode eventually hit a poignant note, but with the character of Ben finally old enough to have both lines and storylines, the armadillo episode was a great way to grow Ross and Ben's on-screen relationship.

Originally, as 'The One with the Holiday Armadillo' was the last episode before *Friends* took a break for the festive season, the writers planned to close the episode with a Christmas song. In keeping with telling a Jewish story, they instead opted to use 'Tradition' in what might have been a jarring musical note for the viewers not familiar with *Fiddler on the Roof*. The most memorable image from the episode is the hilarious tableau of Chandler as Santa, Joey as Superman and Ross as Armadillo sitting together on the sofa. *Friends* rarely went fully ridiculous, but when it did, it did it well.

The ridiculous and the conceptual had become a rare thing in sitcoms by the year 2000. Possibly one of the last of the nineties sitcoms to embrace the 'wacky' was *3rd Rock from the Sun*, which came to an end in the 2000/2001 season. *3rd Rock* had struggled throughout the entirety of its run with NBC's habit of shifting schedules. John Lithgow, who starred in the show as Dick Solomon, complained to the *New York Times* in the weeks leading up to the show's final episodes that 'it almost takes ingenuity to do away with a show like this'. *Friends, Seinfeld* and *Frasier* were the shows that most marked the shift in the sitcoms of the early nineties. Sitcoms had become low- or no-concept, and *3rd Rock* was an anomaly with its alien characters and deep sense of silliness. The show was originally a ratings success, used for promotional stunts including, in 1998, a post-Super Bowl hour-long episode about sinister supermodels and, of course, the episode shot in 3D.

Jeff Zucker, the man responsible for cancelling *3rd Rock*, told the *New York Times* that he was grateful to the producers and 'out-of-this-world cast', and that 'their loopy and creative humour will make this one of the classic series of the 1990s'. The show has become a beloved classic, but at the time it aired it was as out of place on the schedule as aliens in Ohio. In some ways, *3rd Rock* was behind the times. The show had the same sense of conceptual quirkiness that had powered much older sitcoms like *Bewitched* and *I Dream of Jeannie*. In another sense, *3rd Rock* was ahead of the zeitgeist. Sitcoms centered on just family or friends were beginning to fade out of fashion, and more experimental concepts were about to become the norm.

While many of the shows airing on broadcast networks like NBC, CBS and ABC were fairly low-key, cable networks had begun taking risks with shows that had more complex structures. In October 2000, just as *3rd Rock* was beginning its final season, a new show began on cable network HBO – *Curb Your Enthusiasm*. The mostly improvised show starred Larry David, co-creator and one of the lead writers of *Seinfeld*, as a fictionalised version of himself. *Curb* was as focused on everyday minutiae as *Seinfeld* had been, but this improvised and almost mockumentary style show was a new way of making comedy. Premium cable was pulling ahead of broadcast networks when it came to conceptual television.

Outside of cable television, that growing teen market continued to mark the changes to come. *Malcolm in the Middle* was growing more and more popular and receiving praise from critics for its fresh, dynamic feel. The teenage audience had become a huge draw for advertisers, and as television grew less communal with the rise of multi-set households, networks were looking for new ways to bring audiences together. The rise in reality television and game shows allowed for now-rare unifying experiences as families gathered together to watch 'event' television. Comedies and dramas just didn't have the same effect. The growth in teen markets was further pushed by the development of online fandom spaces. Where teenagers would have once found it necessary to watch identical shows to their peers in an effort to keep up with the school equivalent of water cooler conversation, now it was easier than ever to reverse engineer the process: finding a show to love first then seeking out fellow fans in online spaces. Collective fandom wasn't a new thing, but the ease of access to it was a game changer for viewers with more freedom to choose than ever before.

Shows aimed purely at teens didn't entirely dominate the younger market. *Friends*, and even reruns of *Seinfeld*, remained popular with the younger generation, and *Sex and the City* was finding an audience in teens with access to cable. However, the opportunity to see teen content on primetime television had grown massively over the previous five years. The WB were so confident in their programming that they were occasionally willing to challenge the bigger networks. *Gilmore Girls* never posed a major threat to the *Friends* audience share, but was popular with critics from the get-go, and continued to build up viewers despite being in the same Thursday night slot as *Friends* and, later in the season, *Survivor*. *Gilmore Girls* went on to become famed for rapid-fire, reference-filled dialogue and was an excellent example of what teen programming could become – willing to take risks with the mildly surreal and unwilling to patronise its young audience, even if they couldn't catch all of the references to David Lynch's *Twin Peaks*.

Despite the ratings disappointment of *Freaks and Geeks* the previous season, NBC tried to get back into the teen market with *Tucker*: a new sitcom aimed at younger viewers. The show – starring Katy Sagal and occasionally featuring Seth Green as a fictionalised version of himself – failed to capture audiences, was considered bland and uninteresting by critics, and was unsurprisingly cancelled early into its twelve-episode run.

In the UK, Channel 4 was finding its own way to appeal to the younger market. The channel had long been home to *Friends* on terrestrial television, along with a handful of other hit American sitcoms. In 2001, they expanded into the digital market with the launch of E4 – a new service aimed primarily at teens and young adults. Channel 4 had become the centre of its own TV-based cultural zeitgeist in the summer of 2000 when the first season of *Big Brother* became a massive hit, but the terrestrial channel was risking irrelevance in a new era of television as audiences had access to more choice than ever before. E4 mixed an extended version of Channel 4's popular teen programming block – featuring shows such as soap opera *Hollyoaks* and American import *Dawson's Creek* – with the shows that had formed an essential part of Channel 4's primetime schedule in the nineties. While Channel 4 itself had, by 2001, changed the structure of its Friday nights – shifting from a block of American sitcoms (imported almost directly from NBC's 'Must See' line up) to a focus on British comedy, reality television and animated hit *South Park* – E4 was being touted as the home to all of the US imports that had brought its older terrestrial sibling success. E4 filed its primetime schedule with a prestigious mix of American television. Not just NBC stalwarts like *Friends*, *E.R.* and *The West Wing*, but also popular cable dramas like *The Sopranos* and *Sex and the City* featured on the schedule alongside edgier British comedies like *Trigger Happy TV* and *Smack the Pony*.

Some critics pointed out that shows like *E.R.* and *Friends*, both now in their seventh seasons, were yesterday's news and didn't fit the edgy, contemporary feel that E4 was supposed to represent. Channel 4 managed to create buzz around these shows, a necessity after a huge bidding war to claim the digital rights from Sky the previous year, by airing them on the new channel months before they reached terrestrial television. The first three seasons of *Friends* aired solely on Channel 4 but the fourth, fifth and sixth seasons all appeared on Sky1 first. In 2001, after a multi-million pound spend, E4 was able to reclaim the 'Must See' label that Sky originally adopted from NBC.

In E4's first year on air, *Friends* was by far the most-watched show week to week for the entirety of the show's seventh season, with *E.R.* the only other American import to reach the top ten once *Big Brother* began its second season. While the British press still largely viewed *Friends* as a tired disappointment, it was proving to be a huge hit for the fledgling channel. The finale of the seventh season had almost as many viewers on E4 – a channel to which less of the population had access – as it later did on the terrestrial Channel 4.

That finale episode was planned from the beginning of the season. The writers knew that Chandler and Monica's wedding would be the big set piece for the end of the season, but that presented problems. *Friends* had already done a wedding finale, and that one had room for an unexpected outcome. In *Friends'* seventh season, there was little the writers could do to raise the stakes after spending so much time establishing Monica and Chandler as a solid couple. Any conflict, any risk to the eventual 'I Do's' ran the risk of being schmuck bait – unnecessary problems building to a foregone conclusion. Adding to the difficulty of presenting a compelling end to the season was the expectation that the finale would be an hour long. Since the fourth season, *Friends* had been given an hour in the schedule to conclude each season, and that time could be challenging to fill. According to David Crane in commentary for the episode, there was 'a lot of pressure on the script ... the bar was really high'.

The moment the pregnancy storyline entered the episode the writers were invigorated. They had a secret to play with. The writers tended to approach the end of each season looking for a cliff-hanger, something to hook the audience for the following year. In early drafts of the finale the positive pregnancy test found at the end of the first half of the finale belonged to Monica. The writers rapidly realised how little that created in the way of tension for the following year – Monica being pregnant was very much an expected outcome. Giving Rachel the pregnancy storyline provided a huge drive for the upcoming season.

Creating tension and urgency within the episode itself fell well into schmuck-bait territory. It was a given for most viewers that Chandler, a character repeatedly shown to be scared of commitment, would get cold feet. The case of the missing groom built slowly in the first half of the finale. With that longer runtime, there was more of a challenge to keep the stakes of the story alive while stalling the resolution until as close to the end of the episode as possible. Plenty of room was given to the B-plot: Joey filming a movie with fictional actor Richard Crosby, played by Gary Oldman. Two-part episodes such as this season finale were usually shot over two weeks, each week just filming a single half of the episode. Things were complicated by Oldman's availability as he was only available during the first week. The veteran actor's incredible scenes of expectoration and inebriation were all shot alongside the rest of the scenes for the first half of the finale. Gary Oldman and Matt LeBlanc had previously worked together on the 1998 film *Lost in Space*, and their past working relationship was instrumental in getting Oldman to appear on *Friends* despite his unfamiliarity with television work. The stakes of Joey's unfortunate work day, preventing him from making it to the wedding he's supposed to officiate on time, were believable and funny enough to stop the momentum of the episode from stalling completely.

The Chandler story was harder to maintain across the full hour. The scariest moment of his doubt came towards the end of the first half when he disappeared, having left a note. As the rest of the group conspire to hide his absence from Monica, the audience never really doubts that the couple will eventually make it down the aisle, despite the writer's best efforts. There was a challenge for the creators of the show, having built up such a likeable character with Chandler, in raising the stakes high enough without making the audience hate him.

Behind the scenes things were further complicated by Matthew Perry's health, and there was a real risk the actor wouldn't be available to shoot the end of *Friends'* seventh season. Perry was in the process of seeking treatment for his struggles with addiction, and was living in a residential rehabilitation centre while the last few episodes were being filmed. Thankfully he reached a point in his recovery where he was able to continue performing as Chandler, and the writers weren't forced to contend with the actor's absence.

Despite the lack of tension generated by Chandler's disappearing act, by the time he and Monica made it down the aisle there was a sense of relief in the episode. As a string arrangement of 'Everlong' by Foo Fighters plays, there's a sense that the audience can let out a sigh, that they've been tricked into a comfortable conclusion. Chandler expressed his acceptance of the new baby to Monica only for the episode to finally get the cliff-hanger it needed. The live studio audience was cleared from the set when the last reveal was shot. Monica tells Chandler the pregnancy test wasn't hers and the camera slowly pans to a quietly crying Rachel.

With the wedding as a logical conclusion to Chandler and Monica's role as the central emotional part of *Friends*' story, the Rachel pregnancy was a much-needed way to reinvigorate the show for the next season. Both Kauffman and Crane were incredibly satisfied with the result, with Crane calling it the best cliff-hanger they ever did. Despite the rumours spreading in both the British and American press, *Friends* wasn't ready to come to an end. Building a story around a new chapter in Rachel's life was a way to bring new energy to the show while almost going back to its beginning. Across American television sitcoms were shifting, changing and falling out of favour. *Friends* had found a way to stay exactly the same.

Chapter Eight

The One with the Baby

The US network television season usually begins around the middle of September. At the time of writing, there have only been three times that the beginning of the season has been delayed across all of the networks. In 1988 it was due to a writer's strike. The 2020/2021 season saw severe delays due to the Covid-19 pandemic. In 2001, a world changing tragedy happened in New York. The consequences of the terrorist attacks on the World Trade Centre were far grander and further reaching than just a change in television schedules. Television, however, has often been an arbiter of bigger shifts in the world.

In the immediate aftermath of the attacks, networks aired rolling news coverage twenty-four hours a day. Premieres of new shows and first episodes of new seasons were delayed for weeks, and some shows and films were cancelled altogether. Multiple films featuring the Trade Centre towers or plots about plane crashes and terrorism were delayed or heavily edited. A teaser trailer for the first instalment of Sam Raimi's *Spider-Man* trilogy featuring the titular hero spinning a web between the towers to capture a helicopter was rapidly taken out of circulation. A *Law & Order* mini-series featuring the casts of both the show and its two spin-offs dealing with an escalation of terrorist attacks in New York was cancelled by NBC. The response across television in the wake of the attacks was fearful. Individual episodes of television like *The Simpsons'* 'The City of New York vs Homer Simpson', which prominently featured the towers, were pulled from syndication. ABC's *The Runner*, a new reality television show about an individual attempting to move secretly around the country while performing spy-like tasks and being tracked by the viewers, was delayed indefinitely.

There were big questions around how dramas that had a foot planted heavily in the real world would handle things. *24* on Fox was one of the most hotly-anticipated dramas of the new season; a political thriller taking place in real-time. The show's premiere was delayed and a scene involving terrorists hijacking and exploding a plane was removed from the pilot. *The West Wing*'s third season premiere was one of the many shows postponed. A special episode addressing the reality of terrorism in America was hastily written in the wake of the attacks and aired at the beginning of October. The stars of the show appeared at the beginning of the episode to explain to the audience that it was not part of *The West Wing*'s official continuity. The episode received a mixed critical reaction as the show struggled with the line between reality and close-to-the-bone fiction.

Friends, shot in LA but set in New York, faced the challenge of how to reflect real-world events without dramatically shifting the tone of the show. Immediately, changes were made to both the initial title card and the interstitial shots of the New York skyline scene in the show to remove all images of the towers. The first episode of the eighth season, 'The One After I Do', featured a title card dedicating the episode 'To the People of New York'. David Crane and Marta Kauffman, native New Yorkers themselves, found themselves reeling as they processed not just the tragedy itself but how to handle it in their own fictional universe. A B-plot in the third episode of the season, 'The One Where Rachel Tells…', showed Monica and Chandler's honeymoon facing delays after Chandler makes a joke about bombs while going through airport security. The storyline had to be removed and replaced, preferably with a new story that could use the same sets and still match a phone conversation with Joey. The replacement story, Monica and Chandler becoming jealous when another pair of newlyweds claim perks on their honeymoon, was maybe not the writer's best work but it certainly filled the gap.

On the day of the terrorist attacks, the cast of *Friends* were due to begin rehearsals for the sixth episode of the season – 'The One with the Halloween Party'. Production shut down temporarily as the cast, crew and creators dealt with the news. The return to set a week later was minus a live studio audience due to security concerns. Instead, extras and Warner Brothers employees filled the seats to watch the episode shoot. Sean Penn joined the cast for the Halloween party as Phoebe's twin sister's boyfriend, gamely dressed as the solar system. The most memorable costumes of the episode, however, were David Schwimmer as an unfortunately scatological sputnik and Matthew Perry's giant pink bunny costume. In a 2012 interview with the Television Academy, Lisa

Kudrow recalled that herself, Matthew Perry and others kept the mood up on set with 'tickling war games', with her chasing after Perry in her Supergirl costume to tickle him. At one point, during a break in filming, Perry flinched as Sean Penn walked by, certain that the veteran actor was about to join in the fun.

Perry even pitched a fourth-wall breaking episode tag to the writers, in which he (the actor, not his character Chandler) would approach Penn behind the scenes to ask for advice. Perry described the pitch in his book *Friends, Lovers and the Big Terrible Thing*: 'I'm smoking the cigarette myself as I say this, and as I put the cigarette out with my huge bunny foot, I say "I've been looking to transition myself into dramatic work."' The suggestion got laughs at the initial table read, but the *Friends* writers weren't willing to risk something as conceptual as acknowledging the world outside of the fictional reality of the show.

When audiences were once again allowed to attend live tapings, Marta Kauffman pitched an idea to the production company. She wanted to know if it was possible to fly around 400 people in to form the audience for an upcoming episode. The people in question were family and friends of firefighters and others who had lost their lives in the World Trade Centre Attacks and subsequent rescue efforts. The studio agreed, and the audience on set for the thirteenth episode of the season – 'The One Where Chandler Takes a Bath' – was full of people who were, as Kauffman remembers in commentary for the episode, 'really grateful for the opportunity to laugh'. The attendees brought sweatshirts and t-shirts for the cast and crew and in the episode, Joey wore an FDNY t-shirt specifically honouring Captain Billy Burke, a firefighter who sadly lost his life while rescuing survivors.

Throughout the season, *Friends* made nods to the tragedy and the lives lost. Characters often wore clothes that celebrated New York's emergency services. A small American flag appeared in the background of the Central Perk set. The messages on the board in Joey's apartment varied from 'I [heart] NY', to clever sketches of the New York skyline. *Friends*, however, never acknowledged the attacks openly. Neither did other sitcoms set in New York at the time. The general consensus was that audiences wanted escapism, not to watch characters they considered old friends experiencing the same grief as the rest of the nation. In that same Television Academy interview, Lisa Kudrow remembered landing on an episode of *Will and Grace* while channel-hopping and found herself thinking 'God, I wonder who they've lost', before remembering that, like *Friends*, *Will & Grace* existed in a world not gripped by tragedy. *Everybody Loves Raymond*, set in Long Island, took a similar track. The show didn't acknowledge the attacks directly but a small American flag appeared on the set along with a photograph of Stephen Hoffman, a long-time friend of lead actor Ray Romano who died during the attacks.

Sitcoms weren't considered the place to bring home the reality of what had happened. Michelle Nader, co-executive producer of *Spin City*, told the *New York Times* that 'We could never, as a sitcom, handle this in a real authentic way that would be satisfying to us, or America.' Marta Kauffman, in the same article, explained that 'I don't think it's appropriate for our comedy' to show the reality of what New Yorkers were dealing with.

Frasier was one of the shows hit hardest by the tragedy. David Angell, co-creator of the show, and his wife were passengers on American Airlines Flight 11 and were killed during the attacks. The first episode *Frasier* to air after the attacks also didn't mention them directly in the universe of the show, but ended with the tribute 'In loving memory of our friends Lynn and David Angell'.

Dramas, especially those set in New York, were better positioned to handle the news from the real world with grace. *Third Watch*, the NBC show about emergency services in New York, created specific episodes showing the aftermath of the attacks and the toll it took on workers. When the after-effects of the attacks were used in television shows it was done carefully, and with a great deal of thought.

The big prevailing feeling was that comedy was a necessary form of escapism and that any attempt to show recent events would, in a way, trivialise them. Audience numbers reflected the fact that sitcom creators had made the right decision. As more people looked inward for comfort and normality, families began to gather around television sets again and old favourites experienced a huge uptick in ratings. *Frasier* and *Everybody Loves Raymond* were among the shows growing in audience numbers, but it was *Friends* that people seemed to be turning to the most. In October almost thirty million people were tuning in to *Friends* each week, and the show was consistently number one in the ratings. *Friends* was experiencing its highest numbers since the show's second season. While in previous years sitcoms seemed to be declining in popularity, in the 2001/2002 season these established shows had become 'Must See' again.

Newer shows, comedy or otherwise, weren't managing similar success in the early months of the TV season, and it seemed to be familiarity that people were craving. Part of the problem was that new shows needed heavy publicity in the run up to premieres. By the time many shows launched after an aggressive twenty-four-hour news cycle and war with Afghanistan looking likely, audiences didn't have the energy to care.

NBC's roster of popular sitcoms had been dwindling dramatically over the previous few seasons. While *Friends*, *Frasier* and *Will & Grace* were still reliable ratings draws, the network was facing more competition than ever. NBC had, by 2001, long given up on making Monday an essential night of sitcoms. Instead, Monday evenings became home to *The Weakest Link*, based on the British quiz show of the same name, and *Third Watch*. CBS, the network that had posed the biggest threat to NBC during the previous season with *Survivor*, had made Mondays the home of their comedy programming. *Everybody Loves Raymond* was the cornerstone of the night. The show never quite managed *Seinfeld* numbers but *Raymond* was ranked fourth overall for the season and it was more than enough to build an evening of comedy around. *The King of Queens* – another family sitcom – was also a comforting draw for newly nostalgic viewers, and Ted Danson was continuing to charm viewers with his misanthropic doctor in *Becker*, now in its fourth season and another ratings hit. On Thursday nights, both *Survivor* and *CSI: Crime Scene Investigation* continued to challenge NBC for 'Must See' status. NBC executives remained publicly confident, but it was clear CBS had become a real challenger.

Other networks faced their own battles as The WB and UPN found themselves in a rivalry. The WB had built a large part of its reputation as the network for innovative primetime teen drama thanks to the success of *Buffy the Vampire Slayer*. The UPN was beginning to follow The WB's lead in building up teen programming. A contract dispute between seasons had almost spelled the end for *Buffy*, and the new season saw the vampire drama landing on UPN; a network away from spin-off show *Angel*. The WB countered and gained viewers by moving *Gilmore Girls*, the surprise hit of the previous season, away from Thursdays and the big NBC/CBS ratings battle – instead putting it directly against *Buffy* on Tuesday nights.

Most impressively, in a time when audiences were after the familiar, both networks premiered new series that – thanks in part to their connection to existing IPs – would go on to have die-hard fan bases. *Smallville* aired on The WB immediately after *Gilmore Girls* on Tuesday nights. Unsurprisingly, especially considering it was on at the same time as *Frasier*, *Smallville* didn't manage amazing ratings. However, the teen Superman story was revolutionary as part of a new wave of comics-based storytelling on the small screen that would grow massively in the years to come. *Smallville* might not have risen to great heights in the ratings, but the show quickly built up some devoted fans. On UPN, *Star Trek: Enterprise*, a prequel series set before the original sixties *Star Trek*, had the benefit of a built-in fandom. As with *Smallville*, *Enterprise* couldn't compete against the ratings heavyweights on other networks, but it was a surprise success for UPN as it became the top new drama for viewers aged 18 to 34.

One of the biggest threats to NBC's heavyweight status was the risk of losing a cornerstone series. The future of *Friends* regularly remained in doubt as the core cast continued to negotiate their contracts as a group. The last set of discussions about the actors' salaries had taken place during the sixth season, with the final deal made close to the wire. A particular point of tension between the cast and the network was that in 1998, Paul Reiser and Helen Hunt were each getting $1 million per episode for the final season of *Mad About You* – a show that hadn't come close to earning *Friends*-like figures for NBC and Warner Brothers. Those sixth-season negotiations led to a pay raise for the actors – $750,000 per episode in exchange for a guarantee of two more seasons of the show, ensuring that *Friends* would last at least eight seasons.

By the time the eighth season was on the air, negotiations had begun again. Lisa Kudrow was reportedly one of the biggest holdouts in the group, not sure if she wanted to sign on for a ninth season considering how side-lined her character had become. The cast insisted on, and eventually received, that $1 million per episode figure for a ninth and – the creators assumed at the time – final season. NBC's willingness to spend on *Friends* was due in large part to the fact that, in the years since the show began, the network hadn't successfully built anything up to take *Friends*' place as a ratings leader. Other networks had big shows approaching the end of their run in 2002 and NBC weren't ready for their own big finale episode.

On Fox, two cornerstone and (at one point) critically acclaimed series were coming to an end. Both *Ally McBeal* and *The X-Files* aired their final episodes in 2002, with the former criticised for having long since jumped the shark, and the latter having never really recovered from the departure of David Duchovny. As popular shows from recent years ended and with the news in the air that the *Friends'* stars were only contracted for one more year, cultural conversation turned to whether or not a show could successfully end before the audience grew tired of it.

ABC faced a similar quandary that season as two of the network's biggest sitcoms drew to a close with nothing there to replace them. Just two years previously, both *Dharma & Greg* and *Spin City* had enjoyed huge ratings boosts thanks to the success of *Who Wants to Be a Millionaire*. However, the quiz show that had dominated the Nielsen ratings in its first year had faded in popularity. Game shows were no longer a heady mix of new excitement and old nostalgia. Instead, they'd become a network standard so commonplace that even the eighth season of *Friends* had Joey preparing for a game show host audition. *Dharma & Greg*'s ratings had dropped dramatically since its third season when *Millionaire* was at peak popularity. The problems with the show were compounded by a sour critical response to the fourth season's car-crash cliff-hanger, and the fifth season would be its last.

Dharma & Greg and *Spin City* both aired on Tuesday nights as part of ABC's attempt to build a comedy programming block that could rival NBC. The network had little success. *Spin City* struggled in the wake of the World Trade Centre Attacks due in part to the show's depiction of an incompetent New York City mayor. *Spin City* failed to provide escapism or entertainment, instead feeling out of touch. Some executives felt the show was reaching the natural end of its run anyway, and the ratings had certainly dwindled after Michael J. Fox left the show. The co-creator of *Spin City*, Gary David Goldberg, insisted that the poor ratings were due to shifting schedules, complaining that the show had moved to too many different time slots. The Tuesday block on ABC changed often throughout the season as *Bob Patterson*, a new and ultimately unsuccessful vehicle for Jason Alexander, struggled for a while before being replaced by ratings safe-bet *NYPD Blue*. *Spin City* was regularly moved as the network tried to find a line-up that worked.

There were similar issues with ABC's Wednesday night programming, and a move there did little for *Bob Patterson* – the show was cancelled by the end of October 2001. Only relative newbie *My Wife & Kids* and long-established *The Drew Carey Show* got consistent times in the schedule. Reviewers were optimistic about *According to Jim*, a new family comedy starring Jim Belushi that also aired on Wednesday nights. *Jim* never got impressive ratings, but nonetheless managed to continue being completely adequate for the next eight years. ABS were still doing some quick cancellations, but the network had less dominance in the comedy arena than NBC and was more willing to wait and see if an audience could grow for a promising show.

NBC, on the other hand, was far less willing to take risks, especially on shows holding a Thursday night slot. The network's first attempt that season to fill the post-*Friends* half-hour was *Inside Schwartz*. The conceptual show starred Breckin Meyer (of *Clueless* fame) as a sportscaster whose dating life was depicted as ESPN style highlight reels, featuring various sports personalities. The show managed to consistently hold on to a good percentage of the *Friends* audience, but it wasn't good enough for NBC, who believed something new could get more viewers in the same slot. By January, *Inside Schwartz* had been cancelled.

It was replaced by *Leap of Faith* – NBC's answer to *Sex and the City*. *Leap of Faith* starred Sarah Paulson as the well-behaved friend in a foursome completed by Regina King, Lisa Edelstein and Ken Marino. The show was briefly lauded for allowing some salaciousness on usually buttoned-up network television, but it was criticised for its predictability. *Leap of Faith* was a success in the schedule, reaching ninth in the ratings for the season, but it wasn't successful enough for NBC. The show was cancelled after just six episodes, and the post-*Friends* time slot was filled with more *Friends* – repeats which ultimately gained more viewers than either *Schwartz* or *Leap of Faith* could manage.

NBC's Tuesday line-up became a rotating mess of attempts at new programming for most of the season. Briefly, the block of shows began with *Emeril* at 8 pm – a sitcom based on the life of, and starring, TV chef Emeril Lagasse. Although the creators of the show blamed *Emeril*'s struggle to find an audience on the new coverage of the terrorist attacks and a subsequent lack of promotion, it was likely that the consistent panning from critics and the fact that the show just wasn't good led to it being cancelled after just seven episodes. *Emeril* was replaced by *Imagine That*, a new series originally called *The Hank Azaria Show* starring, funnily enough, Hank Azaria. *Imagine That* was originally created by Seth

Kurland, a former *Friends* producer, but by the time the show had reached the air Kurland had left due to creative differences. The show was based around Azaria playing a comedy writer whose fantasies materialised on screen. It could have been a new and unique concept if *Ally McBeal* hadn't been doing something similar for the last five years, and if *Dream On* had never happened. NBC only scheduled five episodes of *Imagine That* to air – a short run for a new show, but room was needed in the schedule for television coverage of the winter Olympics in Salt Lake City. The first two episodes of *Imagine That* were positively reviewed – sort-of. Caryn James, writing for *The New York Times* called the show 'a labored premise given wit and liveliness by glittering performances'. The ratings didn't agree and, in the end, those first two episodes were the only ones to make it to the screen. *Imagine That* quickly faded from cultural memory, replaced in the schedule by repeats of *Frasier*.

Joining the struggle for Tuesday night ratings on NBC was *Watching Ellie* – a new show featuring *Seinfeld* star Julia Louis-Dreyfus. There was doubt if Louis-Dreyfus could succeed as the lead in her own show; both Michael Richards and Jason Alexander had struggled with theirs. *Watching Ellie* was a rarity in the early noughties. It was shot single-camera style, had no laugh track and each episode took place in real time. Jeff Zucker, still President of Entertainment, was highly enthusiastic about the show and was the one to suggest a clock appearing in the corner of the screen to show the minutes of the episodes counting down. *Ellie* also starred Steve Carell, best known at the time for his work as a correspondent for *The Daily Show*. Louis-Dreyfus and her husband Brad Hall, who came up with the original concept for *Watching Ellie*, pitched the show to multiple networks. It was turned down by ABC, CBS, Fox and HBO before it found a home at NBC.

Julia Louis-Dreyfuss and Brad Hall's demands contributed to the struggle of getting *Watching Ellie* on the air. They were contracted to earn $350,000 per episode, and insisted on each season being only fifteen episodes long. The cost of producing the show was much higher than the average sitcom. The single-camera style meant each episode took eight days to shoot, as opposed to the two or three expected of most multi-camera sitcoms. These extensive costs led to the original production company, Carsey-Werner-Mandabach Productions, dropping out of the project early in the show's conception. NBC Studios stepped in, which might have contributed to the network's very public enthusiasm for the new show.

Watching Ellie wasn't exactly highly anticipated, or loved by critics. An early *Entertainment Weekly* review described the show as 'a sitcom that actually prides itself on not being funny'. Thirteen episodes were filmed for the first season and only ten made it to air before, in April 2002, *Watching Ellie* was placed on indefinite hiatus due to its poor ratings. When it eventually came time to make the second season, *Watching Ellie* was revamped into a traditional multi-cam sitcom, complete with laugh track. This new version of the show proved to be even less of a hit with audiences and *Ellie* was, unsurprisingly, cancelled.

There was one new success story on that Tuesday night line-up. In October 2001, the pilot episode of *Scrubs* aired immediately after *Frasier*, and proved that there was some hope for sitcoms outside of the traditional mould. Until this point, *Malcolm in the Middle* had been an anomaly – a single-cam sitcom filled with clever cuts that actually succeeded with both critics and the ratings. As *Scrubs* became popular, it was a sign that sitcoms were ready to take a new shape. The show was the brainchild of Bill Lawrence, best known at the time for co-creating *Spin City*. The idea for the show, following the lives of young doctors working at Sacred Heart Hospital, stemmed from anecdotes Lawrence had heard. Two of his school-age best friends had gone on to become doctors, and anecdotes from their work life provided plenty of sitcom material. One of those friends, Jonathan Doris, worked as a regular medical advisor for *Scrubs* and the main character, John 'J.D.' Dorian was named in his honour.

The cast of *Scrubs* featured an impressive mix of unknowns and well-knowns. Zach Braff had only a handful of roles to his name when he was cast as J.D. On the other hand, there was Donald Faison, who played J.D.'s best friend Turk and was already well known for his supporting role in the film *Clueless*, as well as the spin-off sitcom of the same name. Sarah Chalke, who played Elliot Reid, had possibly the most sitcom experience going into the show, having appeared as the 'Second Becky' on *Roseanne*. John C. McGinley, on the other hand, was best known for his film work – especially 1986's *Platoon*. *Scrubs* was his first major television role.

Scrubs stood out for its great soundtrack and lack of laugh track, but there was more that made it a groundbreaking sitcom. Workplace sitcoms weren't new, but the workplaces in comedy were often low-stakes; a background setting that served to get all of the characters into the same room. In *Scrubs* the hospital was very much the driving force of the show. *Scrubs* was filmed entirely on location in an abandoned hospital. Old patient rooms became dressing rooms for the performers, and while renovations did take place to make filming easier, the production team intentionally left the building in a state of disrepair to give the show a scruffier, darker appearance. The tone of the show was much darker than other sitcoms of the time. Bill Lawrence compared it to classic comedy-drama *M*A*S*H*, a show where – in Lawrence's words when talking to *The New York Times* – 'you had two funny stories and then the young pianist who loses his hands'. *Scrubs* also stood out for its fantasy vignettes, something which drew a constant comparison to Ally McBeal but paid off far better than those in *Imagine That*, and its willingness to dive into the difficulty and hardships of a career in medicine. The humour of the show was punched up by a constant background of the grim threat of illness, and critics responded well to early episodes.

Scrubs was in a strange position, produced by ABC but airing on rival network NBC. NBC originally ordered thirteen episodes of the series, and although it couldn't hold on to all of *Frasier*'s audience it was enough of a success for that order to swiftly become a full season. From the first episodes, it was thoroughly successful with critics. Some of that success was down to the excellent mix of casting. While some characters were destined to be leads from the beginning, the writers of the show were constantly willing to let more material develop for actors that impressed them. The show had the diversity that had been sorely missing from sitcoms for a while, and it had the good sense not to become too trapped in a tight ensemble with no room for new characters. Early in the first season Bill Lawrence cast his wife Christa Miller, who had been starring on *The Drew Carey Show* for six years, to play Dr Cox's wife for a single episode. Her chemistry with the rest of the cast was so impressive that by the second season she had a recurring role as the acerbic Jordan. *Scrubs* was also willing to take a bigger risk with its own Ross and Rachel, pairing up J.D. and Elliot then separating them again in a single episode. It was a far cry from the slow burn of *Friends*, but it allowed more than a single relationship to be the engine that drove the early episodes. *Scrubs* wasn't yet a ratings hit, but it had the drive to get there.

In the eighth season of *Friends*, the 'will they, won't they?' question was still being asked, but the writers had introduced new obstacles for Ross and Rachel. As the creators of the show didn't know at the

actor, he had solid comedy chops and had been appearing regularly on *Saturday Night Live* since 1990. Just like Steve Carell, Baldwin would go on to play a fantastic sitcom character later in the noughties. His character Parker on *Friends* dated Phoebe for just a single episode, 'The One in Massapequa', before the pair broke things off due to his ridiculous and overwhelming enthusiasm for … well everything.

It was understandable, in the eighth season of *Friends,* that Lisa Kudrow was so frustrated with her role. While Ross and Rachel moved apart and drifted back together, Monica and Chandler had settled into married bliss and even Joey got a romantic storyline, Phoebe's romantic life had long been side-lined. Phoebe had only been given two brief opportunities for romance in the eighth season and there seemed to be little else on the horizon. While pairing her with Joey would have been far too obvious and convenient, despite the chemistry between the pair, bringing a new character on to the show for any kind of serious relationship with one of the core six was a difficult prospect – forcing the ensemble to accommodate a seventh member. Phoebe's relationship paucity was eventually solved in the following season, but in 2001 and 2002 she was still very much pushed to the side.

The relationship between Chandler and Monica didn't have much to do after the previous season ended in marriage, and the pair that had driven the show emotionally for the previous few seasons had to take a more supportive role. There was very little the writers could do to create any serious conflict between the pair, and they were regularly relegated to B-plots as Rachel's pregnancy became the dominant storyline of the season. Nonetheless, they provided a solid emotional satisfaction in the season finale as they agreed to try for a child of their own. Previously commitment-phobic Chandler took the lead in the decision after Monica's attempt to terrify him with broodiness as they waited in the hospital for Rachel to give birth. The eighth season of *Friends* ended on another cliff-hanger as new mother Rachel accepted an accidental proposal from Joey, and Ross considered his future with the mother of his daughter. Setting up Monica and Chandler's plans to have a family was a clever way to ensure that there was more to carry the next season emotionally than just a love triangle between Rachel, Joey and Ross.

When the writers concluded *Friends'* seventh season with the reveal of Rachel's pregnancy, they were excited to have an engine that could drive forward the eighth. *Friends* had struggled in the ratings in recent years. Struggled is a relative term in this case; *Friends* never left the Nielsen top ten but it had begun to dip in ratings as reality television began to dominate. The eighth season propelled the show into the number one spot for the first time in its run, and it was the second most-watched season of the show overall. The drive among viewers for familiar television in the wake of the September 11th attacks was a major contributing factor towards the high ratings early in the season. Over thirty-one million people tuned in to watch the first episode, 'The One After "I Do"'. There was, however, more than just comfort-watching to keep viewers engaged as the season went on.

The writers spoke avidly about how much the pregnancy storyline had given *Friends* a new burst of energy. So many sitcoms fell off in ratings during their later seasons, limping towards their finale finish-lines. Sometimes this was due to the interference of the networks, but more often than not it was down to the stories themselves. Trying to keep some kind of status quo among main characters would often turn shows into stale imitations of their former hit selves. *Friends*, on the other hand, was applauded for being bold enough to let its characters change. Imagine an alternative *Friends*, one in which Chandler remained a stunted man-child and Rachel never outgrew her early-twenties incompetence and learned to take responsibility for her own life. That wasn't a show that thirty-one million people wanted to watch.

In the first episode of the eighth season, Rachel took another pregnancy test at Monica's behest. Phoebe was the one to read the result, and she lies to Rachel, telling her that she's not pregnant. For a second or two, as Rachel reacts with an unexpected amount of emotion and Jennifer Aniston gives an incredible teary performance, it feels like a cop-out from the writers – a set-up from the previous season with no pay-off. When Phoebe reveals that the test was positive after all, and this was a way to see how much Rachel really wanted the pregnancy, there's a sense of relief as Rachel chides Phoebe, telling her 'That's a risky little game'. The audience was reassured that *Friends* was willing to take the risk and embrace another big change in the characters' lives; allowing Rachel to come to the forefront for the season in the process. Rachel's future with Ross was now confirmed. With the baby, they'd always be in each other's lives. However, the show took the time to let their chemistry settle, only occasionally flaring up as a background story to the pregnancy and Rachel's personal growth.

Frasier had experienced a similar resurgence the previous season by bringing Niles and Daphne to the centre of the story, having kept their potential romance as a running B-plot for the majority of the show's run. New sitcoms struggled to manage any audience interest during a time when viewers wanted comfort and nostalgia, but even long-established shows weren't guaranteed good ratings. To keep eyes on the screen, the shows that did best pushed their own status quo and took risks, and *Friends* found success in letting its characters grow up.

As the end of the season approached and May Sweeps began, NBC devoted their efforts to cashing in on audience nostalgia; 2002 marked NBC's seventy-fifth anniversary of broadcasting, and the network spent May celebrating its history. Sitcoms went cameo heavy. An episode of *Frasier* contrived to bring as many *Cheers* characters back to the screen as possible, while on *Scrubs* a group of actors from NBC's eighties' medical drama *St Elsewhere* appeared as a group of ill doctors. NBC aired reunion shows for many of its previous hits, including *Laverne & Shirley* and *The Mary Tyler Moore Show*.

The network embracing its history led to John Kiesewetter of the *Cincinnati Enquirer* wondering which shows airing in 2002 would become classics brought back for a reunion in 2020. He said that *The West Wing* cast reuniting was a certainty, while few people would want to see the stars of *That '70s Show* again. He referred to a *Friends* reunion as a 'no-brainer'. His prediction was off by only a year.

Friends itself was absent from the cameos and flashbacks of NBC's anniversary celebrations and sweeps stunts, but it still ended the season on a high. The biggest moments that roped audiences in during that final sweeps period of the season were all about how far the characters had come, and over thirty-four million people tuned in to watch the finale – 'The One Where Rachel Has a Baby'. As Monica and Chandler took a step towards the future and Rachel accepted an inadvertent proposal, it was clear that the writers had successfully rejuvenated the 8-year-old show. In the Emmy awards immediately after the season, *Friends* won the award for 'Outstanding Comedy Series' for the first time and Jennifer Aniston took home the award for 'Outstanding Lead Actress in a Comedy Series'. There was a sense that these awards weren't just for the season itself, but also a retrospective reward for eight years of a job well done. With an absolute certainty all around that the next season would be the last, *Friends* was poised to go out on a high.

Chapter Nine

The One Where Things Get Real

T he ninth season was definitely going to be *Friends'* last. The actors weren't contracted for anything further and the show was getting more and more expensive to produce. David Crane and Marta Kauffman had been quietly informed that there was almost no chance *Friends* would continue past its ninth season, and neither NBC nor Warner Brothers would be interested in stumping up the cash for a tenth. Of course, *Friends* did continue on. NBC proved willing to pay after all and by the end of 2002, after a series of negotiations that took place on the set itself between takes, a tenth season of *Friends* was confirmed. As with the previous season, there was a change in momentum as the writers stopped working towards a conclusion and began working towards a cliff-hanger. Before any of that, however, there was a new milestone to celebrate.

If reaching 100 episodes was a rarity for a sitcom, then reaching 200 was a landmark achievement, especially back in the early noughties. For a sitcom to reach 200 episodes it either had to be such a big ratings hit that the network wouldn't dream of cancellation, or exactly the right balance of bland and inoffensive content that a network could continually air to a small but consistently loyal fan base. Audiences watching shows purely out of habit, rather than because they were good, was a reliable source of income for the networks.

Before *Friends*, both *Cheers* and its spin-off *Frasier* managed to reach the 200th episode milestone. Considering how close *Cheers* had come to cancellation in its early seasons, reaching 200 episodes was no mean feat. In 1990, with twenty-two Emmy awards to show for its long run, *Cheers* celebrated its 200th episode and its first-time landing at the top spot in the Nielsen ratings for the season. The episode, a celebratory clip show in which political pundit John McLaughlin interviewed the cast and creators, was watched by over forty-five million people.

Frasier, the *Cheers* spin-off, reached its 200th episode in 2001, a year before *Friends*, but the show didn't experience the same level of ratings success as its predecessor. Moving *Frasier* to Tuesday nights had initially proved successful for NBC as it formed the basis for a second night of 'Must See' comedy, but by the show's 200th episode many of those other sitcoms from Tuesday nights had either failed or come to rely on *Friends* for an audience, and *Frasier* had begun to languish. Still consistently enjoyed and loved by critics, the show had thoroughly dipped in ratings. The milestone episode, in which Frasier searched for a missing tape of his radio show and discovered the lengths that fan obsession can reach, was watched by less than twenty million people. It's a respectable number when compared to modern audience figures; the 200th episode of *The Big Bang Theory*, arguably the most popular sitcom of the 2010s, was only watched by around fifteen million people. Compared to the hits of the nineties and early noughties, however, *Frasier* was beginning to miss.

The Simpsons, Fox's long-running animated sitcom, hit the rare 200-episode milestone in 1998 with 'Trash of the Titans'; an episode which featured Homer Simpson entering the race for garbage commissioner, a 'Candy Man' musical parody and a guest appearance from U2. By 2002 *Simpsons* creator Matt Groening had begun semi-regularly threatening to end the show and take Fox's most consistent hit off the air. *The Simpsons* still lives on today, however, and recently celebrated its 700th episode. Early on in Fox's time on air, the network had little choice but to continue showing even the most mildly successful shows they had. That might have contributed to *Married ... with Children* airing its 200th episode, a clip show special, in 1995 to an audience of twenty-one million.

The *Friends* creators didn't do a clip show or retrospective episode for the show's 200th, or even a big event like the triplet-birth storyline from the show's 100th. Instead, the milestone was marked with a super-sized episode – 'The One with the Male Nanny'. It was an episode that showed *Friends* at its most *Friends*; funny, emotional and a little bit problematic. Much of the episode followed Phoebe, caught in a love triangle. After eight seasons of Lisa Kudrow not getting much to do in the show's main emotional stories, the ninth and theoretically final season of *Friends* introduced a new love interest for her in the form of Mike, played by Paul Rudd. Rudd had risen to fame as step brother-turned-boyfriend Josh in the seminal nineties teen movie *Clueless*, had recently appeared in *Wet Hot American Summer* – a movie that failed miserably at the box office before going on to find a devoted audience – and had done very little television work before appearing on *Friends*. According to Kevin Bright, Rudd fit in with the cast seamlessly. He did the unthinkable on *Friends*, successfully becoming a seventh member of the ensemble without taking anything away from the other six.

One of the main goals of *Friends'* ninth season was to give Phoebe a solid, long-term relationship – and with Mike the writers succeeded, but there needed to be room for tension in the seemingly perfect pairing. In the 200th episode, David the Scientist Guy – Phoebe's brief but intense fling from the first season played by Hank Azaria – returned and attempted to rekindle the sparks between them. Originally, the story of Phoebe torn between two men was planned as a two-episode arc, but the super-sized 200th episode allowed for a three-act structure and plenty of time to resolve things between the threesome, at least temporarily. The creators of the show really weren't sure who Phoebe would end up with, and in 'The One with the Male Nanny' they faced a struggle, trying to keep Phoebe a character the audience could root for while she swung between the two men. Five or six different versions of David and Mike's confrontation were written but it wasn't until the pair set against each other in a childish attempt at a fight that the writers found the comedy among all of the emotion in the scene. Having had little to do with love during the previous seasons, Lisa Kudrow finally got the chance to play big emotions centered on her future instead of her past, and it paid off as the love triangle resolved and Phoebe made a commitment to Mike.

Paul Rudd's ability to slip in as an extra member of the cast was helped in the early episode of the ninth season by Chandler literally being removed to a distance from the rest of the group. Matthew Perry's character was briefly sent to work in Tulsa, Oklahoma, and while the writers still found a way to keep Chandler in every episode, there was more breathing room to establish a new character. In the 200th, Monica and Chandler were relegated to a background story as Chandler obsessed over the fact that Monica had an extremely funny co-worker. David Crane named the unseen character 'Jeffrey', after his long-term partner Jeffrey Klarik. In fact, there are quite a few random Jeffreys scattered throughout *Friends* thanks to Crane. Chandler's panic at not being the funniest – despite performing meaningless Seinfeld-esque comedy for his wife –

might seem overblown to the average viewer, but it was relatable for the writers. All twelve members of the writer's room admitted that they also wouldn't be able to cope with their partners finding someone else funnier than them. Chandler's insecurities were resolved in the episode when Monica lies that she no longer finds Jeffrey funny after hearing him tell a particularly sexist joke. At one point in the episode, there was a knowing wink to the audience as Monica pointed out the irony of David turning up just as Phoebe had found happiness in a committed relationship. The irony of Monica finding sexist jokes a turn-off alongside a storyline about toxic masculinity remained unacknowledged.

Friends regularly suffered from a tendency to use gender roles and sexuality as a punchline. Any hint of 'femininity' from the men, such as showing too much emotion or taking a bath, came with a belittling suggestion of homosexuality or womanhood. This wasn't out of the norm for the time, and *Friends* was still more progressive than plenty of its contemporaries. In 'The One with the Male Nanny', that unpleasant flavour of judgemental masculinity was put entirely into Ross's character. To give the show its due, Ross is treated as fairly ridiculous.

The episode saw Ross and Rachel hiring a male nanny to take care of new baby Emma. Freddie Prinze Jr. guest-starred as Sandy, the overly sensitive 'manny'. Prinze Jr. had made a name for himself in the *I Know What You Did Last Summer* franchise, and had just appeared as Fred in the live-action *Scooby Doo* movie before his appearance on *Friends*. His entrance was cheered by the studio audience, clearly familiar with his work, and he gave a game performance – teaching both Emma and Joey with puppets, and even taking on-set recorder lessons for a single scene. The writers debated exactly what would be the cause of Ross's intense dislike and discomfort around a man in touch with his 'feminine side', and how deep they should dive into his issues. As Kevin Bright put it in episode commentary: 'We think of the characters as liberal but occasionally this conservative side popped out.' The issues were resolved, although Sandy was still fired, when Ross admitted to a difficult relationship with his father in a scene that was played for laughs more than it interrogated the problem. Earlier drafts saw Ross going much further into his problems, but they just weren't as funny as David Schwimmer screaming 'tank top' while Freddie Prinze Jr. looks on in kind sympathy.

'The One with the Male Nanny' was watched by over twenty-seven million people, and positively received as another sign that the show was on the up after a slump in quality during its middle years. A review of the episode in the *Evening Standard* suggested that 'whoever kicked those scriptwriters up the butt in the off season deserves an award for resurrecting this once moribund show'. The 200th episode did what *Friends* did best. The laughs landed (even if it all looks a bit different through a modern lens), there were emotional beats that didn't threaten to overtake the episode and none of the guest actors – be it Paul Rudd, Hank Azaria or Freddie Prinze Jr. – got in the way of the core group during the episode's thirty-two minutes; the longest run time of a single *Friends* episode.

In September 2002, just two months before 'The One with the Male Nanny' aired, Freddie Prinze Jr. celebrated his wedding to Sarah Michelle Gellar. He had co-starred with Gellar in both the slasher films that made him famous and in *Scooby Doo*, but Gellar was far better known for her work on *Buffy the Vampire Slayer*. In the 2002/2003 season, after seven years and a network switch, *Buffy* was coming to an end. The teen vampire drama had never had amazing ratings, but it was a beloved show with a devoted fandom and a hit with critics for its depth of storytelling. *Buffy* remains a fantastic example of how a show can have a far greater reach than its viewing figures suggest, and the fan engagement with the show to this day demonstrates just how long something well-loved can last.

Buffy wasn't the only long-running series coming to an end. Long-running ABC sitcom *The Drew Carey Show* began its eighth and penultimate season in September 2002. It was pulled from the schedule in January 2003, with half the season left to air. This wasn't technically the end for the show. The rest of the season was 'burned off' in the summer of 2003, and a half-hearted ninth season aired – largely out of order – in the summer of 2004. It was clear, however, that ABC had given up on the once-popular sitcom.

ABC had, in general, lost any dominance in the sitcom market by the early noughties, and the glow of the network's success with *Who Wants to Be a Millionaire* had faded. ABC had all but lost interest in decent comedy programming, instead committing more and more airtime to reality television, and they wouldn't be the only network to do so. Only a handful of new sitcoms aired on ABC that season, and it looked like the network felt little need to replicate the success of previous season's comedy hits. *Less Than Perfect*, starring Sara Rue, was a painfully out of touch sitcom. The title referred to Rue's character Claude being mildly plus-sized (read: a normal healthy weight) compared to many of the women seen on television. ABC had slightly more success with *8 Simple Rules* ... starring John Ritter – well-known for his work on ABC twenty-five years prior in *Three's Company* – and Katey Sagal of *Married ... With Children* fame, as well as a young Kaley Cuoco pre-*Big Bang Theory*.

The Drew Carey Show was the last of ABC's popular nineties sitcoms to leave the air, and while criticisms of the show were justified there was also a sense that the network had found a more lucrative genre with reality television. One element of *Drew Carey*'s eighth season was the lazy, unceremonious write-off of the character Kate – married off-screen and never seen again. Kate was played by Christa Miller, who had to leave *Drew Carey* due to her new commitments on *Scrubs*, having been promoted to a recurring actor for the medical sitcom's second season.

Scrubs had a gift for bringing in talented guest actors who often stole the show. The world of sitcoms and network comedy was a small place, and *Scrubs* had a noticeable overlap of guest actors with its contemporaries. Late in the ninth season of *Friends*, Ken Lerner appeared as a dull palaeontology professor foisted on Ross. Lerner was best known for his work on *Happy Days* and his brief run on *Buffy* as a high school principal who was tragically eaten by hyenas. In 2005, he appeared on *Scrubs* in the fourth season episode 'My Life in Four Cameras' as fictional *Cheers* writer Charles James. His name was an amalgamation of the three *Cheers* creators: James Burrows, Glen Charles and Les Charles. The *Scrubs* episode was an homage to the classic multi-cam sitcom complete with laugh track, studio-style sets and a brightened colour palette. It was a great demonstration of just how much *Scrubs* stood apart from the classic shows of the eighties and nineties. 'My Life in Four Cameras' was a loving tribute to the television that came before, completed with a settled status quo finish in the sitcom fantasy that perfectly encapsulated the classic multi-cam sitcom need for happy endings.

Elsewhere, *Scrubs* made fantastic use of Phill Lewis – an excellent comic actor who had been appearing in brief roles across film and television since the eighties – as Hooch, the 'crazy' surgeon. Lewis also appeared in three episodes of *Friends*' ninth season as Steve, an ad executive who served as part of Chandler's career changing storyline. John Ritter took a break from *8 Simple Rules* ... and made two guest appearances on *Scrubs* during the show's first and second seasons as J.D.'s father, having been specifically requested by Zach Braff.

In 2002, as the ninth season of *Friends* began, *Scrubs* was just entering its second year and rapidly growing in the ratings. NBC opted to put the show in the choice post-*Friends* slot on Thursday nights rather than using the time to launch another new and doomed-to-failure series. The choice paid off and *Scrubs* finished thirteenth in the Nielsen ratings for the year, a significant increase from its first season and a much-needed success for NBC.

Another actor who impressed in a long-running guest role on *Scrubs* was Scott Foley. Foley was best known for his work on *Felicity*, the long-running drama on The WB created by J.J. Abrams. *Felicity* came to a close at the end of the 2001/2002 season and Abrams moved on to create sci-fi thriller *Alias* on ABC starring Jennifer Garner – Foley's wife at the time. Foley himself impressed in his brief appearances during the first season of *Scrubs* and there was clearly room for him to take the lead somewhere. NBC snapped him up, and in February 2003 the Foley-led *A.U.S.A* appeared in the not-so-coveted post-*Frasier* slot on Tuesday night.

Frasier had fallen in the ratings, and the show dropped down to twenty-sixth in the Nielsen rankings in its tenth season. For a new sitcom, that would have been an impressive ranking. For a previous high point of NBC's sitcom programming, it was a hard fall. *Frasier*, a show that had once won the Emmy Award for 'Outstanding Comedy Series' five years in a row, had faded in popularity. The show faced the opposite problem to many series cancelled before they could grow an audience – it had gone on too long. After ten years on the air and with the romantic tension between Niles and Daphne resolved, *Frasier* was getting tired. The stories were getting repetitive and while the show had matured over the previous decade, the characters hadn't. Robert Bianco, in an article for *USA Today* called the tenth season a 'drastic quality dip' for the series. Until 2016, *Frasier* held the record for most Emmy wins for a single show, with thirty-seven awards to its name. (The record was beaten when *Game of Thrones* won its thirty-ninth award.) While *Frasier* was sinking in the ratings, in 2002 NBC had no plans to force an end to the iconic series. They had nothing in the bank to replace it with.

In the late nineties, comedy had absolutely dominated the ratings. By the 2002/2003 season, that was no longer the case. The slide that had begun a few years earlier with *Who Wants to Be a Millionaire* was well and truly underway. Just two comedies made it into the Nielsen top ten for the season. *Friends* remained high on the list in second place, and CBS were still enjoying success with *Everybody Loves Raymond* in seventh. Monday night football held a consistent position in the top ten and *CSI: Crime Scene Investigation* remained CBS's most popular scripted drama, taking the top spot. NBC had a similar crime drama success with *Law & Order* claiming ninth place, and *E.R.* remained popular, coming in fourth. So only two sitcoms, football and two dramas in the top ten. The rest was all reality television.

The remaining sitcoms on network television in no way matched the heights of the genre in years gone by. CBS had a successful Monday night sitcom line-up that largely traded off the success of *Raymond*, with new spin-off *CSI: Miami* as a late evening draw. NBC's success was limited to Thursdays, with satellite 'Must See' evenings thrown out of the window. *Will & Grace* continued to hold on to an audience in the Thursday 9 pm slot and the show's creators, David Kohan and Max Mutchnik, launched a new series at 9.30 pm – *Good Morning Miami*. Their new show couldn't quite manage *Will & Grace*'s ratings, but it was just successful enough to avoid cancellation in its first season. In fact, when the end of the show came the following year, it had little to do with ratings and a lot to do with Kohan and Mutchnik's relationship with NBC. With *Friends* coming to a close soon, *Will & Grace* star Eric McCormack pointed out in an interview with the *Guardian* that 'NBC are really going to need us'. Comedies like *Will & Grace* that could pull in any kind of consistent audience had become essential to the network that had been so heavy-handed with cancellation in previous years.

Scripted dramas were also struggling across the networks. NBC were confronting fears of a drop in quality for *The West Wing* after Alan Sorkin announced that he would be leaving the show at the end of its fourth season. John Wells, overseer of both *E.R.* and *Third Watch* became the sole overseer of *The West Wing*, but if the show couldn't do well without Sorkin, then NBC was going to be left with a gap in its previously successful drama line up.

On The WB, both *Gilmore Girls* and *Smallville* had developed solid fan bases, but the end of *Dawson's Creek* was coming and the network didn't have much to replace the teen classic. UPN found that despite a lead-in from *Star Trek: Enterprise*, a new reboot of *The Twilight Zone* wasn't going to pull in audiences. Even Jason Alexander as a psychopomp couldn't boost the ratings and the network cancelled *The Twilight Zone* in 2003 after a single season. *Buffy* was ending, but its creator Joss Whedon had a new show to focus on and in 2002 the first episode of *Firefly* aired on Fox. The space-western was cancelled just eleven episodes later, although not before building an intense fandom that would eventually see the series resurrected as a movie in 2005.

Sitcoms and drama had been huge sources of income for the networks in previous years, but now they were falling by the wayside. *A.U.S.A* – Scott Foley's show – was highly anticipated by critics but like so many sitcoms before, it didn't survive the season. It was replaced in April 2003 by the unsuccessfully retooled second season of *Watching Ellie*. Much of the critical anticipation for *A.U.S.A* was less for the show itself and more for a break from the relentless tide of reality television. Allessandra Stanley, reviewing the show for the *New York Times*, acknowledged that while it lacked the originality and clever writing of *Will & Grace* or *Friends*, it at least wasn't a reality show and 'that alone should be honored as an extraordinary act of will by NBC'. She went on to suggest that viewers should 'march en masse to Rockefeller Center [the New York home of NBC] and festoon the gates with bouquets, balloons and messages of thankful praise'. There was a distinct lack of good scripted television on networks and with good shows coming to an end, critics were willing to take what they could get.

In those all-important ratings for the season, Fox claimed multiple top spots with *Joe Millionaire* – in which women competed for the attention of a bachelor pretending to be a millionaire – and *American Idol*, the singing contest inspired by the British *Pop Idol*. This was the season of *The Bachelor* on ABC, the enduring popularity of *Survivor* on CBS and hopefuls competing across networks in repetitive format for a chance at riches, love, fame, or all three. Television trends are cyclical. In the early noughties media scholars drew comparisons between the high-drama soap operas that had been so popular in the early eighties and this new wave of reality shows that focused on intense emotional reactions and bitchy backstabbing. In a time of economic uncertainty reality television was a safe bet for networks, just as game shows had been a few years before.

The cycle continues into the current streaming era. Netflix, the streaming service that made its name with prestigious dramas like *House of Cards*, *Orange is the New Black* and later *The Crown*, has in recent years put out more and more reality television. Dating shows, fashion competitions and inane contests based on drama and deception dominate the streaming service. Across the shows the same aesthetics, music and even hosts are used to mark the shows as part of a cohesive brand of reality TV. Scripted work losing out to reality shows isn't new, and hopefully the cycle will come around again, just as it did after the early noughties.

In the UK, reality television didn't surge in quite the same way, but *Big Brother* remained a huge part of Channel 4 and E4's flagship programming. Channel 4 was troubled after a significant dip in profits. E4 in particular was under scrutiny for its reliance on a mix of *Big Brother* and imported American shows. Channel 4's public remit was to bring attention to lesser-heard voices and promote home-grown programming, and by the beginning of the millennium, there was a shift in focus across both channels to more original British comedy. *Frasier*, long a part of the Friday night primetime schedule, moved to Mondays. Shows like *Peep Show* and *Smack the Pony* became more prominent, replacing American sitcoms. *Friends* still had its place, but there was a sense that American imports were becoming less of a priority. E4 had more to prove as the channel faced direct competition with the newly launched BBC3 – a channel also aimed at the youth market and home to *The Mighty Boosh*.

British viewers had also become frustrated with the long wait between an American show completing a season in the US and its airing in the UK. This was a time when technology had just developed enough for piracy to be effective. Just as Napster had challenged the music industry at the end of the twentieth century, now the television industry had to reckon with a new way to watch. In 2003, *Friends* was apparently the fourth most illegally downloaded show in the UK according to the *Guardian*; coming in behind *24, Buffy* and *Star Trek*. The article admittedly provided no source for that data, and claimed the sixth in the list to be 'Japanese Anime shows (mostly involving robots)'. It might not have been the most accurate reporting, but it was clear that new file-sharing technology was creating an unexpected challenge for television-makers.

The challenge NBC faced was more obvious. The network needed *Friends*, or at least it needed some good, profitable sitcoms. If reality television was such an easy profit-maker for the networks, however, why did the lack of decent sitcoms matter? The problem was, networks still needed scripted television just as much as they needed reality. There was a lot more money to be made in selling the rights to syndication. Scripted shows like *Friends* and even less popular hits like *Just Shoot Me* could continually bring in money as they aired over and over in reruns and were sold for home entertainment. The beginning of the millennium was the time of the DVD boxset. Reality television might have been a big audience draw in the moment, but it didn't have the same rewatchability value – people didn't care about watching old episodes of *Survivor*. There was so much choice fatigue at the time of the reality boom. According to Nielsen Media Research, in 2002 the average television household had eighty-nine channels available, up from twenty-two in 1990. Reality television was the 'easily watchable' option, but it didn't have any profitable longevity for networks. Viewers were compelled at the time, but critics were complaining. They were tired of shows like ABC's *The Search for America's Sexiest People* – a show too ridiculous to be made-up – and there was hope that as networks looked again to the long-term, a comedy revival was imminent.

It was in this landscape that NBC began to look for a solution to the problem of *Friends* ending. While *Will & Grace* had a decent audience and *Scrubs* had potential, there was no new big show to take the place of those six people in a coffee shop. Warner Brothers had lost interest in spending heavily on the show, and a cast of six each earning $1 million per episode was expensive. That's why it had been so firmly established that the ninth season of *Friends* would be the last. At least until Jeff Zucker decided that NBC really needed one more season.

David Crane and Marta Kauffman were surprised, but glad to have more time to play with. The cast of *Friends*, on the other hand, had their doubts. Many of them had begun to look again at the big screen. *The Whole Ten Yards*, a sequel to Matthew Perry's hit film with Bruce Willis, was due to be released in 2004 and there wasn't any sign yet that the movie would be a box office flop. Jennifer Aniston had received a slew of good reviews for her performance in *The Good Girl*, a 2002 indie movie in which she starred with Jake Gyllenhall, and had recently signed on to appear as Jim Carrey's love interest in *Bruce Almighty*. Matt Leblanc was so determined to develop a movie career that he spent two months commuting between Los Angeles and Eastern Europe to film 2001's *All The Queen's Men*, a cross-dressing comedy that failed dismally at the box office. Hollywood was beckoning, with varying degrees of success on offer, but NBC wanted the stars of *Friends* to wait. Those down-to-the-wire negotiations on set, with Kevin Bright pulling the cast into a dressing room between scenes, led to an agreement reached at the eleventh hour. According to Matthew Perry, Jennifer Aniston was the biggest hold-out and the one most focused on her post-*Friends* movie career. Finally, the cast settled on a truncated final tenth season.

That decision meant another shift in momentum for the show. As with *Friends'* eighth season, the promise of one more year gave the writers room to breathe as they found new stories for the characters. Having created a happy, long-term relationship for Phoebe, there was now time to throw more conflict into the mix. Phoebe was always the most out-there, least conformist member of the group. The writers had played with her lack of interest in commitment during the fifth season and her short-lived relationship with Gary. In the ninth season, there was a chance to give Phoebe a growing-up moment as she made a commitment, moved in with Mike and began to get hopeful about marriage, children and a picket-fence life. It's tiring that the ultimate moment of growth for a female character was based on a romantic relationship, but it was a welcome change for Lisa Kudrow to be so at the forefront. Her character had so often been side-lined as an observer and advice-dispenser that her arc in the ninth season wasn't just nice, but needed.

With a tenth season on the cards there was space for roadblocks in Phoebe and Mike's relationship. The sixteenth episode of the season, 'The One with the Boob Job'. showed the pair first moving in together then choosing to part when Mike admits that, after a previous divorce, marriage will never be on the table for him. Unlike the earlier relationship with Gary, concluded off screen and never mentioned again, in the ninth season the writers allowed Phoebe time to grieve and process what could have been before reintroducing Hank Azaria's David for the last few episodes. David Crane and Marta Kauffman took a while to decide who Phoebe should end up with, but bringing David back into the picture built up to them finally using the dual-proposal plot they'd previously imagined for Chandler and Monica at the end of the sixth season.

The room to explore new challenges for Chandler and Monica as the season progressed stopped *Friends* from getting predictable. The aim to start a family faded into the background during those Tulsa episodes. There was a hint of schmuck bait to Chandler's relocation storyline as the second episode of the season set up Monica also moving to Oklahoma. There was no real risk that the show would continue without the pair and, of course, by the end of 'The One Where Emma Cries', Monica had a reason to stay in New York. While the Tulsa plot allowed Matthew

Perry to take some time away from the *Friends* set as he continued seeking treatment for his addiction issues, the commute storyline was ultimately unsustainable for *Friends* alongside Chandler and Monica's plan to have a baby. In the tenth episode of the season, 'The One with Christmas in Tulsa', an unfortunate clip show was saved by a brief appearance from Selma Blair – known at the time for her appearances in *Legally Blonde* and *Cruel Intentions* – as a co-worker who makes a pass at Chandler and, in the process, reminds him that some things are more importance than work. Returning Chandler to New York but removing his barely comprehensible job was a risk to the status quo of *Friends*. His eventual move to advertising, however, served as a handy emotional weight in 'The One with the Lottery', as Chandler waited for a call about a desperately needed job while the rest of the group fought over lottery tickets.

With Chandler out of Tulsa the show could focus on impending parenthood for him and Monica. In the season's Thanksgiving episode, 'The One with Rachel's Other Sister', Chandler faced his fears of fatherhood directly, neatly clearing up any doubts the audience might have had about his willingness to take the next step. Thanksgiving episodes had often been an opportunity to work with just the core six in a room together, but after the success of Brad Pitt's appearance in the previous season the writers had realised that there was room for an extra seat at the table. In the ninth season that was filled by Rachel's other sister Amy, played by Christina Applegate. The story was originally conceived for Jill, the sister introduced in the sixth season, but Reese Witherspoon was unavailable. The writers liked the story so much they forged ahead anyway and decided this was the perfect time to introduce Rachel's briefly mentioned 'other' sister.

Bright, Kauffman and Crane had a previous working relationship with Applegate thanks to their short-lived sitcom *Jesse*. Where, often, guest stars would struggle to keep up with the performances of the core group, Applegate was able to go above and beyond. It was unusual to give a guest star that much comedy, according to David Crane, but having seen what Christina Applegate could do they were confident she could deliver. Applegate went on to win an Emmy for 'Outstanding Guest Actress in a Comedy Series' for her performance as the spoiled, obnoxious sister throwing a tantrum at the news that if Ross and Rachel passed away their daughter Emma would go to live with Chandler and Monica. It was that promise that gave the episode its emotional resonance as Chandler reacted to learning that his friends trusted him as a future parent. There was conflict, of course, when they suggested he couldn't do the job solo, but it was swiftly resolved as Chandler took on the role of disciplinarian and broke apart the fantastically silly slap-fight between Rachel and her sister. Showing Chandler and Monica making a real commitment to parenthood after their impulsive decision at the end of the eighth season made what was to come for the pair even more heartbreaking.

Friends had spent nine years setting Monica up as a character destined for motherhood, and if the ninth season had been the last it would have been the obvious thing to end with a baby Bing on the way. Instead, with another season to develop the story, the writers took the less obvious route and established fertility problems for the pair late in the season. It was a topic rarely seen at all on light-hearted sitcoms, and Courtney Cox and Matthew Perry were both superb as the couple learned that they'd have to take a non-traditional path to having a family.

It was a particularly difficult storyline for Cox, having suffered two miscarriages herself while working on *Friends*. Speaking to Matt Lauer for *NBC News* in 2004, she recalled the difficulty of filming the episodes where Rachel gave birth, remembering that 'it was terrible having to be funny'. Happily for Cox, by the final season of *Friends* she was going through a successful pregnancy, carefully hidden in the classic sitcom manner with generously sized coats and carefully placed lampshades, and she gave birth to her daughter in June 2004.

Monica, on the other hand, had to look for alternatives. One option she considered was John Stamos – of *Full House* fame – who appeared in the episode 'The One with the Donor', the last before the two-part season finale. Stamos played a colleague of Chandler, unwittingly brought to dinner as a potential sperm donor. The episode ended with the pair deciding to adopt instead and tidily wrapped up Monica and Chandler's emotional story for the season, leaving room in the finale for romantic geometry.

Juggling a love triangle, a square entanglement and a trip to 'Barbados' (or at least, to some sets that looked like a Barbados hotel) was a massive amount of work. The writer's had a tricky amount of relationship chaos to navigate, but it was the set designers who faced the real struggle as they worked to set up two episodes' worth of artificial rainfall outside the tropical hotel sets without interrupting the sound design of the show.

For the writers, the difficulty came in setting up the final piece of the Ross/Joey/Rachel puzzle – the introduction of Charlie.

Aisha Tyler's appearance as Charlie on *Friends* marked the first time a speaking black character had both a name and a recurring role. *Friends* wasn't alone in facing criticism for its overwhelming whiteness, and racial diversity was still sorely lacking across sitcoms at the time. Comedy was still quite segregated, both in casting and in viewing, with predominantly white shows unlikely to be a hit with black viewers. At the time, Marta Kauffman thought that *Friends* was being unfairly singled out for its lack of diversity, but in 2022 she experienced a huge change of heart. Speaking to the *LA Times* she admitted that the show's 'failure to be more inclusive' was a sign of her own internalisation of systemic racism. As a result, she pledged $4 million to Brandeis University, her alma mater, to establish an endowed professorship in the school's African and African American studies department.

Charlie Wheeler was a breakout role for Aisha Tyler, who had done little television acting before *Friends*; although she had hosted a couple of short-lived reality television series. Tyler worried that her character would come across as callous for her behaviour in the ninth season finale 'The One in Barbados'. Similarly, David Schwimmer had concerns that the audience would judge him for Ross's actions with Charlie, and Jennifer Aniston needed the audience to understand Rachel's attraction to Joey was a crush, not a deep love.

The resulting romantic chaos on the Barbados trip was paused at the end of the first half of the finale to resolve the separate love triangle between Phoebe, David and Mike. The resurrected double-proposal didn't have both David and Mike on one knee, but the decision felt tangibly difficult. While both writers and audience found themselves rooting for Mike – due on the writers' part to Paul Rudd's availability for the following season – Hank Azaria played David with such genuine sweetness that there was a resounding sympathy on set for his character after Phoebe made her choice. Ending Phoebe's emotional story halfway through the episode made more room for the quadrangle in the second half. In the process, the rest of the characters not in the square were relegated to a table tennis tournament in the bowels of the hotel in an attempt to cram some laughs into the heavy emotional story.

The writers had already toyed with the idea of Joey and Rachel together during the eighth season, and returned to it in the first episode of the ninth when Rachel accepted Joey's accidental proposal. With one more season on the way the story of Ross and Rachel needed one last roadblock, and Jennifer Aniston's easy, natural chemistry with Matt Leblanc made the Joey relationship the best option. The writers were tentative about how far they could take the relationship. They had to do it in a way that would protect Ross and Rachel – still the planned endgame for *Friends*.

Bringing Charlie into the show for an extra layer of drama made sense, but her relationship with Joey was one of the weaker parts of the story. Early in the ninth season, Joey admitted that he wanted to explore a committed relationship, but that plot was rapidly thrown out. Briefly pairing Charlie and Joey was a good cliff-hanger for 'The One with the Soap Opera Party', an episode filled to the brim with *Days of our Lives* cameos, but there was very little chemistry between the pair. The couple had nothing in common. Charlie was a palaeontology professor and clearly meant for Ross, and Joey was unable to engage in her interests. That was the reason for their inevitable finale break up and also the reason that audiences struggled to buy into a schmuck bait relationship that clearly only existed as a convenient obstacle in the plot. Bringing Ross and Charlie together, on the other hand, made sense. It was refreshing to see Ross in a potential relationship of equals and attraction, especially after the eighth season's bland Bonnie.

The later moments in the finale when Rachel admits her feelings to Joey would have been more satisfying if the writers hadn't spent the season dumbing Joey back down after his brief burst of maturity during the time he was in love with Rachel. Nonetheless, the audience cheered as the two of them finally came together. It was obviously not going to last, but in the moment, there was a real sense that those characters were the best for each other, and the mystery of how things would fall apart was enough to compel viewers to watch *Friends'* final season. The Barbados finale was far from the highest rated of *Friends* closers and the show was clearly past its prime. *Friends* was, however, one of the last surviving bastions of quality comedy on network television, and having survived its middle-aged slump, its ninth season was highly rated and celebrated in reviews. All that was left now was to stick the landing.

Chapter Ten

The One with the Finale

'It's just the perfect way to say goodbye.' The quality of sitcom endings varies wildly. Television comedy has always suffered the most in an industry focused so intensely on ratings, and a sitcom getting the chance to end on its own terms is a rarity. When looking at what gave *Friends* such an impressive life beyond the show's ten years on television, it's impossible to ignore how well it ended. The end of *Friends* had been a long time coming, predicted repeatedly during the previous few seasons. In the show's tenth year, it had been solidly established that this was it. There was no more to come. Jeff Zucker, still presiding over entertainment at a struggling NBC, saw the writing on the wall. The end of *Friends* would irrevocably change the nature of the network's programming.

Super-sized sitcom episodes, especially *Friends* episodes, were Zucker's promotional brainchild and in the final season of *Friends* he made sure that every possible extra minute of the show filled up network airtime. Rumours ran rampant before the finale was even filmed that the cast would reunite for a 'Where are they now?' special as early as the following television season, less than a year after the end of *Friends*. Jeff Zucker told *Entertainment Weekly* that he was 'here to offer them $4 million' to reunite on air. Unfortunately for him, it would take a lot more time and money – and a different network – to bring the cast back together. Before the end of *Friends* however, the show had some laughs to celebrate.

One of those lasts was 'The One with the Late Thanksgiving'. The holiday specials had been a favourite way for the writers to gather the cast in a single room for an episode. In this last Thanksgiving episode, however, they were locked out. It was a difficult episode to write, especially as the bar was set so high after years of celebrated Thanksgiving episodes. 'The Late Thanksgiving' was the first hint of a victory lap feeling that ran through the tenth season as writers found ways to echo the stories that had come before.

In the very first Thanksgiving episode, 'The One Where Underdog Gets Away', a younger Monica found herself hosting the holiday meal for the first time, unwillingly making a feast that ultimately got ruined after the group got locked out of the apartment. In the tenth season, after a decade of celebratory dinners, Monica was once again the unwilling host, making a meal that the group failed to arrive on time for. The biggest and best examples of character growth in *Friends* came from unspoken moments. Monica had gone from newly grown-up and hosting for the first time, to an obsessive insistence on being the best at hospitality, to finally being mature enough to accept that hosting wasn't an act she was obligated to perform. Chandler's growth was simpler, going from a man that refused to eat traditional Thanksgiving food, instead opting for childish favourites of grilled cheese sandwiches and tomato soup, to a man genuinely willing to help his wife prepare the holiday meal.

A side plot of Rachel and Phoebe entering little Emma into a beauty pageant horrified Jennifer Aniston, but led to a fantastic scene as the group crammed their heads into a gap in the apartment doorway and tried to apologise for their late arrival. The final moment of chaos, as a trapped Joey burst through the door and destroyed a carefully placed table of food was a moment of glorious slapstick, although a friend of David Crane's believed it to be a giant birth metaphor. The last moment of the episode, when Monica receives a phone call and finds out that she and Chandler are close to becoming adoptive parents, was the 'beginning of something that really re-energised the season' according to Kevin Bright, speaking in the episode commentary. 'The One with the Late Thanksgiving' was the episode that really set the final season of *Friends* in motion. There was a clear end in sight, and the show had the momentum to get there.

Friends wasn't the only show moving towards a finale in the 2003/2004 season. After eleven years, Kelsey Grammer was ready to leave the character of Dr Frasier Crane behind him, and the Seattle-based sitcom was coming to an end. Grammar had, by 2004, been playing the same character for twenty years, having first appeared as Frasier during the third season of *Cheers* in 1984. The announcement that the eleventh season of *Frasier* would be the last came in January 2004, midway through the season. The show's ratings had steadily diminished in previous years, and though the writing felt newly invigorated that season, the numbers weren't adding up. The licensing costs for *Frasier* had risen and with both Grammer and David Hyde Pierce – who played Frasier's brother Niles – receiving over $1 million per episode, it wasn't financially viable for NBC to keep the show.

As the *Frasier* writers built towards the finale, they were determined to end the show with Frasier romantically content. Laura Linney, fresh from a starring role in *Love Actually*, joined the cast as matchmaker Charlotte in the eighteenth episode of the season. Her character's move to Chicago and the apparently doomed nature of her relationship with Frasier set the show up for a big finale. Where *Friends* opted to keep its last episode simple and focused on the main characters, *Frasier* embraced big events. The story was framed with scenes of Frasier on a plane apparently headed to begin a new job in San Francisco. As the episode unfolded there was a wedding, a birth, cannon fire and fantastic guest appearances from Robbie Coltrane and Richard E. Grant as Daphne's brothers. The final minutes of the episode were, comparatively, an oasis of calm as Frasier finished telling his story to his seatmate – played by Jennifer Beals – and it was revealed that he'd travelled to Chicago, having chosen romance over work. Frasier Crane wouldn't be the only character to make such a choice in a series finale that season.

Kelsey Grammer received the Emmy for 'Outstanding Lead Actor in a Comedy Series' for his work in the final season of *Frasier* – his eleventh nomination and fourth win. The award was as much a celebration of his twenty years playing Frasier Crane as it was an award for the season itself. Grammer used his speech to acknowledge the 'extraordinary life' he'd lived on television, but he also took the time to honour another nominee for the award. John Ritter had received a posthumous nomination for his work on *8 Simple Rules*…. Ritter had passed away suddenly in 2003, while in rehearsals for the family sitcom. Grammer opened his acceptance speech by paying his respects to the late Ritter, who was sorely missed 'not just for his kindness, but for his work'.

The shocking passing of an actor who'd been a huge part of American comedy had ripples across television. Production on *8 Simple Rules* paused as the creators of the show worked out how to cope with the loss of their lead actor, both emotionally and within the show itself.

Eventually, *8 Simple Rules* was retooled to acknowledge his passing, giving his fictional family and real fans a chance to grieve. Stephen McPherson, president of Touchstone Television (the company that produced the show), told the *New York Times* he felt that 'dealing with the tragedy on-air was the right thing to do creatively and cathartically'. John Ritter had also been scheduled to make another guest appearance on *Scrubs*, and Bill Lawrence had to make new plans when Ritter passed away just days before he was due to shoot the episode. An episode was instead dedicated to Ritter's memory, and the characters grieved on screen as J.D. and his brother, played by Tom Cavanagh, mourned their fictional father.

Endings and losses were a huge part of that particular season of television. There were more shows than just *Frasier* and *Friends* approaching the finish. *Sex and the City* came to an end the same year, and among all of the big finales was a quiet end for one of NBC's newest shows. The second season of *Good Morning Miami* began in September 2003. The show was pulled from the air in December, just a few months later, leaving over half of the season unaired. This wasn't an uncommon occurrence for an NBC show, but this time the decision had less to do with ratings, and much more to do with the actions of David Kohan and Max Mutchnik. The pair were best known as the creators of *Will & Grace*, which at that point in time was one of the few popular sitcoms left on NBC's roster and, more importantly, was produced by NBC Studios.

In December 2003, Kohan and Mutchnik filed a multi-million-dollar lawsuit against NBC. They claimed that NBC Studios had failed to negotiate a fair licensing fee for *Will & Grace* with its parent network, costing the two of them about $65 million in lost revenue. The complaint read that 'While [NBC Studios] purported to engage in arm's length and good faith negotiations with NBC, NBC in fact effectively sat on and controlled both sides of the "bargaining" table.' The pair also claimed that James Burrows, the sole director of every *Will & Grace* episode, had received preferential financial treatment from NBC.

Kohan and Mutchnik approached both the network and the production company via their legal representation before the suit was filed and invited them to participate in pre-filing negotiations. NBC, the network, responded with veiled threats. According to the lawsuit, an NBC executive spoke to a higher-up at Warner Brothers – the studio that produced *Good Morning Miami* – and reminded them that 'NBC would not support shows from persons who sued it.' Pulling *Miami* from the air and letting the show die a quiet death was only part of NBC's response. The network went on to countersue, claiming that Kohan and Mutchnik themselves were supposed to be the independent voices in the room during those negotiations. The deal between NBC and NBC Studios involved a licensing fee of $5 million per episode for the fifth, sixth and seventh seasons of *Will & Grace*. No part of that deal required Kohan or Mutchnik to remain involved with the show. Early in 2004, they were removed from their showrunner positions at *Will & Grace*. The show remained on the air as the legal battle continued, but Kohan and Mutchnik were no longer a part of their own project. The pair briefly returned as writers for the show's finale in 2006, but it would be just over a decade before they worked with NBC again.

The legal case and complex countersuing weren't settled until 2007. The settlement itself was, as with the rest of the case, a messy little drama. Originally, the case was settled in court, with a jury voting to award a payout of $48.5 million to Mutchnik, Kohan and their agent Scott Schwartz. Then followed the dismissal of a juror and a motion for mistrial, and the verdict was thrown out. That night, the two parties hunkered down with Lou Meisinger – former general counsel for Walt Disney – as a mediator, and finally reached a settlement. They announced the agreement the following morning, just minutes before Warren Ettinger – the judge on the case – was due to announce whether he was declaring the mistrial or sending the case back to court with a replacement juror. Although the jury's verdict was never officially entered, it was a landmark case – the first in which a jury determined that a studio had committed fraud by licensing a show to a related network. It was a messy few years for Kohan and Mutchnik, but the pair were eventually able to properly return to their creation when NBC revived *Will & Grace* for three more seasons in 2017.

Will & Grace had been a rare success for NBC, and it was one of the few sitcoms guaranteed to survive beyond the end of *Friends* and *Frasier*. The network hadn't totally given up on being a home for quality comedies in 2003, and a solid handful of new shows aired on the network that year in the hopes that a new hit could be found. None of those shows survived the season. Whoopi Goldberg was the biggest name to come to the network in *Whoopi*, a sitcom where she played a boozy, loud-mouthed hotelier. Omid Djalili – the beloved Irani-British actor – also starred in the show, but even his comic talents weren't enough to save *Whoopi* from cancellation. The show was one of the most anticipated of the season, but it failed first with critics, then with audiences. *Whoopi* attempted to be groundbreaking and daring as it tackled racial and ethnic discrimination, but the energy was lacking and clever social satire was available elsewhere in more exciting packages. The ratings dwindled and cancellation came.

The same gate fell to *Happy Family*, a completely unremarkable sitcom starring John Larroquette and Christine Baranski. Despite the big names attached, there was just nothing exciting about a family sitcom focused on empty nesters reluctantly forced to continue parenting their adult children. The show was cancelled after a single season.

A more interesting failure was *The Tracy Morgan Show*. The vehicle for Morgan, looking for a new challenge after a nine-year run as a cast member on *Saturday Night Live*, began in December 2003 and lasted only until March the following year. It was another ratings failure, part of a shifting Tuesday night schedule that NBC still couldn't settle on. There was little excitement for *The Tracy Morgan Show* before it began, it received less of a push from NBC than other new shows on the network, and the show generally seemed doomed to failure from the start. Few sitcoms that traded largely off the star's name found success, and just like with *Whoopi, The Tracy Morgan Show* was no exception. It did, however, do the job of proving Morgan's comic abilities outside of *SNL* and, more importantly, in sitcoms. Morgan would go on to star as Tracy Jordan in the hit NBC sitcom *30 Rock* just a couple of years later.

NBC's biggest hope for the new season was *Coupling*. Despite the fact that very few adaptations of British sitcoms did well on American television, *Coupling* promised a particularly sexy brand of success. The original English *Coupling*, created by Stephen Moffat, was a hit – often referred to in the press as a sexier *Friends*. Jeff Zucker promised in an announcement of the season's new shows that the American *Coupling* was going to 'push the envelope'. There were hints of big changes coming to previously-prudish network television, and *Coupling* was NBC's biggest hope for a *Friends*-size hit.

The network's hopes were soon dashed, with the *New York Times* calling *Coupling* 'a spasm of insecurity by a network desperate to find a potent successor to *Friends'*. The original British version of the show was airing on BBC America at the time, and with the chance to compare the two shows easily available to the audience, the American version couldn't live up to the original. Despite NBC's best efforts and a lead-in from *Will & Grace*, *Coupling*'s panning from critics led to dire ratings. Thirteen episodes of the show were commissioned, only ten were filmed and only four of those made it to air before the show was cancelled at the end of October 2003. Stephen Moffat blamed the failure on NBC's constant interventions. Jeff Zucker later admitted that the American *Coupling* just wasn't any good.

Other networks had more luck that season, or better-quality shows. CBS had by far the most successful new comedy of the season with *Two and a Half Men*. The show starred Charlie Sheen as a bachelor forced to take in his brother, played by Jon Cryer of *Pretty in Pink* fame, and his nephew. The show was the brainchild of Chuck Lorre, his first major project after the end of *Dharma & Greg*. The pilot was directed by, of course, James Burrows. While media publications across America were donning black veils and weeping at the graveside of sitcom-as-they-knew-it, *Two and a Half Men* was quietly proving them wrong as it found a comfortably high spot in the ratings, boosted by its proximity in the schedule to *Everybody Loves Raymond*, and continued to get fairly decent ratings for twelve seasons.

Two and a Half Men is best remembered now for Charlie Sheen's very public breakdowns and eventual termination from the show – he was replaced by Ashton Kutcher in the ninth season – or for young actor Angus T. Jones leaving after becoming a Seventh Day Adventist and decrying the show as filth. At the time of its first season, it was just remarkable that a new, comedy of errors and manners, multi-cam sitcom with a laugh track could find success amid a sea of reality television and network cost-cutting.

Fox had a surprise hit on their hands when *Arrested Development* began in September, 2003. If *Two and a Half Men* had a surprisingly traditional sitcom shape, then *Arrested Development* was a breath of fresh comedy air. Shot almost mockumentary style, with Ron Howard narrating the story, the riches-to-rags comedy was far from a ratings hit. There was plenty of critical acclaim to make up for that though, and *Arrested Development* took the Emmy for 'Outstanding Comedy Series' after just one season on the air. The show starred the infamous

Jessica Walter as matriarch Lucille Bluth, alongside a wealth of both established actors and unknowns. Even Liza Minelli made regular guest appearances. The Russo Brothers, who made a name for themselves in cult sitcoms before graduating to Marvel movies, directed the pilot and a handful of episodes across the first season. The success of *Arrested Development* – among critics if not in the ratings – showed where television was going. There was still room for comedy, and there was definitely room for shows that thought outside the box.

Sitcoms might have fallen in popularity, but the boom of reality shows couldn't last and networks once again were looking for decent, scripted television that could plug gaps in the schedules. Sci-fi and fantasy stories had long been popular in teen dramas, and teenagers were now one of the most desirable demographics. As a result, more and more genre television began to appear on networks. On Friday nights, CBS had *Joan of Arcadia*, a fantasy drama about a teenager regularly spoken to by God. *Arcadia* began airing just as *Touched by an Angel* had ended after nine seasons, and the show was viewed by critics as a grittier and more compelling alternative. It was a mild hit, one of the most successful new shows of the season, and it gave critics hope that there was still some good scripted television left in the world.

Fox also entered the supernatural realm. They daringly scheduled new series *Tru Calling*, starring Eliza Dushku of *Buffy* fame, in the Thursday night time-slot directly up against *Friends*. Unsurprisingly, the supernatural drama struggled in the ratings against the hit sitcom, but it was still a promising sign that the networks were willing to try these riskier prospects.

A safer show, and a bigger hit, was Fox's new teen soap opera *The O.C.* Created by Josh Schwartz, *The O.C.* was a slow burner in the ratings, up against *The Bachelor* on ABC and *The West Wing* on NBC. It was a lead-in from *American Idol* that really pushed up the teen drama's audience numbers. On the surface, the show was one in a long line of teen soaps that had only recently become successful in primetime positions, but the popularity of *The O.C.* has long since been attributed to its fresh take on teen drama and the meta-humour of the show. Show-within-the-show *The Valley* allowed the creators of *The O.C.* to mock critical perceptions of soapy teen storylines. *The O.C.* proved to be more than just a vehicle for Peter Gallagher's magnificent eyebrows. Teen drama had grown from a niche market to something big enough to laugh at itself, and *The O.C.* was a herald of playful new styles of storytelling on television.

Even NBC began to branch out with its offerings, but reality television remained the safest bet. In a not totally unsuccessful attempt to claim viewers from CBS on Monday nights, NBC sandwiched a new drama between reality shows. The fourth season of *Fear Factor*, a hit in recent years for the network, continued to draw in viewers willing to be disgusted, and plenty of them stuck around for the new thriller *Las Vegas*, starring Josh Duhamel, at 9pm. A handful of those viewers stayed on to complete the night with *Average Joe* – a reality dating format that attempted to buck the trend of only pretty people on television – at 10pm.

Thursdays remained the most important night for NBC. The evening was still being marketed with that 'Must See' tagline, but after the failure of *Coupling* NBC took a risk and temporarily tried something other than a sitcom to pull in viewers. In January 2004, the first episode of *The Apprentice* aired at 9 pm on a Thursday night. The show was an instant hit, unfortunately making a household name of previously unsuccessful Donald Trump. Trump would go on to be fired by NBC after beginning his campaign for the American presidency with a racist tirade (one of many), eventually winning the presidency, and then becoming the first American president to be impeached twice, and the first former American president to be indicted and face criminal charges. At the time *The Apprentice* began, he was just a businessman capable of faking success.

As with many shows, *The Apprentice* is a show remembered now for the appalling actions of its star, but at the time it was just the ratings smash that NBC needed and the show went on to finish fifth overall in the Nielsen ranking for the season. It was renewed for the following season, giving NBC something to fill the dwindling Thursday schedule after the departure of the network's biggest hit. It was a huge change, scheduling reality television on what had, for years, been a devoted night of sitcoms. With *Friends* and *Frasier* ending, NBC needed anything that could conceivably be called 'Must See'. Other than *The Apprentice*, there was only one show in NBC's future that had any real hope of getting big ratings – the planned *Friends* spin-off.

The spin-off series, *Joey*, was a beacon of hope for Jeff Zucker in the wake of *Friends* ending. It looked like a sure-fire way to keep viewers on a Thursday night. Within *Friends* itself, Joey became the only character whose story seemed worth continuing past the end of the show. Where the rest of the group were given emotionally satisfying conclusions, Matt LeBlanc's character was side-lined in the final season of *Friends*, with any character development apparently waiting for his fictional move to L.A. The ninth season of *Friends* had ended with Rachel and Joey finally getting together, a move that got a mixed response from both the fans and the actors themselves. Matt LeBlanc complained to David Crane that the relationship felt wrong, like dating his sister. With the end in sight and Ross and Rachel a foregone conclusion, Joey's brief opportunity to be in a mature relationship was taken off the board in the third episode of the final season.

Similarly, Ross's romance with Charlie had to be taken out of the equation, and in the sixth episode of the season Greg Kinnear made a guest appearance as Charlie's ex-boyfriend in a story that ended her relationship with Ross. With ten episodes to go, Ross and Rachel were once again single and the show was ready to rekindle their chemistry.

While the rest of the group spent the season with goals and conclusions to work towards, Joey's role became similar to Phoebe's in earlier seasons – a comic relief sidekick whose own growth would have to wait. The character briefly got the chance for a bit of emotional depth as he came to terms with Chandler and Monica moving out of the city, but the writers had to force him into the role of emotionally immature man-child for the story to fit.

Phoebe, on the other hand, had the chance for a truly satisfying ending. At the end of the ninth season, she was newly reunited with Paull Rudd's Mike but had turned down his proposal. In the tenth season, the proposal took place for real, admittedly after a series of mishaps. In other shows, the wedding itself could have made for a grand finale to bow out on. That was the route that *Frasier* took. *Friends* had already done the wedding finale thing, though, and instead Phoebe's wedding was a unique standalone episode. It allowed the focus to be on Phoebe and not the end of the show itself.

'The One with Phoebe's Wedding', the season's twelfth episode, is such a perfectly-shaped sitcom story that the extra runtime (it was one of Zucker's super-sized episodes) goes almost completely unnoticed. At the beginning of the episode, Phoebe asks Joey if he would be the one to give her away, reminding the audience of the family that the character didn't have. Obstacles sprung up through the episode as Phoebe railed against Monica's incessant planning, and a last-minute blizzard threatened to put an abrupt end to the festivities. The most important thing was the happy ending: Phoebe embracing Mike as her new family as they celebrated out in the snow. While marriage as the ultimate conclusion for a woman often feels like lazy writing, for Phoebe the satisfaction was truly earned as the most unsettled *Friends* character finished her story with a future of emotional security ahead of her.

Before a wedding, however, there must be a bachelorette party. The preceding episode, 'The One Where the Stripper Cries', was one of the rare late *Friends* episodes written by David Crane and Marta Kauffman, and the one that most encapsulated that farewell tour feeling. The main story was Phoebe's hen party and an incredible guest appearance from Danny DeVito. DeVito got an Emmy nomination for his performance as 'Officer Goodbody', the titular stripper. The storyline was casting dependent, written specifically for DeVito once the creators knew they could get him for the role. His wife Rhea Perlman, herself a sitcom star, came to watch the episode taping as DeVito gamely sobbed before tearing off his police uniform to 'You Make Me Feel' and the whooping cheers of the audience.

In one of the episode's side stories, Joey appeared on the popular game show *Pyramid*, hosted by Donny Osmond. The *Pyramid* scenes were pre-shot on the set of the actual game show using the quiz's usual live studio audience. There was impressive attention to detail, with the live question scenes shot on video tape, as they would have been for the real game-show, and the usual film used for the interactions and his unfortunate co-contestant. The *Pyramid* story was the impetus for the *Joey* spin-off. To the creators it was proof that the character could carry a standalone story.

'The One Where the Stripper Cries' also carried the most intensely nostalgic story of the season as the creators took one last opportunity for an eighties flashback. Unfortunately, this meant the reappearance of the fat suit, requested by Courtney Cox who had great fondness for her time playing 'Fat Monica'. It's understandable that an actress forced to live up to unrealistic Hollywood beauty standards would find liberation in playing a character who's able to actively enjoy food without restriction, but it's a shame that the character was once again a mean punchline – the audience almost snickering as she dances with a slice of pizza in hand. The flashbacks, however, did manage to dive into the theme of endings running through the season. This was the last time the audience would see Ross's unfortunate facial hair, Rachel's first nose and Chandler's *Flock of Seagulls* hair. It was an unexpected goodbye, but an entertaining one as Ross and Chandler fought over girls from their college years.

The structure of the story, set at a university reunion, gave Crane and Kauffman a chance to get in one last moment of name-dropping. As Ross and Chandler discuss past alumni, Crane's partner Jeffrey Klarik gets another mention, along with the creator's Rabbi, assistants and various family members. Many of those whose names were used in the episode also appeared as extras in the series finale. The eighties flashback led to a series of horrifying revelations as Chandler admitted to kissing a drunk Rachel, and Ross discovered that his first kiss with Rachel was actually with his sister. The writers revelled in the fact that after ten years with these characters, there were still secrets that the audience didn't know.

The final season of *Friends* continued to celebrate quiet goodbyes as the show revisited past characters, stories and relationships. Christina Applegate returned in the fifth episode of the season as Rachel's spoiled sister Amy, and made a brief reference to Barry – Rachel's almost-husband – in a story that showed just how far Rachel had come from the first season's runaway bride. Monica and Phoebe got the chance to revisit their history as roommates thanks to an incredible guest appearance from Jennifer Coolidge, sporting a British accent so terrible that it's fantastic, in the season's third episode. There was even one last clip-show in the season's tenth episode – 'The One Where Chandler Gets Caught'. The cloying nostalgia was almost forgivable in the episode where Chandler and Monica reveal their plans to finally move out of the purple apartment. While clip-shows are usually a lazy option, just filler episodes, in this one the flashbacks felt earned as the characters reminisced together, ending on a moment from that first Thanksgiving before jumping to the show's present and reminding everyone that it was time for the characters to move on.

The ninth episode of the season, 'The One with the Birth Mother', was one of the most nakedly emotional stories outside of the finale. Anna Faris – famous for her role in the *Scary Movie* franchise – played Erica, the birth mother considering Chandler and Monica as adoptive parents. David Schwimmer directed the episode, which also saw Ross accidentally wearing women's clothing and Joey refusing to share food. The main story of Chandler and Monica finding out that Erica has mixed up their file with that of a reverend and a doctor, is memorable for a beautiful performance from Matthew Perry as Chandler explains to Erica that she should choose him and Monica as parents, and that Monica is 'a mother without a baby'. It was an emotional beat that gave the audience a cause to celebrate even as the characters prepared to move on to a new phase in their lives.

The new house and baby for Chandler and Monica allowed *Friends* to post a clear end point for the show. Their apartment would eventually be empty, and big events in the lives of the six would no longer all take place in one central city. The house story set up the saccharine clip show and gave the characters a chance at closure. Joey's storylines might have been lacking for the final season, but there were some solid emotional moments in 'The One with Princess Consuela' when he visited Chandler and Monica's new home and received some sage advice from a young Dakota Fanning.

In the following episode, 'The One Where Estelle Dies', the final season continued saying goodbye with another house visit and a final appearance from Maggie Wheeler as Janice. No other guest character was quite so iconic, or so beloved by the fandom, and the final nasal 'Oh My God' felt like a nod to all of the laughs that came before as the show cleared the runway for the last few episodes.

As *Friends* wound towards the end, the show looked further and further back into its history. In the fourteenth episode a brief cameo from Steven Eckholt as Mark, the focus of Ross's intense jealousy in the third season, became the catalyst for the final drama between Ross and Rachel. Rachel loses her job at Ralph Lauren only to, be offered a job, thanks to Mark, in Paris. In the fifteenth episode Ross frantically attempts to keep her from leaving before magnanimously accepting that she truly wants to take the opportunity. It is a sweet sentiment, but one that undermines the weight of the finale when watching the episodes back-to-back. It's the clearest sign that this was never a show intended for bingeing.

The season began bringing Ross and Rachel back to the forefront in the thirteenth episode, 'The One Where Joey Speaks French', when Rachel visited her father after he had a heart attack, and then sought comfort from Ross. Unsurprisingly, this resulted in an argument but the episode ended with an important point from Rachel – to her, the subject of her and Ross is never entirely off the table. Originally, the writers planned an episode that sent Ross and Rachel on a romantic trip to Paris together before the finale, but the idea never came to fruition. It was tough to reinvigorate the Ross and Rachel relationship with so little time left in the season. The pieces fell into place close to the wire, but as the finale loomed the stage was finally set to reunite the pair.

The penultimate episode of the season, 'The One with Rachel's Going Away Party', was a subdued little story as the characters said their goodbyes and Rachel prepared to leave for Paris. There was a silly side plot about furry handcuffs that reminded the audience just how many members of the group had lived in Monica's apartment, but the main focus was on simple emotional moments. There were only a handful of laughs across the episode, and even the music remained consistently quiet. There was a brief funny moment early in the episode as Rachel demonstrated how thoroughly organised she was for her impending flight and Monica cries that 'I've got nothing left to teach you.' The runaway bride had grown up, and now she had something to run towards.

The climax of the episode set up the cliff-hangers before the finale. Erica went into labour and parenthood was imminent for Monica and Chandler, while Ross and Rachel fought over Rachel's inability to say goodbye until emotions came to a head, and the episode ended on a kiss. In the lead up to the final episode, NBC aired overwhelming amounts of promotion featuring sombre music and hushed tones more suitable to adverts for an animal rescue. The advertising was so relentless that many found it off-putting, but it worked. Between the cliff-hanger kiss and the efforts of the network, on Thursday, 6 May 2004, over fifty-two million people were in front of their television sets, ready to watch 'The Last One'.

The pressure was on for David Crane, Marta Kauffman and Kevin Bright to deliver a perfect goodbye. They began the writing process by watching the final episodes of other sitcoms, keeping an eye on what worked and what didn't. Speaking to the *San Francisco Chronicle*, David Crane dubbed the end of *The Mary Tyler Moore Show* 'the gold standard', and Kauffman noted that 'the ones we really like are the ones that stayed true to what the series was'. The creators wanted the finale to feel like a pure episode of *Friends*. They wanted no flash forwards to the future and no gimmicks or big guest stars. It was an emotional time as they came close to the show's final moments; all anyone had to say to Kauffman was 'empty apartment' and she'd burst into tears. After a frantic period of co-writing over the phone during the festive season, a final draft of the finale was completed early in January 2004.

The weeks of the final taping – two-part episodes were shot over a fortnight – were marked with a series of both planned and unexpected wrap parties. The episode was written to only use the Central Perk set during the first half, allowing room for the airport scenes in the second. After filming was finished and the coffee shop came down, an impromptu crew party took part on the stage. A few days before the final taping, Jennifer Aniston hosted a dinner party of the cast and executive producers at her $13.5 million home. The wine served was vintage, bottles of Haut-Brion purchased by Kevin Bright ten years previous during *Friends*' first season. There was a dinner for the cast at a favourite West Hollywood restaurant, again just a couple of days before the final taping. Finally, there was a giant official wrap party the day after the last taping, featuring a live performance of 'I'll Be There For You' by The Rembrandts and a surprise re-enactment of the pilot episode's opening scenes from the cast.

It was the day of filming itself that had emotions running highest for the cast and crew. The day began with a sky-written thankyou to Crane and Kauffman from the writers. Maggie Wheeler was in the audience for the taping, and later recalled the cast crying so much when they appeared in front of the audience before the taping began that they had to go back and have their make-up redone. The producers gifted the six *Friends* stars with diamond earring and designer cufflinks, and in return the cast gave the producers inscribed Cartier watches. The cast and crew signed special *Friends* yearbooks, David Arquette ran around backstage filming everything on a video camera, and every tear on screen in the episode was absolutely real.

There was a conversation, before the taping, about keeping the live audience out of the room during key scenes to avoid spoilers being leaked. This was not the time of the internet we know today, however. In the end, the creators felt that the energy a live audience gave the show was more important than keeping a few plot details secret. Despite that, there were surprisingly few leaks, and the viewers were generally able to go in blind when the finale aired in May.

'The Last One' needed a handful of things to make it the perfect way to say goodbye. There had to be one last surprise, every relationship needed a satisfying end, and the audience needed to be reminded one last time of why, exactly, they loved *Friends*. Phoebe's marriage to Mike had given her a satisfying enough ending that she was free to act as a foil to others throughout the episode, although Paul Rudd came back one last time to remind the viewers that she was landing in a good place. As a result, she acted as a sidekick as Ross processed the imminent loss of Rachel and made one last ditch effort to save whatever might be there between them. Before Rachel could leave for the airport, however, there was that last surprise as Monica and Chandler found themselves with twins to parent. The writers did argue about how believable they could conceivably make the unexpected twins storyline, but eventually came to the conclusion that there was no good reason to let realism get in the way of a good story.

With the tricky-to-film infants firmly tucked away off screen and Rachel sent off to one of New York's airports, there was time to resolve a relationship that had received little attention in *Friends*' later seasons. The platonic romance of Joey and Chandler was arguably the longest running relationship of the show, and with the birth scenes out of the way there was time for one last goodbye for the two of them as they destroyed the football table from what was once their shared bachelor pad to save a baby chick and duck. The writers took the time to wrap up a dangling plot hole as the characters mention the wonderful farm the original chick and duck were sent to live on – one last preservation of Joey's naivete. For all the valid criticisms, and there are many, of *Friends* and its handling of toxic masculinity, it was a rare sitcom from that era that allowed two straight men to share a meaningful and emotional relationship at all. It was even more unique that *Friends* gave them a chance to acknowledge the depth of their feelings as they shared a meaningful goodbye.

The most important goodbye, of course, was Gunther's admission to Rachel when he finally, very sweetly, confessed his undying admiration for her after years of pining. It was a stand-out moment, a rare bit of levity in the emotionally heavy story. Almost as important was Rachel's admission to Ross. After spending the night together, she uttered that 'perfect way to say goodbye' line. The audience in the studio was dead quiet as the expected reunion seemed to be taken permanently off the table. At the halfway point of the episode, when Ross announced his intent to run to the airport and convince Rachel to stay, the screaming from the stands went on far longer than the episode's run time could take.

What followed was an excellent echo of the first season's finale, a role-reversed airport dash full of missed opportunities. Phoebe delays Rachel's plane with a phone call about a damaged 'falange', a nod to her often-used pseudonym and a way to add some comedy to a scene that had the writers worried; the threat of something wrong with a plane was a difficult joke to pull off post 9/11. There's finally a moment of confession, a 'Don't Go.' from Ross to Rachel at the airport. The original draft of that airport scene was much longer, but a quietly stunned Rachel getting on the plane to Paris worked far better in one of the most plainly dramatic scenes of the finale. Of course, the pair couldn't stay apart. The writers brought them back together with a message on Ross's answering machine – a plot point that placed *Friends* firmly in its era.

The question of whether or not Rachel should have gotten off the plane is one that's haunted *Friends* ever since its conclusion. Only a handful of episodes before, Rachel had explained to Ross in great detail why the move to Paris was so essential for her. Only months earlier, *Sex and the City* had ended with a similarly aborted move to Paris, and drew criticism as a result. Objectively, Rachel's decision made very little sense. Rachel had a career to move toward, and only an ex whose behaviour looks less and less sympathetic on rewatches of the show to keep her in New York. Such is the enduring popularity of *Friends* that the finale has been held up to repeated scrutiny throughout the years, and Rachel's choice has often been found wanting. Who, in their right mind, would choose Ross over Paris? If a friend in the real world made a similar decision, it's not hard to imagine frog-marching them back to the airport and telling them not to be so silly.

That endless scrutiny, however, misses the most important factor. *Friends* was always a wild fiction, a fairy-tale version of New York with magically cheap apartments and a wealth of convenient job opportunities. Post *Friends* sitcoms would learn to mix gritty realism into the happy endings, but that wouldn't satisfy the audiences of the early noughties. Rachel and Ross reuniting allowed for a conclusion that was satisfying in the moment, even if thinking about it deeply destroys the illusion of a happy ending.

The One with the Finale

In the last moments of *Friends*, the apartment was empty, ready to be vacated as Chandler and Monica moved into the next phase of their life. The six gathered together on that big purple set one last time, leaving keys on the counter one-by-one as they headed out of the door. In *Friends, Lovers and the Big Terrible Thing*, Matthew Perry recalled taking Marta Kauffman to one side before taping the episode and asking her for a favour: 'Nobody will care about this except me. So, may I please have the last line?' In the show, Rachel suggested one last coffee and as the six friends turned their backs on the audience and Chandler got his last quip in as he asked 'Sure. Where?' and Perry got his final word.

It might not make sense in the real world, but in the last moments of that *Friends* fantasy it was the perfect emotional landing. The six keys and the six characters walking away together were essential, and it couldn't happen without Rachel. For that, she got off the plane.

Chapter Eleven

The One with the Aftermath

When the dust had settled after the *Friends* finale, American network television looked remarkably different compared to the beginning of the show's ten-year run. NBC had reached impressive heights during that decade, but by 2004 the network had fallen from grace. The season after *Friends* ended, running from 2004 to 2005, was the worst in the network's recent history. No NBC shows reached the Nielsen top ten that season; the network's highest rated show was *E.R.,* which fell to twelfth place. Things had changed for more than just NBC. Sitcoms had fallen off their pedestal across the board, and now it was reality television and scripted dramas taking the lead.

That season, ABC debuted three big new shows, two of which reached the ratings top ten. None of them were sitcoms. *Grey's Anatomy* began as a mid-season replacement in March 2005. It went on to become a television phenomenon, at the time of writing running for twenty seasons with no sign of stopping. *Desperate Housewives* began in October 2004 with a pilot watched by twenty-one million people – the best performance for an ABC pilot since *Spin City* began in 1996. *Desperate Housewives* was a rare female-led drama that stood out for its soapy storylines and dark comedy, and it remained a hit throughout its eight-year run. In July 2004, at San Diego Comic-Con, the attendees got the opportunity to watch the pilot for another new ABC drama two months before it aired on television. *Lost* went on to debut on the network in September 2004. The two-part pilot of the supernatural mystery-box drama – created by JJ Abrams and Damon Lindelof after ABC jumped on the idea of a *Castaway* meets *Survivor*-style show – was the most expensive pilot in ABC's history, with the costs coming in at around $14 million. *Lost* went on to become a gigantic critical success, ranked by multiple outlets as one of the top TV shows of all time – despite its contentious ending. Reality television might have been taking over, but big dramas were still a strong daw. It was sitcoms that had fallen by the wayside.

The only sitcoms to rank in the top twenty Nielsen ratings for the season both belonged to CBS. The final season of *Everybody Loves Raymond* reached a ninth place, one last triumph for the sitcoms of the nineties. Thanks in large part to the *Raymond* lead-in, *Two and a Half Men* landed eleventh in the ratings and would continue on for another ten years despite being consistently unloved by critics. These structured multi-cam sitcoms had, in 2005, begun to look like relics from a bygone era.

The new, more exciting and more critically acclaimed comedies were those that had taken new shapes. *Scrubs* was an early single-cam hit and continued to develop a devoted fan base and receive strong reviews thanks to the show's emotional honesty and willingness to play with its established form. *Arrested Development* never became a ratings giant, but the critics loved it and it was even called 'the best sitcom on TV' by *Entertainment Weekly* during the show's second season in 2004.

The short, six-episode first season of a surprising future hit aired on NBC late in 2005. There was little evidence that a 'mockumentary'-style sitcom could be a success, and remakes of British shows usually seemed to crash and burn on American network television. Somehow, though, those six episodes of NBC's *The Office* grew into an outstandingly successful sitcom that would go on to run for nine seasons and inspire countless other comedies. When Apple updated iTunes to include support for purchasing and viewing video content in 2005, *The Office* was one of the first shows available for download. Not only was the show's structure different from the sitcoms that came before, the ways to consume content were also changing; and *The Office* was there at the beginning.

While *The Office* would eventually become a sitcom colossus, in 2005 it was little more than a plug to fill a gap at the end of an incredibly lacklustre season for NBC. In a single year, the network had fallen from first place among its competitors to last. All of the major networks were struggling as cable television became more accessible to the average American household but NBC, now lacking two of its flagship shows, fell furthest and hardest. Nowhere was this more obvious than Thursday nights.

Thursdays were still the big night for advertisers, but where NBC had previously dominated in ratings, now CBS were the ratings' stars. The network's line-up of *Survivor*, *CSI* and *Without a Trace* were all top ten shows that season, with *CSI* taking first place. By contrast, NBC was almost non-existent. *E.R.* still held sort-of strong, and would for a further four seasons. *The Apprentice*, the first reality show to get a 'Must See' time slot had a successful enough second season, though it had dropped in ratings compared to the previous year and would continue to fall throughout the rest of its run. *Will & Grace* had begun to slip down in the ratings without a powerful show to serve as a lead-in. At that point, it was in the penultimate season of its original run. The show was still getting good reviews, but it didn't have the power to draw in viewers when it was standing alone. The most surprising ratings failure of all, however, was the new show in the Thursday evening, 8 pm slot – *Friends'* replacement.

While *Joey* was already planned at the beginning of *Friends'* final season, it wasn't anyone's first choice for a spin-off. At one point there was an idea for a follow-up show centered on Monica and Chandler, but neither Courtney Cox nor Matthew Perry wanted to stay on in those roles. In 2005 the rest of the cast were ready to move on and only Matt Leblanc seemed willing to continue on in the world of *Friends*. Among the people not interested in a *Friends* spin-off were David Crane and Marta Kauffman. Instead, Scott Silveri and Shana Goldberg-Meehan, both of whom had written on *Friends* for the bulk of its ten-year run, created the new vehicle for Joey. Kevin Bright signed on to executive produce the spin-off. Where Bright's collaboration with Crane and Kauffman had been an easy working relationship, this new set-up felt more forced – a risk when the trio had such an established and beloved character to work with. The results were decidedly unsuccessful.

NBC had high hopes for *Joey*, pushing the first season aggressively in promos during coverage of the 2004 Summer Olympics. Drea De Matteo, already a big name in television, joined the cast as Joey's sister Gina. After five years as the tragic Adriana on *The Sopranos*, De Matteo spoke openly in interviews at the time about looking forward to being in a funnier, less intense role. The actress has since admitted in an interview with *Vulture* that she had very little interest in the project and 'had such animosity towards that whole experience at the time', but was 'pushed' into taking part. The lack of interest and enthusiasm on set wasn't solely De Matteo's, and the resulting show was a drab attempt to keep what was so great about *Friends* alive. Even David Schwimmer, who didn't appear in a cameo but did direct a couple of episodes in the first season, couldn't liven up the comedy. Goldberg-Meehan left at the end of the first season with little explanation. Presumably, as she went on to marry Scott Silveri in 2006, there wasn't any animosity between her and her fellow co-creator. Kevin Bright stuck with *Joey* until its bitter end – and there was ample bitterness as it limped towards the inevitable.

Despite the failings of the first season of *Joey*, NBC remained optimistic that the right combination of Thursday night shows could bring the network back to its former glory. *Joey* was given one more chance in the 2005/2006 season, once again airing at 8 pm on Thursday nights. However, the show didn't get quite the same promotional push that it had the year before. Instead, the centrepiece of NBC's line-up for the season was new comedy *My Name is Earl*, starring Jason Lee, which would go on to easily trump *Joey* in the ratings. *Joey* failed to match even its previous season's audience numbers, and went on hiatus in December 2005. It returned in a Tuesday time slot on 7 March 2006. Only four million people tuned in to watch, and the show was cancelled immediately after, leaving eight episodes unaired in the US.

Even the cast of *Joey* knew the end was coming. Before the cancellation was official, cast member Andrea Anders had already signed on for a new show the following season: *The Class*, created by David Crane and his partner Jeffrey Klarik. Sadly, *The Class* was another show destined for cancellation, lasting only a single season despite the involvement of James Burrows, who liked it so much that he directed every episode.

Speaking on the failure of *Joey*, Kevin Bright has since admitted that he was unhappy with the direction the show took, and blamed the interference of the network for its failings. On *Friends*, Bright had a fairly equal partnership with Crane and Kauffman, as well as a decent amount of say in the shape of the show. On *Joey*, he was relegated to executive producer and director only, and had little control over the show. In an interview with *The Age* eight months after the show's cancellation, he explained that 'Joey ... became a pathetic, mopey character. I felt he was moving in the wrong direction, but I was not heard.' Much later, when speaking to the *Hollywood Reporter*, he complained that the network and the studio had their 'imprints' on the show, and that the storyline 'did not do service to the character'. *Joey* became an unfortunate footnote to a beloved sitcom, one best forgotten.

After *Joey*'s cancellation, Kevin Bright stepped away from television. After twelve years of working on *Friends* and its spin-off, and heavily neglecting his personal life as a result, he took a calmer approach to his future. Bright went on to return to his alma mater, Emerson College, as a visiting professor; beginning with teaching a course on directing comedy for television. He went on to teach a filmmaking class at Perkins school for the blind, and that led to the creation of his 2017 documentary *Best and Most Beautiful Things*. Bright never returned to producing television, instead focusing on teaching and the occasional documentary. He revisited the world of sitcoms just once when, in 2019, he reunited with Matt LeBlanc when he directed a single episode of the CBS sitcom *Man with a Plan*.

After *Joey*, Matt LeBlanc also chose to step away from television, although not for as long as Kevin Bright. He returned just five years later, this time in the company of David Crane and Jeffrey Klarik. *Episodes* began in 2011 and was Crane and Klarik's first show after the abrupt end of *The Class*. The Showtime cable network provided a home for the show in the States, but it was produced by a UK company – Hat Trick Productions. As a semi-British creation made for the BBC and a US cable network, *Episodes* was a departure from Crane and Klarik's previous work. The subject matter, however, couldn't have been closer to home for the pair. *Episodes* showed an English couple played by Tamsin Grieg and Stephen Mangan – no strangers to working together after their brilliant performances in Channel 4's *Green Wing* – struggling with the Hollywood television scene as they attempt to get an American remake of their successful sitcom *Lyman's Boys* on the air.

While British and cable television might have been new territories for Crane and Klarik, the development hell, smirking network executives and heads of comedy with no sense of humour were all part of a reality that they'd suffered through and were ready to send up. At the end of the pilot episode Kathleen Rose Perkins as Carol, the network's head of programming and an artful bullshitter, squealingly announced to Grieg and Mangan's character that they have the chance of scoring none other than Matt LeBlanc himself to star in their pilot. From the second episode of the show, LeBlanc played a hilarious pastiche of himself – arrogant, wealthy and appalling. After the flop of *Joey*, Matt LeBlanc got to be funny again as he played an egotistical has-been version of himself. *Episodes* didn't land on the air as a highly-anticipated show, having been lumped in with the 2011 season's failed crop of British imports and remakes, but the show rapidly grew an audience both sides of the Atlantic, and the deserved love from critics came soon after.

It wasn't just David Crane and Jeffrey Klarik who stepped away from network television. In 2014, Marta Kauffman moved to streaming when she signed a deal with Netflix for a thirteen-episode order of *Grace and Frankie*. Kauffman co-created the show – starring Jane Fonda and Lily Tomlin as the titular characters – with Howard J. Morris, an old colleague from her *Dream On* days who had gone on to work on *Home Improvement, According to Jim* and a handful of other renowned sitcoms. *Grace and Frankie* quickly became a hit, praised for its unflinching depictions of age, queer relationships and the depths platonic friendship can reach. The situation part of the sitcom was established in the opening five minutes of the episode. Frankie and Grace's respective husbands Sol (Sam Waterson) and Robert, (Martin Sheen in a massive departure from his time on *The West Wing*), announce their twenty-year affair over dinner. They intend to leave their wives for each other and get married because, in Sol's words, 'We can do that now.'

In fact, plenty of fantastic actors appeared in *Grace and Frankie* in both regular and guest roles. A brief *Friends* reunion took place in the show's fourth season when Lisa Kudrow appeared for a handful of episodes as ditzy manicurist Sheree. RuPaul Charles, host of the iconic *RuPaul's Drag Race*, appeared in the fifth season in a campy set of cameos. Even Dolly Parton, who appeared in *9 to 5* with Fonda and Tomlin back in 1980, made an appearance in the show's finale.

Grace and Frankie ran for a total of seven seasons, although the last was delayed due to the Covid-19 pandemic, making it one of Netflix's longest-running original series. It seems a miracle that *Grace and Frankie* was able to continue for as long as it did before ending on the creator's terms. Netflix has regularly been criticised for cancelling original productions far too soon, instead spending money on nostalgic safe-bets to pad out its catalogue.

One such safe bet was *Friends*. In 2015, Netflix paid Warner Brothers $100 million for the rights to stream the full *Friends* back catalogue. (Unsurprisingly, no such deal was made to acquire *Joey*.) As the full series became available to binge on streaming for the first time, there was a huge resurgence in *Friends* fandom alongside a wealth of nuanced criticisms that might have been missing during the show's first airing. For perhaps the first time, *Friends* was available to a whole new generation of potential fans, many of whom fell in love with the show despite it originally airing long before they were old enough to watch. *Friends* has become such a cornerstone of pop culture that literacy in the show is just assumed, and it still provides constant material for listicles and discussions. Multiple rankings of Rachel's outfits of the show have appeared online: a 2015 *Bustle* article ranked them all, *ScreenRant* published a top ten in 2020, and *Buzzfeed* chose twenty-seven of the best in 2021. There have been celebrations of the best moments, jokes, stories, couples, outfits and more, but alongside those has come a new era of criticism.

Some of the people watching *Friends* for the first time hadn't grown up in the era when the casual sexism, homophobia and erasure of people of colour that formed part of *Friends'* fabric were common on mainstream television. There was confusion about why the show was so beloved. Alongside the celebrations, more articles came out dissecting the show. A piece from *Entertainment Weekly* in 2019 headlined '"Fat Monica" is the ghost that continues to haunt *Friends* 25 years later' dove into the problematic nature of the storyline and the failure of those jokes to land, pointing out that it was 'an incredibly lazy part of *Friends'* comedic relevance'. The same year, *Buzzfeed* took a broader view in an article simply headlined '*Friends* Hasn't Aged Well'.

Friends does deserve the criticism, and in places the humour of the show seems like an ancient relic. The same is true of many of the shows from that era of television. However, few of those shows continue to occupy space in the cultural consciousness the way *Friends* does, remaining so present as to be consistently discussed over a decade after they came off the air. In a 2023 *Variety* article, Jennifer Aniston was quoted complaining about the modern reactions to older comedies, saying, 'There's a whole generation of people, kids, who are now going back to episodes of "Friends" and find them offensive.' She wasn't wrong. What Aniston might have missed is that *Friends* is so often discussed as a problematic part of sitcom history because the show is so often discussed, full stop. *Friends* wasn't more or less problematic than its contemporaries, but the show has come under scrutiny because it's survived long enough to still be incredibly popular. While many have, especially since that 2015 Netflix deal, been rightfully pointing out the problems that were always present in *Friends*, many more have simply grown more and more in love with the show, warts and all.

Without that devoted fandom, the inevitable *Friends* reunion would have been a waste of money, falling on deaf audiences. That clearly wasn't the case, however. The reunion was first announced late in 2019, planned as part of the launch of HBO's new streaming service HBO Max. Along with the reunion, the streaming service – more recently renamed to Max – was going to put up all ten seasons of *Friends*, having claimed the show from Netflix in a $500 million deal. While some parts of the reunions did film early in 2020, the full show was delayed due to the Covid-19 pandemic, eventually making it to screens in May 2021.

The original sets were reconstructed on Stage 24 of the Warner Brothers lot, named 'The Friends Stage' since the show's end in 2004. There were genuinely sweet moments of reminiscence among the cast members, alone on the sets, as they recalled hiding scripts in Monica's fruit bowl and spotted the inexplicably reconstructed 'Burrows Beam'. They found their signatures from the last day of filming, scrawled on the back of the set's flats, and revisited old dressing rooms and the spot where they would 'huddle' before every episode. There were table reads in the special – emotional re-enactments of beloved scenes. There was a quiz, styled after the apartment-swapping contest from 'The One with the Embryos', featuring cameos from the barbershop quartet that appeared in season three and Tom Selleck; glorious moustache intact. There was genuine warmth in the moments between just the original cast members, which unfortunately only served to make much of the rest of the special feel like too much, and a bit surreal.

The reunion featured clips from fans around the world expressing how *Friends* changed their lives and a series of pre-recorded celebrity interviews in case audiences were curious about David Beckham, Malala Yousafzi or Kit Harrington's favourite *Friends'* episode. There was a brief appearance from Lady Gaga, performing the famous 'Smelly Cat', while a baffled Kudrow watched, looking as if she was politely accepting an unwanted gift; and a fashion show featuring Cara Delevingne in the infamous Armadillo costume.

The centrepiece of the reunion was an interview with the main cast, led by James Corden, held outside so that a live, socially distanced audience featuring beloved members of *Friends'* history could attend. David Crane and Marta Kauffman were there, as well as featuring in pre-filmed featurettes. Christina Pickles and Elliot Gould appeared, James Michael Tyler featured over a Zoom call and both James Burrows and

Kevin Bright were in attendance; although anything they said during the interview was cut for time.

The reunion special was almost two hours long, and each member of the original cast was paid around $2.25 million to take part. It was an odd mix of the heart-warming and the unnecessary, something that could only work for a show that still possesses a broad and intense fandom. *Friends* never stopped being adored, and the numbers proved it – 29 per cent of US streaming households watched as soon as the special landed on HBO Max. Over half of those viewers were in the 35 to 54 demographic – the ones most likely to have caught the show's initial run. In the UK, the reunion aired on Sky One to 5.3 million viewers, making it the channel's most watched show ever.

Sadly, the original six Friends won't be reunited again. In October 2023, at the age of just 54, Matthew Perry tragically passed away. In the days after his death, the internet filled with outpourings of grief from his friends and fellow actors, as well as thousands of devoted *Friends* fans. Perry had never shied away from speaking of the difficulties he'd faced throughout his life, outlining his struggles with addiction in painstakingly honest detail in his memoir *Friends, Lovers and the Big Terrible Thing*. In interviews, he was clear that while he knew *Friends* would always be the thing he was most known for, he truly wanted his legacy to be the people that he'd helped throughout his life. Realistically, his ten years as Chandler Bing are a huge part of his legacy. The character that he put so much into was very much another way he helped people, from the laughter and energy he brought to sets to the fantastic amounts of joy he brought to the *Friends* audience. *Friends* would have been a very different show without him, possibly one not so beloved or well-remembered, and the world won't be the same without him in it, helping.

During that HBO reunion, Crane and Kauffman were asked if they'd ever consider making a reboot of *Friends*, or a sequel. Obviously the idea of doing such a thing now, without Matthew Perry, is completely unthinkable, but even at the time of the reunion the answer was an emphatic 'No'.

Other sitcom creators from the *Friends* era have been more willing to revisit their work. In the last few years, reboots and sequels have become bread and butter for networks and streamers as executives pursue safe bets. *Will & Grace* was one of the first shows from the nineties to make a triumphant return to screen when a reboot of the show began airing on NBC in 2017. Three new seasons, all overseen by David Kohan and Max Mutchnik, gave viewers a chance to revisit the old favourite and gave writers the opportunity to tackle a new realm of politics before leaving the characters in a much better place than the hastily retconned original finale.

The Fresh Prince of Bel-Air got a gritty reboot on Peacock, NBC's streaming platform, in 2020. After two movies, one of which was widely panned, three quarters of the original *Sex and the City* gang returned to the screen in *And Just Like That…*, a sequel to the original series which began on HBO Max in 2021. Frasier Crane returned to screens on streaming service Paramount+ in late 2023, in a sequel that featured none of the original cast bar Kelsey Grammer. James Burrows, however, was attached to the *Frasier* reboot and directed the first two episodes. While some reboots and sequels have been successful, most have been criticised for being little more than transparent cash grabs. It's possible that the *Seinfeld* cast had the right idea in 2009, performing a faux reunion that genuinely brought the cast back together on *Curb Your Enthusiasm*.

David Crane and Marta Kauffman have given their reasons for that 'no'. At the end of *Friends* all of those characters were in solid, happy places in their lives. To open the world back up would be to undo all of that work, forcing conflict back into those fictional lives for the sake of entertainment. The end of *Friends* has repeatedly been dissected and fairly criticised, but it was exactly what a sitcom should be. Something that wrapped up the lives of the characters and left them uninteresting, not still compelling to follow. The legacy of *Friends* would live on in memories of a purple apartment with a yellow picture frame around the door. Nothing more was needed.

Epilogue

The Concluding One

Will, Grace, Dharma, Greg, Raymond, Ellen, Seinfeld, Frasier. The decade that *Friends* spanned was filled with big names and unforgettable shows. Surrounding those were a wealth of other comedies that, for good or bad, lived short lives and left little more than a stub on Wikipedia. *Friends*, somehow, still stands head and shoulders above it all.

There's plenty of reasons why *Friends* has remained so incredibly popular. That decade covers such a specific snapshot of time. Those ten years saw the birth of the internet as a commonplace tool, the rise of cell phones and all of the new avenues of connection and communication that came with them. They saw one of the biggest tragedies the world had ever experienced, the political ramifications of it, and all of the new ways that people could close themselves off to each other. There was the beginning of a new millennium and, above all, there were some truly heinous fashion choices. *Friends* was, through it all, a constant; an unchanging happy little bubble of time. The world changed in that decade, and the world of television changed along with it. Multiple TV sets became the norm, sitcoms adjusted to suit new audiences, premium cable television rose and networks had to fight for viewers harder than ever.

In 1994, American television was the land of comic opportunity. By 2004 it was a place of network uncertainty and numbers' panic. The long-running love for *Friends* exists, in part, because the show got to last. Who knows how many of those shows that didn't quite pull in the first season numbers could have gone on to become cultural phenomena? Bright, Crane and Kauffman were beyond lucky to get that full decade, to be able to keep telling stories.

In that time of uncertainty *Friends* didn't just end, it ended well. Finales written hastily after a network and studio fail to come to an agreement, or open-ended series-enders after cancellation comes too quickly, have never been satisfying endings. The creators of *Friends* knew that the tenth season was it, the very last. Admittedly they also knew that the sixth, eighth and ninth seasons might have been, but by the tenth it was definite. They took the time to end the show on good terms, with no lingering doubt about the fates of the characters. Yes, getting off the plane might not have been an ideal choice, and staying on the plane might be the bittersweet decision made in a more modern show, but *Friends* wrapped up every character emotionally. The audience was left with fond memories, instead of frustration at a job poorly done. It's impossible to overstate the importance of getting the end right. Shows that fail the audience in their last episodes stick around the cultural consciousness unpleasantly. *Friends* just stuck.

Friends was unique. That cast, at that time, in that place, was like nothing else and could never be recreated. There have been ensemble sitcoms since, and New York sitcoms, and ensembles in New York, and all of those things existed back when *Friends* was airing. No other show, however, has managed to capture an audience in quite the same way. *Friends* became safe from the rounds of reboots and sequels because there was never a need for it. The show remains so beloved that merchandise, Lego sets and in-person *Friends* experiences are available now for the millions of fans still bingeing the show, using quotes as pop culture short-hand (could *Friends* BE any more culturally relevant?) and sometimes discussing its shortcomings at length.

There will be more comedy in the future. Sitcoms didn't end with *Friends*, although they were waning. But these things come around. There will be new shows, and some will be about groups of twenty-somethings, and some will be set in big cities, and some might even go on to last ten years and cover another distinct snapshot of changing times. Hopefully, those sitcoms yet to come will be better than their predecessors, resorting less and less to cheap humour and sharp digs. The chance of any of those new shows reaching fifty million viewers in a single night is, in a time of content overload, miniscule. They will find their audiences, however, and they'll be loved and discussed and endlessly dissected. A whole new golden age of television awaits, but there will never be another *Friends*.

Friends, however, will always be there for you.

Bibliography

Books

Austerlitz, Saul, *Still Friends* (Trapeze, 2019)

Burrows, James, Friedfeld, Eddy, *Directed By James Burrows* (Ballantine Books, 2023)

Gordon, Aubrey, *What We Don't Talk About When We Talk About Fat* (Beacon Press, 2020)

Littlefield, Warren & Pearson, T. R., *Top of the Rock* (Doubleday, 2012)

Perry, Matthew, *Friends, Lovers and the Big Terrible Thing* (Headline, 2022)

Susman, Gary, Dillon, Jeannine, Cairns, Bryan, *Friends Forever* (Harper, 2019)

Newspapers, Magazines and Periodicals

The Boston Globe

Cincinnati Enquirer

Chicago Tribune

The Directors Guild of America Quarterly

Entertainment Weekly

Evening Standard

Forbes Magazine

Guardian

Hartford Courant

Hollywood Reporter

The Independent

Los Angeles Times

NBC News

New York Observer

New York Times
People Magazine
Rolling Stone
San Francisco Chronicle
The Spokesman Review
The Telegraph
Time Magazine
TV Guide
US Weekly
USA Today
Vanity Fair
Variety

Online Resources

TheAge.com.au
Barb (Broadcasters' Audience Research Board)
The Conversation (BBC World Service)
Bustle.com
Buzzfeed.com
Catapult Magazine
DavidandMaddie.com
DigitalSpy.com
Fake Doctors, Real Friends Podcast
TheFutonCritic.com
IndieWire.com
ISNA.org (The Intersex Society of North America)
Jumptheshark.com
Nielsen Media Research
Off the Beat Podcast
ScreenRant.com
Snopes.com
The Television Academy
Them.us
TVTropes.org
Vulture.com
Wired.com